LAND OF LINCOLN

Also by Andrew Ferguson

Fools' Names, Fools' Faces

LAND OF LINCOLN

Adventures in Abe's America

ANDREW FERGUSON

Atlantic Monthly Press
New York

Photo credits on p. 281

Published simultaneously in Canada
Printed in the United States of America

FIRST EDITION

Library of Congress Cataloging-in-Publication Data

Ferguson, Andrew, 1956–
Land of Lincoln / Andrew Ferguson.
p. cm
ISBN 10: 0-87113-967-7
ISBN 13: 978-0-87113-967-2
1. Lincoln, Abraham, 1809–1865—Influence.   2. Lincoln, Abraham, 1809–
1865—Public opinion.   3. Lincoln, Abraham, 1809–1865—Miscellanea.
4. Ferguson, Andrew, 1956—Travel—United States.   5. United States—
Description and travel.   6. Presidents—United States—Biography—
Miscellanea.   7. Public opinion—United States.   I. Title.

E457.2.F47 2007
973.7092—dc22   2006052634

Atlantic Monthly Press
an imprint of Grove/Atlantic, Inc.
841 Broadway
New York, NY 10003

Distributed by Publishers Group West

www.groveatlantic.com

07 08 09 10 11 12 10 9 8 7 6 5 4 3 2 1

To Denise

CONTENTS

PREFACE

More books have been written about Abraham Lincoln than about any other American—nearly fourteen thousand in all—and at least half of those books begin by saying that more books have been written about Abraham Lincoln than about any other American. This book, you'll notice, is one of them. Yet its subject matter is not Lincoln directly, or Lincoln exclusively. Its subject is really the country that Lincoln created and around which, I think I can show, he still putters, appearing here and there in likely and unlikely places, obtruding, stirring things up, offering consolation, dispensing bromides and bits of wisdom and otherwise making himself undeniable.

So even though this is a Lincoln book and not a book about me— sorry to disappoint you—it might help explain some things that happen in the book later on if I explain at the outset my own association with Lincoln, which runs pretty deep.

I was born in a midsize town in northeastern Illinois, the state that sells itself (to itself, among others) as the Land of Lincoln; its convicts stamp the claim right there on the license plates. My father worked as a lawyer in Chicago, in a firm founded after the Civil War by Robert Todd Lincoln, the only one of Abraham Lincoln's sons to survive childhood. I grew up in a drafty old Victorian house on Lincoln Street, a mile or so from another drafty old Victorian where, legend has it, Lincoln himself had spent the night in the 1850s. Riding in our family's Oldsmobile as a boy, I saw this house nearly every day, turning in my seat as we passed, always picturing the tall stooped figure climbing the front porch, removing his stovepipe hat to greet the lady of the house as he crossed the threshold into the cool of the parlor, until the Olds took the bend in the road and the house was out of sight.

During the long humid summers, on visits to grandparents and cousins downstate, my parents would sometimes break the boredom by taking my brothers and me on side trips to the state capital of Springfield, an exhausted city of liquor stores and parking lots but to me a place full of wonders. There in the heat we would run a well-worn path from the Lincoln tomb to the "Restored Law Offices of A. Lincoln" to the only home A. Lincoln ever owned, a clapboard house tucked behind a picket fence in a down-at-the-heels neighborhood not far from the Capitol building. Once or twice we drove twenty miles out of town to New Salem, the village on a bluff above the Sangamon River where Lincoln spent his young manhood. Its inhabitants abandoned New Salem long before Lincoln died, and a commemorative collection of log cabins had been rebuilt on the site a century later, as a tourist draw. Already, by the time of our first visit, the splintered logs of the new buildings had grown gray and brittle from the weather, taking on the faded look of historical artifacts themselves. Our Lincoln diversions climaxed in a long car trip the family took one bright, blissful week along the then new, and soon to be defunct, Lincoln Heritage Trail.

Having been where he'd been, and walked where he'd walked, I became a Lincoln buff, junior division, privileged to indulge (I thought) in a special intimacy with greatness. I cleared my schedule—not so hard to do when you're ten—whenever *Abe Lincoln in Illinois* or *Young Mr. Lincoln* was to show up on TV. My favorite book was a photographic album as thick and heavy as a plank of oak, called *Lincoln in Every Known Pose*. My second favorite was a Yearling children's book called *Abraham Lincoln,* by Ingri and Edgar D'Aulaire, a beautifully illustrated biography whose only defect was that it ended before his dark and splendidly heartbreaking death. Photographs of Lincoln hung on the walls of my bedroom. Sometimes at night, wakened by a bad dream, I'd rise from my bed and go to my desk and pull from the center drawer a sheaf of papers written in Lincoln's own hand. I'd bought a packet of these yellowed, crinkly reproductions, reeking of the rust-colored dye that was meant to make them look antique, at a cavernous gift shop near his birthplace. The words carried the force of an incantation—entrancing, if not, to me, thoroughly comprehensible. By the light of the desk lamp I'd read the "Letter to Mrs. Bixby" or the last paragraph of the Second Inaugural, the one beginning "With malice toward none . . ." I memorized the Gettysburg Address and his sublime "Farewell" to the people of Springfield.

What I mean is, I had a great deal of Abraham Lincoln growing up. I was a buff, and I was not alone.

And then I wasn't a buff anymore. The country had undergone a Lincoln boom in the early 1960s, following the 150th anniversary of his birth and coinciding with the centennial celebrations of the Civil War, and not long after the centennial passed my interest in Lincoln waned too. On my bedroom walls Lincoln was replaced by the Beatles, who were themselves replaced in a few years by the languid Susan Dey. *Every Known Pose* sat stoutly on the shelf, unconsulted, passing eventually to a box in my parents' garage, doomed. I don't know what happened to it, or to the sheaf of Lincoln papers. I seldom recalled Springfield or New Salem. Something similar was happening in the country at large, I think. The great historical amnesia, certified and lamented nowadays by professional educators and tut-tutters of all kinds, was just settling in. Fewer and fewer courses in American history were taught less and less frequently, and those that survived were recast as exercises in multicultural special-pleading or litanies of political grievance. The tut-tutters took surveys and compiled the sad data of what has come to be called "historical illiteracy": fully two-thirds of graduating high school seniors can't name the half century in which the Civil War was fought, another third can't identify Thomas Jefferson, 65 percent think Stonewall Jackson was a bass player for the Funkadelics, and so on. Historical tourism, another marker, declined too. The historian Barry Schwartz checked the figures and found a steady decline in attendance at Lincoln sites from the 1960s to the end of the century. More than a million people a year visited New Salem in the mid-sixties, for example; twenty years later the number was reduced by half.

But more than simple amnesia was at work. There was something willful in the forgetting. Americans, particularly the well off and overschooled, were entering a wised-up era, where skepticism about the country, its heroes, and its history was a mark of worldliness and sophistication. The historian C. Vann Woodward called this loss of innocence—if that's what it was—the "fall of the American Adam." Even in Springfield, which clings to Lincoln's memory like a rosary, road signs that directed tourists to the "Lincoln Shrines" were replaced by signs listing the "Lincoln sites." I recall one episode in particular from the 1970s. Talking after class one day, a college friend and I discovered that we had both been buffs as boys, both in thrall to the same Lincoln children's book by the d'Aulaires. I mentioned the climactic scene, in which young Abe witnesses a slave auction and announces: "Someday I'm going to hit that, and I'm going to hit it hard."

"Yeah," my friend said. "What a load of crap." Historians had discovered that the incident was wholly fictitious, he said—a fantasy. In fact Lincoln had been as much a racist as . . . as . . . Jefferson Davis! His official policy, as president, was to ship the slaves back to Africa. The Emancipation Proclamation was a cynical, empty act that didn't free the slaves Lincoln could have freed and "freed"—here his fingers wiggled air quotes—only those that were out of his reach. All this was, he said, common knowledge, and in the face of it I realized that the very thought of being a buff indicated a hopeless lack of sophistication—the mark not only of an ignoramus but of a dweeb. You might as well wear a pocket protector and highwater pants.

Of course, Lincoln didn't fall from the nation's esteem altogether. We can't shake him. Indeed, he's fared better than many other of our traditional heroes. He's still on the penny, for one thing. You can still find discussion groups and clubs devoted to him in many large and midsize cities, and you can subscribe to half a dozen periodicals with names like the *Lincoln Herald* and the *Rail Splitter*. The books continue to pile up. Occasionally one or two of these will prove popular; Doris Kearns Goodwin's Lincoln book was a best seller in 2005 and may even serve as the basis of a movie by Steven Spielberg. But you can't help noticing, in most of the Lincoln books, an air of narrow self-justification—a wan parochialism. Mario Cuomo, the politician, published a polemic called *Why Lincoln Matters*, proving that if Lincoln were alive today his political views would be pretty much indistinguishable from Mario Cuomo's. The gifted journalist Joshua Wolf Shenk, who has struggled with clinical depression, wrote *Lincoln's Melancholy*, proving that the key to Lincoln's achievements was his struggle with clinical depression. Most memorably of all, in 2005, a sex researcher and gay rights activist named C. A. Tripp published *The Intimate World of Abraham Lincoln* in hopes of proving that Lincoln was an active homosexual—the point being, as another activist put it, "He's ours."

For a century or more, generations of Americans were taught to be like Lincoln—forbearing, kind, principled, resolute—but what we've really wanted is for Lincoln to be like us, and this has never been truer than the present day. Lincoln hasn't been forgotten, but he's shrunk. From the enormous figure of the past he's been reduced to a hobbyist's eccentricity, a charming obsession shared by a self-selected subculture, like quilting or Irish step dancing. He has been detached from the national patrimony, if we can be said to have a national patrimony any longer. He is no longer our common possession. That earlier Lincoln, that large Lincoln, seems to be slipping away, a misty figure, incapable of rousing a reaction from anyone but buffs.

Or that's what I had assumed, anyway. Then one wintry morning a while back I fetched the local paper from the front stoop and saw a headline: LINCOLN STATUE STIRS OUTRAGE IN RICHMOND.

I thought: Lincoln? Outrage? And I felt the first stirrings of the fatal question, the question that, once raised, never lets go: "Huh?"

I took off for Richmond a week later. I spent a lot of time there, off and on—long enough to see the statue unveiled and to imbibe the outrage in deep drafts. The chapter that follows this preface, "When Lincoln Came Back to Richmond," is the result. I left Richmond convinced that I was at the beginning of a story rather than at its end. I decided to keep looking for Lincoln.

Richmond did something else to me, too. My time among the Lincoln haters, and the briefer time I spent with the Lincoln operators who had commissioned and financed the statue, made me uncomfortably aware of how little I really knew about Lincoln—and made me wonder, more to the point, how we know what we think we know about Lincoln. How was it that a single historical figure, and a single set of historical facts, could inspire such wildly divergent views, held with equal certitude by seemingly sensible people? So the first place I went looking for Lincoln was in books, and in one book in particular. There I discovered a wild and woolly character—the overworked phrase is perfectly appropriate—who stands as godfather to every Lincoln buff, and to every Lincoln hater, too. Learning the story of Billy Herndon constituted a kind of refresher course in Lincoln Studies, which I happily pass on in chapter 2.

Then I started moving again, and I didn't really stop till I reached the steps of the Lincoln Memorial—and this is where, conveniently enough, I wind up in chapter 10. The curiosity that pushed me along was part personal and part professional, which accounts, I suppose, for the strange commingling in what follows. Lincoln means a lot to me. He means a lot to the country—or he should if he no longer does. By the end of my travels I was more convinced of that truth than I'd been since I was a boy, reading beneath a pool of light in a darkened bedroom on Lincoln Street.

LAND OF LINCOLN

1

WHEN LINCOLN CAME
BACK TO RICHMOND

braham Lincoln, with his son Tad in tow, walked around Richmond, Virginia, one day in April 1865, and if you try to retrace their steps today you won't see much that they saw, which shouldn't be a surprise, of course. The street grid is the same, though, and if you're in the right mood and know what to look for, the lineaments of the earlier city begin to surface, like the outline of a scuttled old scow rising through the shallows of a pond. Among the tangle of freeway interchanges and office buildings you'll come across an overgrown park or a line of redbrick town houses, an unlikely old bell tower or a few churches scattered from block to block, dating to the decades before the Civil War and still giving off vibrations from long ago.

Richmond rests on a group of hills above a bend in the James River. Along the riverbank at the east end of town, where Lincoln began his tour that day, is a long rank of tobacco warehouses, abandoned now, and from behind them the land rises steeply through the commercial district for perhaps half a mile. The Capitol, built from a design by

Thomas Jefferson in the eighteenth century, sits on the crest of the hill, and back of it, seven blocks away, is a Georgian mansion that served as the White House of the Confederacy, official residence of President Jefferson Davis. Walk due west from there, past the parking lots, through the plaza surrounding the new glass-and-concrete convention center, and then head south, and before too long you're back at the riverbank, at the ruins of the Tredegar Iron Works, where the cannon and shot were forged that sustained the South through four years of rebellion.

No one knows for sure whether Lincoln and Tad visited Tredegar, or whether they passed by the ironworks during a carriage ride they took later the same day, but they're there now—so a romantic would say—in the form of a bronze statue. The statue, showing both father and son, was installed in April 2003, at the headquarters of the National Park Service's Richmond Civil War battlefield park, which is housed in Tredegar's surviving buildings. In the months leading to its unveiling, the statue created a controversy that reached far beyond Richmond, beyond the United States even, to become an object of international interest—improbably enough, during that season when the world's attention was diverted by another war looming in Iraq. One Richmond official, traveling through Barbados a few months before the statue arrived, picked up a newspaper on an excursion plane. LINCOLN COMES TO CONFEDERATE CAPITAL, read the headline on the back page.

What made the controversy newsworthy was that there should be a controversy at all. Members of the Richmond establishment—the businessmen, journalists, politicians, rich people, and other well-wired doers of public good, who unanimously supported the statue as both a tourist attraction and a statement of civic virtue—were caught unawares. It came as a surprise to them, as it had to me, that anyone should find a tribute to the sixteenth president so objectionable. Who could object to Lincoln? He seems too big even to have an opinion about. It would be like objecting to the moon.

Yet many people do object, as Richmond's big shots discovered, and these Abephobes, it turns out, are almost always well spoken and well read and, in percentage terms, not much crazier than the general population that tends to accept Lincoln's presence as a fact of life. When I first visited Richmond, a month before the statue's unveiling and two months after I read the story in the *Washington Post*, I went to see Bragdon Bowling, who had been stoking the controversy like a steam engine. Bowling popped up in every story I read. He was gathering petitions, setting up Web sites, pestering politicians with mail and phone calls, and encouraging others to do the same. He had enlisted Thomas DiLorenzo, the author of a recently published anti-Lincoln book called *The Real Lincoln*, to help him gather scholars and authors for a public conference, with the title "Lincoln Reconsidered," to lay out his case as soberly and comprehensively as possible.

This was his sworn duty. Bowling is division commander of the Army of Northern Virginia, Sons of Confederate Veterans, and at those moments when he decides that the heritage of the South is being abused, as it was with the placement of a Lincoln statue in the former capital of the Confederacy, he becomes an agitator ex officio. "It's a responsibility you have," he said. "You've got to try to stop it."

He's a tall man with a scholarly air, due largely to an unruly shock of white hair and the wire spectacles that are always slipping down his nose. I met him in the stripped-down living room of one of the rental properties he owns, in a working-class suburb north of Richmond. He had to repaint the place and it was covered in tarps. "Sometimes you end up renting to people who simply do not know how to keep house," he said. He turned a paint tub upside down and sat on it, and gestured for me to sit on a butt-sprung couch across from him.

Bowling said he was a native of Virginia—but of *Arlington*, Virginia, which many native Virginians consider less a part of the commonwealth than a satellite of Washington, D.C., or worse, liberal Maryland, with all its inevitable corruptions.

"It's a zoo now, but it wasn't so bad then," he said of his hometown. "I got a good education. See, you could still do that in those days. I got taught the usual liberal history, but my teachers were smart people who had high standards. They taught me to think for myself, and that's what I've done.

"Ten years ago I started to learn about my family. I read intensively, everything I could—not just politically correct history but also other history that's been suppressed. That's the way this learning process often starts. My great-grandfather served in the Army of Northern Virginia as a private under General Robert E. Lee. He was at Sharpsburg—Yankees call it Antietam—at Chancellorsville, other places. And like ninety percent of the soldiers who fought for and served the South, he never owned a slave. So—just to show you how the thought process works, for people who are still capable of thinking for themselves—so I thought, well, why is that? If the war is all about slavery, why's he fighting so hard? It didn't fit, you see, with everything I'd been taught about the Civil War. Like all his comrades, my great-grandfather gave everything he had. Why? He did it for his country. The South had bad everything—bad munitions, bad clothing, bad food. But they had the best men. They gave everything they had. And they did not do that to defend slavery."

The war wasn't about slavery for Lincoln, either, Bowling explained. He ticked off the particulars of his indictment of Lincoln. With his generals he invented the concept of Total War, and waged campaigns of unprecedented savagery against noncombatants and private property in the Shenandoah Valley, Sherman's March through Georgia, and elsewhere. He was the father of Big Government, vastly expanding the reach of Imperial Washington in ways unthinkable to the country's founders. The Northern victory was therefore the triumph of a cosmopolitan, commercial culture, controlled by Big Business, over a Southern culture of farms and small towns that asked only to be let alone.

"It was all about power," he said. "Six hundred thousand dead. All so Lincoln and his friends could consolidate their power to tell other people how to live their lives."

What Bowling learned inspired him to join the Sons of Conferdrate Veterans. He rose through the ranks, and it was in his capacity as division commander that he received a phone call one winter evening from a reporter for the *Richmond Times-Dispatch*.

"This reporter says to me, he wants a comment on the statue of Lincoln they're going to put up in Richmond.

"I said, 'Huh?'

"He said, 'Yeah, a fellow named Bob Kline has donated a statue of Lincoln and they're going to put it up down at the visitor center at Tredegar. You got a comment?'

"Well, I knew right away what was going on here. And I told him so. This is the latest move in a scheme to demonize the Confederate soldier. The Park Service, the politicians, the politically correct historians, they've been doing this all across the country, and now they're doing it right here in Richmond."

I said a statue of Lincoln didn't sound to me like it was demonizing anybody.

"To worship Lincoln, right here, is an insult to the Confederate soldier," he said. "There are forty thousand graves of Confederate soldiers in this city and I will defend their honor. You see, unlike the politicians and these others, I'm a student of history. I know what this man Lincoln did to this country. I know what the army under his command did to the South. You ever wonder why there are no statues of Abraham Lincoln in the entire southern half of the United States? It's pretty simple: people here remember what he did. Used to be, everybody here remembered. Now only some of us do."

Three times during our interview Bowling was interrupted with phone calls from reporters, including one from the *Times* of London, seeking comment on one aspect or another of the controversy. He answered them all with a patient repetition of well-rehearsed sound bites.

"It is an insult to the Confederate soldier," he said. After the third call I got up to leave and he walked me outside. The pickup in the drive-way had an old NRA sticker peeling from its bumper: CHARLTON HESTON IS MY PRESIDENT.

"This thing is not over yet," he said. "There are a lot of people upset over this, and they may still have a few tricks up their sleeves."

I asked him if he meant someone was planning to prevent the statue from going in.

"If there's anything violent or what have you that happens, the Sons of Confederate Veterans will have no part in that," he said. "People do feel strongly. But the statue will go in," he said. "Probably." He laughed.

"Unless it doesn't."

While he was alive, Abraham Lincoln was one of the most intensely hated public figures the country has ever known. The minute he got shot, however, things began looking up for him. Colleagues and sub-ordinates who had considered him dithering or imperious in life fell into inconsolable and very public mourning at word of his death. Political enemies who had prayed for his demise suddenly saw a figure of in-violable moral integrity, farseeing competence, unsearchable wisdom. The historian Merrill Peterson, in his great book *Lincoln in American Memory,* cites the instance of Henry Ward Beecher, the abolitionist preacher in Brooklyn who for four years had lacerated Lincoln from his pulpit for timidity and hesitation in the face of Southern barbarism. Then came John Wilkes Booth, and Lincoln was dead, and when the body passed through New York on its way to the cemetery in Spring-field, Illinois, the old blowhard ascended the same pulpit and became the martyred president's foremost eulogist.

"Dead-dead-dead, he yet speaketh," Beecher said. "Four years ago, O Illinois, we took from your midst an untried man, we return him to you a conqueror. Not thine anymore, but the Nation's; not ours, but the world's. Give him place, ye prairies!"

Everyone was ready to give him place. So quickly and so thoroughly did his countrymen exalt him that causists everywhere found it profitable to enlist his memory. A teetotaler in life, for instance, Lincoln became, once he was safely dead-dead-dead, an unsilenceable advocate of national temperance—or so claimed the Drys of the national temperance movement, which distributed millions of copies of a speech he had made on the subject early in his career. The Drys pressed their Lincoln association for decades, until historians employed by Adolphus Busch, partner of Anheuser and father of Budweiser, discovered a yellowing liquor license that had been issued in the 1830s to a small prairie grocer by the name of Abraham Lincoln. Busch made sure that reproductions of Lincoln's license soon hung on the wall of every tavern in America. They stayed there, consoling drinkers, until the tragic triumph of the Drys in 1919.

By that time Lincoln had been dragooned into causes far more implausible than temperance. On the centennial of his birth, in 1909, the nation's leading white supremacist, a senator from Mississippi named James K. Vardaman, made an unironical pilgrimage to Springfield and claimed "the immortal Lincoln" as his inspiration. "My views and his views," he said later on the Senate floor, "are substantially identical." He would have got an argument, probably, from the American Communist party, which throughout the 1930s put on an annual Lincoln-Lenin Day festival and festooned its Harlem headquarters with his likeness.

Americans laid claim to his spiritual life, too. To his friends, Lincoln appeared to be a man of few and ambiguous religious beliefs. He quoted the Bible often but he never joined a church, and when he ran for president every pastor in Springfield pointedly refused to endorse him. Yet when his soul took flight it was lassoed by every Protestant denomination simultaneously. Unitarians took him as their own, and so, later on, did the Christian Scientists, even though the science of divine healing was not revealed to Mary Baker Eddy until a year after Lincoln's death. In 1891, the famed (at the time) seer Nettie Colburn Maynard published a long study called *Was Abraham Lincoln a Spiritualist?* She answered her question with an emphatic yes, describing dinner parties during the Civil War at which the president had witnessed a grand piano rising mysteriously off the floor, with the president himself perched atop it—a rare treat for a teetotaler. One Christian publicist after another saw in Lincoln's life eerie resemblances to the life of Christ: both Jesus and Lincoln were born of carpenters and rose from lowly beginnings, both were storytellers, both were killed on Good Friday, both were saviors—of the world, in one case, of the Union, in the other. And in the days before his death each made a profound journey of mercy: Jesus to Jerusalem, Lincoln to Richmond.

Robert Kline was working out of a large house on Richmond's Main Street, a brick pile built in the Federal style a decade or two before the rebellion. It lies just far enough west to have escaped the flames that leveled the old downtown in April 1865. A brass nameplate next to the front door identifies it as the headquarters of the United States Historical Society, the company Kline started thirty years ago, after a career in public relations and real estate.

Hairsplitters might complain that the name is a little misleading; Kline's society does not have members or hold conferences in the manner of more conventional historical societies. It is instead "a private nonprofit educational organization," according to its literature, "dedicated to fostering increased awareness and appreciation of America's culture and history." It does its fostering by making and selling "collectibles"—small, heavy things forged of pewter or brass, mounted on polished strips of cherry or little rectangles of marble—that bear a strong resemblance to what many in the nonprofit world call knickknacks.

A first-floor conference room, where I waited for my interview with Mr. Kline, serves as a kind of showroom for the society's handiwork. Collectibles hung from walls and stood in ranks on every available flat surface. The overflow was gathered in piles on the floor. All stages of American history were represented. There were miniatures of World War II submarines, minesweepers, destroyers, and PT boats; gilt-rimmed plates featuring famous American homes—Monticello, Graceland—dappled with sunlight in sylvan settings; reproductions of pewter tankards designed by Paul Revere. President Kennedy was there as a doll delivering his inaugural address, one hand tucked in his coat pocket, the other thrust confidently toward the future.

There were replicas of swords—one worn by George Washington at his inauguration, another surrendered by Cornwallis at Yorktown—and reproductions of famous pistols, and mounted replicas of "famous canes," and tiny cannons adorned with plaques. There was enough stained glass to fill the windows at Sainte-Chapelle, if it were suddenly taken over by Wal-Mart: familiar, multicolored scenes from Norman Rockwell and from the life of Christ, Calvary next to Valley Forge next to the parting of the Red Sea next to Tom Sawyer and the whitewashed fence, plus a spookily detailed rendering of the Elvis postage stamp, Washington on the Delaware, and cozy Christmas scenes. Dolls of Patrick Henry, FDR, Chuck Yeager, and Clara Barton queued up beside a three-dimensional tableau of the angels hovering over the stable at Bethlehem.

I was straining to see who was in the cradle when Kline appeared, wearing a sky-blue suit with a wide tie striped in shades of gray. "This is what the U.S. Historical Society does," he said, sweeping his arm across the room with evident pride. He's a tall man, with a prominent nose, and very slender; Lincolnesque in stature, almost, though his hair is white now and thin as silk. His voice is soft and so is his handshake.

We sat down at a conference table. "This Lincoln idea first came to me twenty years ago," he said. "I had already lived here for many years, knew the city well, and loved it. And I thought: Lincoln in Richmond! What an event! What a symbol!" His voice, though frail, still conveys his unmistakable enthusiasm. "The visit to Richmond should be a big thing in the history of our country—bigger than it is. It stands for peace, for reconciliation, all those things that we need more of. So I brought the concept to Virginius Dabney."

In Richmond there are few weightier names to drop than that of Dabney, now deceased but for forty years a Southern historian of note and, as editor of the *Times-Dispatch*, a legendary defender of the honor of the Confederacy. A *nihil obstat* from Dabney, under normal circumstances, would go far in protecting anyone against charges of carpetbaggery.

"Dabney thought it was a wonderful idea, too," Mr. Kline went on. "From there I went to elected officials, off and on over the years. A year or so ago I went to our lieutenant governor, Tim Kaine, and he suggested the Park Service might be interested in a memorial to Lincoln's visit. And indeed they were very enthusiastic. And now here we are. Sometimes I can't believe it's really about to happen—if we can just get through the next few weeks."

When I brought up the controversy—the petitions and protests—Mr. Kline's enthusiasm seeped away. He had the look of someone who didn't know what hit him. "Sure, of course, we thought perhaps a few diehards might object here or there. But nothing like this . . . this ugliness."

He made a gesture toward the window. Out on the street a well-fed fellow in a black T-shirt and low-slung Relaxed Fit jeans was holding a hand-painted placard: "Lincoln = War Criminal." He was a holdover from larger demonstrations that had been held outside the society's headquarters in previous weeks. None drew more than twenty demonstrators, according to news accounts. Still, twenty good old boys doing the rebel yell outside your window can be unsettling.

"You should see the mail," Mr. Kline went on. "And my e-mail, oh my. Accusing me of everything they can think of. And now, of course, it's reached the newspaper. Anytime a businessman sees the word 'impropriety' and his own name in a headline—even if it says 'cleared of improprieties'—well, it's just not good, is it?"

Together with city and Park Service officials, Mr. Kline announced plans for the statue at a press conference and the controversy began at once, with that first phone call from that first reporter to Brag Bowling. In keeping with the way public disputes play out nowadays, the air was soon thick with motive-mongering, personal vituperation, and allegations of criminality. An anonymous Web site appeared, accusing Kline of exploiting public assets—the Tredegar visitors' center—for financial gain. This in turn generated hundreds of letters to Virginia newspapers, and then to the commonwealth attorney general, demanding an investigation for possible fraud. Some Sons persuaded a local congressman, Virgil Goode, to ask the Park Service itself to see whether the society's activity was legitimate.

The particulars of the accusations against Kline, the Park Service, and local officials—all of whom were supposedly acting in self-dealing collusion—were never made completely clear. At the heart of it all was the odd means by which the relevant parties had agreed to finance the statue, an arrangement that Kline said was not unusual in the collectibles business. The society would commission the statue and pay for its design, forging, and transportation to Richmond and then give it to the Park Service free of charge. To recover its money, the society would sell miniatures of the statue as a collector's item, with prices ranging from $125 to $875. Solicitations were already being made by direct mail and over the Internet, at the Tredegar gift shop, and through an agreement with the Virginia Historical Society.

"We're going to be out of pocket a considerable sum," Mr. Kline told me. "And we're assuming all the risk, for goodness sake." Already, he said, the statue had cost the society $225,000, and sales thus far had totaled only around $40,000.

To the Sons this sounded like profiteering, but the attorney general, the commonwealth's corporation counsel, and the Park Service all said they found nothing improper in the deal. Still, simple arithmetic showed that Mr. Kline wouldn't have to unload too many mini-Lincolns to cover his costs. I asked him what he was going to do if he sold so many that he had money left over.

"Oh my, wouldn't that be nice?" he said. "Well, we'll want to with-hold some funds for a reserve for future projects—we're always coming up with projects. And then any money beyond that we'll give to the Richmond Peace Education Center, a wonderful group of people here in town. They stand for a lot of things Lincoln stood for. Peace. Understanding. Their specialty is conflict resolution."

As it happened, I'd already run across the Peace Education Center during my time in Richmond. In the days leading up to the war in Iraq they had taken to the streets downtown in peace demonstrations they called "Women in Black." Stuck in traffic jams, I'd watch through the windshield as the women in black hoisted signs reading "Jail Bush, Not Saddam" and "Disarm U.S., Not Iraq." It seemed odd to fund a paci-fist group with money from the sale of little statues representing America's greatest, and fiercest, wartime president, but before I could say anything Mr. Kline took me over to a shelf.

"And here it is," he said, holding up a bronze miniature. He gave me a high-wattage smile. Lincoln was ready to take his place in the pantheon. Santa. Jesus. Chuck Yeager. Elvis. Abe.

No one knows why Lincoln came to Richmond. On April 4, 1865, the correspondent from the *New York Herald,* William Merriam, filed a report with a Richmond dateline.

"No incident of all this drama"—he meant the four years of civil war—"will so attract and fix the attention of the American people and the civilized world as the appearance to-day in the city of Richmond—erased capital of the infernal traitors—of Abraham Lincoln."

Unlike most predictions from journalists, this one proved to be al-most accurate. Other memorable episodes from the Civil War are more packed with incident, more gripping in their violence or pathos. In most full-dress histories, however, Lincoln's visit to Richmond stands as the perfect punctuation at the close of the grand narrative, a lingering grace note in the coda of the war, a final eloquent gesture made by the martyr before he leaves the stage. Lincoln in Richmond, wrote James McPherson in *Battle Cry of Freedom,* "produced the most unforgettable scenes of this unforgettable war."

Yet why did he come? In their ten-volume biography of Lincoln, his secretaries John Nicolay and John Hay described the visit in the grandest terms: "Never in the history of the world did the head of a mighty nation enter the chief city of the insurgents in such humbleness." But even they didn't hazard a guess to explain why Lincoln would risk his own safety, and that of his son, in such an excursion. Mere curiosity is a plausible motive; Lincoln always had a fascination with military maneuvers, and the prospect of seeing the vanquished capital might have proved too much to resist.

The war was in its final hours. He had left Washington a week before to visit Ulysses S. Grant at City Point, Virginia, a river port thirty miles downstream of the Confederate capital, from which vantage he could watch at close range the final progress of federal forces. Dislodged from their defenses at Petersburg, south of Richmond, Robert E. Lee's ragged troops zigzagged their way west, in a final attempt to twist free of the enemy. On Sunday, April 2, Jefferson Davis ordered the government to evacuate the capital. That night detonation squads spread along the waterfront, torching warehouses filled with tobacco and munitions. From across the James River a northerly wind picked up the flames and carried them beyond the warehouses. By daybreak, when Union troops arrived to extinguish the blaze, more than half the business district was gone.

From City Point the next evening, Lincoln telegraphed Edwin Stanton, his secretary of war: "It is certain now that Richmond is in our hands. I think I will go there tomorrow." And to calm the skittish Stanton, who fretted always for Lincoln's safety, he added: "I will take care of myself."

Dozens of armed guards were assigned to make sure that he did. Early Tuesday morning they loaded onto a flotilla that included the *River Queen,* the steamer carrying the presidential party of Lincoln,

Tad, and his guide, the naval commander David Porter. They quickly ran into trouble. The Confederates had sown the James with mines and other snares, and one by one the boats ran aground or were abandoned. By the time they reached Richmond, Lincoln and his party had transferred to a scow, with fewer than a dozen marines to row them ashore. They made landfall at Rocketts Landing, on the east end of the charred city, a couple of miles from the Capitol grounds.

For an event so freighted with history, whose symbolic importance was grasped by its witnesses even as it happened, we know for certain remarkably little about Lincoln's time in Richmond. That hasn't kept later generations from speaking about it with great conviction. For Lincoln's admirers the visit is further evidence of their man's largeheartedness. For his detractors it demonstrates a conqueror's arrogance.

No photographs were taken of Lincoln in Richmond, and no sketches made from life by the magazine artists who sometimes appeared serendipitously at key moments of the Civil War. The most complete eyewitness accounts are from the embellishing and unreliable pens of Northern newspapermen, like Merriam, who followed the Union troops into the Confederate capital. Their accounts differ in specifics and vary in plausibility. They disagree even on what time of day Lincoln came ashore. One episode, first put on paper by Admiral Porter in a memoir published twenty years later, is invariably included in histories that mention the visit, in both plain and enhanced versions. Lincoln steps off the barge at Rocketts and is spotted at once by an "aged Negro."

"Bress de Lord, dere is the great messiah!" the old man is quoted as saying, kneeling before his savior and sounding suspiciously like a dispatcher for the Amos and Andy cab company. "He's bin in my heart fo' long years an' he's cum at las' to free his children from bondage! I know dat I am free, for I seen Father Abraham. Glory, Hallelujah!"

Lincoln's response is a mouthful, but it's worth quoting entire, if only to show how quickly the unlikely congeals into fact, when circumstances are right, and then fact into myth.

"Don't kneel to me," Lincoln is said to have said. "That is not right. You must kneel to God only, and thank Him for the liberty you will hereafter enjoy. I am but God's humble instrument; but you may rest assured that as long as I live no one shall put a shackle on your limbs, and you shall have all the rights which God has given to every other citizen of this Republic."

We do not climb out on a limb, historiographically, if we conclude that this quote, recorded with stenographic precision, is baloney. The same can be said of several other episodes reported then and later in the Yankee newspapers. No military escort or even a carriage greeted Lincoln at Rocketts—it's unclear why—and so he set off by foot, with his son in hand, on a two mile trek to the White House of the Confederacy, which then served as occupation headquarters but had also, only thirty-six hours before, been Davis's home. Along the route Lincoln stopped at the notorious Libby Prison, emptied at last of the Union officers who had suffered there for half the war. One correspondent told his readers he'd seen Lincoln linger at the building with "tears pouring down his cheeks," though he must have been the only witness, since no other account mentions this touching detail.

Rising up the hill from the wharves, acre after acre of the city still guttered and smoked. And as Lincoln and his party made their way through the blackened timbers of the business district, word of his presence spread and a crowd gathered around him—jubilant blacks, mostly, freedmen who were now freshly minted citizens of liberated Richmond. On some facts, all accounts agree. The president's bodyguard—the dozen blue-coated marines from the barge—walked with him in a phalanx, alert to sniper fire or violence from the crowd. There was neither. Only women and children and the elderly were left among the city's white residents, and they stayed shuttered in their houses, watching Lincoln pass from behind parted curtains. When he reached the White House just beyond the hill where the Capitol sits, the president found an elated crowd of Union officers spilling out from the mansion onto the front porch and into the back garden. Much of their elation was traceable to the wine and spirits cellar they had discovered below the house. Lincoln climbed onto the porch and moved into the cool of the parlor. Ever the teetotaler, he asked for a glass of water.

After lunch the president received callers. The most significant of these was Judge John Campbell, the highest-ranking civilian left in Richmond, who presented Lincoln with an offer to call the Virginia legislature back to session, whereupon, Judge Campbell said, it would vote to rejoin the Union. Lincoln liked the idea but nothing ever came of it, since Lee's surrender a few days later made it moot. After his meetings, the president and Tad embarked on a carriage ride around town. Where the carriage took them isn't known, though some accounts record a tour of the Capitol, and Lincoln wandering the chambers through drifts of Confederate currency, now worthless. Two accounts suggest he gave a speech to the freedmen on the Capitol grounds, at the foot of a statue of Washington on horseback, though if he did no one reported what he said.

What we know of this momentous visit is laced with such empty spaces, and into them later generations poured their own views of the great warrior-statesman who had spent a handful of hours in the capital of his vanquished enemy. The visit with Judge Campbell is taken as the primary evidence that Lincoln traveled to Richmond to hasten the end of the war. But it was Campbell, not Lincoln, who requested the meeting, and Lincoln did little to follow through on its implications. "He came as a friend," wrote an early historian, "to alleviate sorrow and suffering—to rebuild what had been destroyed." There's not much evidence for or against this proposition. The wife of George Pickett, the major general who had led his men in the charge at Gettysburg almost two years before, later wrote that Lincoln interrupted his tour to stop at her town house. Lincoln had been a distant acquaintance of Pickett before the war. Mrs. Pickett greeted the president at the door, she said in her account, and Lincoln admired her new baby, even planted it with a kiss, and briefly exchanged pleasantries about friends in common. To future generations this vignette has illustrated Lincoln's thoughtfulness and his commitment to letting bygones be bygones, but no one knows whether it's true.

The president and his son spent that night in a boat at anchor on the James. The next day they sailed down to City Point, and from there to Washington.

"He seemed the very personification of supreme satisfaction," a friend remarked when Lincoln returned to his own White House. Ten days later he belonged to the ages.

"Victors write the history," Brag Bowling was telling me, "and when you've got a dumbed-down country like we do now, it's not so hard to make this man appear to be something he clearly wasn't. But we're going to start to correct the record—right here, right now."

We were standing in the lobby of the John Marshall Hotel on a Saturday morning, greeting guests as they arrived for the "Lincoln Reconsidered" conference. The Marshall was put up not long after World War I, and it's still the tallest building in Richmond's old downtown, though there's not much competition. Within days of the conflagration in April 1865, downtown was on the mend, and before too long terraced rows of shops and town houses were spreading across the hilltops above the James. Recent decades have been unkind, however, and the Marshall stands now at the edge of a vast acreage of empty storefronts and parking lots, enlivened here and there by random glimmers of commercial life—a hot dog stand, a shoe repair shop, a check cashing service. Especially on a Saturday morning, downtown gives off a defeated air. If someone decided to burn it down again I don't think anybody would mind.

The Marshall was struggling to keep business up. A hardy band of civic-minded entrepreneurs undertook a bottom-to-top renovation a few years ago, working their way up, story by story, and from what I could see, snooping around, they had decided to catch their breath after the third or fourth floor. Our Lincoln conference took place on the

mezzanine, in the old ballroom, site of generations of Richmond co-
tillions and comings-out. It had been freshly painted in a cheerless taupe,
and the hotel itself was weirdly quiet. The conference was its only activity. Bowling told me that roughly three hundred people had regis-
tered for "Lincoln Reconsidered," drawn from more than a dozen states,
and none seemed to mind the drowsy, languid air of the setting. For
even with modernity's depredations downtown Richmond is hallowed
ground, rich beyond price with associations from the sacred past. Sitting in the Marshall we were only two blocks from Robert E. Lee's town
house, where Mrs. Lee had paced the floor in worry over her absent
husband and sons, and eight blocks from the White House of the Confederacy, where Lincoln had met with Judge Campbell, and three blocks
from the Capitol, where Davis had struggled in vain to stanch his
country's bleeding, and just around the corner from the Presbyterian
church where Stonewall Jackson himself had once served as an elder,
before his martyrdom at Chancellorsville.

Folding tables covered in white linen were set out in the lobby, a long
one for registration, many others heaped with stuff for sale. One booklet ("Arm Yourself with the Truth") had conveniently assembled in a
single, at-the-ready volume all of Lincoln's least attractive remarks on
the subject of race, such as his outburst in the Lincoln-Douglas debates:
"Negro equality, fudge!"—a comment famous among the Sons and
their compatriots, less frequently quoted elsewhere. Next to this stack
was a poster for another Lincoln book: "You think our problems began
in the sixties? You're right: The 1860s!" Said another poster: "What if
everything you knew about Lincoln were false?"

There were stacks of rare videos and audio tapes. "*The Real Lincoln* Home Study Program" had been designed for homeschoolers and
college students. "You read a chapter of Dr. DiLorenzo's ground-
breaking book," the salesman said, "then you watch this video in which
Dr. DiLorenzo goes over the key points and expands his discussion in
new and surprising ways. When you're done with this aspect, you turn
to our *Real Lincoln* home workbook." He ran his hand over a cream-

colored folder from which Lincoln's face stared out, looking unhappy. "The workbook is where you test and hone your knowledge, with questions prepared especially for that purpose," the salesman went on. "Then you return to the book, then the video lecture, and back to the workbook. You see how it works. It's a system," he said, "and we do grant discounts for multiple orders."

Round tables filled the ballroom. At each seat was a pad of paper and a pen, for note taking. These got heavy use as the day wore on. The conference-goers were a studious, earnest group, hungry for information. In certain respects, people who really, really hate Abraham Lincoln get a bad rap. The general view of them—when they are acknowledged at all—is of grizzled hillbillies, a few steps out from the hills and hollers, chewing straw and chain-smoking 'boro Reds. This is inaccurate, in the main. The conference-goers gathered at the Marshall were almost exclusively male, of course, and white, but with their affable demeanor and dress—the suburban weekender's uniform of expensive sneakers, pastel polo shirts stretched smooth across the belly, khaki trousers pleated in front and cut generously at the rear—they could have been airlifted from the clubhouse of any community golf course in America.

Together they bowed their heads when, only a few minutes behind schedule, an Anglican priest rose to give the invocation. "We ask your aid, oh Heavenly Father," he said, in a buttery voice, "in prevailing over the liberal historians who would distort our history and destroy our heritage." Then Bowling introduced himself. He explained to the audience, as he had to me, how appalled he'd been to learn of the Lincoln statue, and how it had inspired him to organize the conference. "So I turned to Dr. DiLorenzo and asked for his help in taking an objective look at Abraham Lincoln," he said. "In the face of so many facts, we cannot allow this myth to continue."

Bowling's remarks were followed, unexpectedly, by a musical interlude, the national debut of a music video made just a week before, as a public protest against Lincoln's uninvited return to the capital of the Confederacy. "Goin' Back to Richmond" is a lament in a minor key, written and recorded by a man from Fort Myers, Florida, named Robert Lloyd. The lights came down and in the front of the ballroom a TV screen brightened to a silver glow. From the speakers came Lloyd's baritone, trembling with anger and regret. "I hear the voice of Jackson," Lloyd sang, "calling out my name / 'Don't let ole Dixie writhe in shame / Don't let our children go on wonderin' / Did their fathers die in vain?'"

The video was filmed in sepia tones, with a herky-jerky handheld camera, the better to suggest antiquity. There were no slithery dancers in it, as in other music videos, no preening guitar players; just old photos of Richmond before and after the fire, along with dour images of Jefferson Davis, Robert E. Lee, and John C. Calhoun. These bled into one another, then faded in and out, in the tempo of a dirge. Occasionally footage of Civil War reenactors filled the screen. They fired their long guns, scampered in mock panic across open fields, and pretended to get shot, crumpling horribly before the camera and rolling their eyes heavenward.

"I'll join hands with my brothers," Lloyd continued, "And guard this precious land / To you, Mr. Lincoln, we take our stand / You're still not welcome, now or ever / At least to this loyal Southern man."

When it was over, the man sitting next to me shook his head, much moved, and said, "Whoa." His first name was Robert. He asked that I not use his last name, because he works for the federal government in Washington. "There's a lot of political correctness up there," he said. "They don't need to know about my interest in Mr. Lincoln."

His manner was quick, energetic, and very friendly. Before long it became clear that he, like every other Son I've spoken to, had read deeply, if not widely, in the nearly limitless literature of the Civil War and its aftermath. During breaks in the conference Robert explained some of what he'd most recently learned. "Objective historians," he told me, now realized that racism had played a much smaller role in Southern history than previously thought.

"You know why Southern legislators enacted Jim Crow laws after the war?" he asked.

I said I could guess.

"Well," he said with a friendly smile, "you'd be wrong."

Southerners accepted Jim Crow only with the greatest reluctance, he told me. Segregation was a response to demands from Northern businessmen following the Civil War.

"The South desperately needed their commerce," Robert explained, "but the Yankees wouldn't do any business down here unless the African Americans were kept segregated. The Yankees wouldn't have anything to do with the black man. And they call the Southerners racist?"

He sat back and folded his arms, case closed. Lincoln haters are touchy on the subject of race; most of them don't want their Abephobia tied in any way to negrophobia, and in fact they are delighted, for this reason and for reasons of general perversity, to confound expectations by condemning Lincoln as a racist. In the same way, it is important for them to assert that the war Lincoln won was not about slavery. During another break, Robert grabbed a fresh piece of notepaper and diagrammed an econometric model that he had lately unearthed from an academic journal of political economy. It demonstrated, he told me, an ironclad law of social relations: When disparities in income and productivity levels between one region of a nation and another region grow too great, the inequality becomes unsustainable, and the result, as night follows day, is civil war.

"It's happened time and again throughout world history, to small countries and big countries and young countries and old countries," he said. Just such a disequilibrium had developed in the United States in the 1850s. He tapped the diagram with the extra-sharp point of his pencil. "Right here is the cause of your War Between the States."

I don't know how many of the conference-goers would have agreed with Robert on the specifics, but the thrust of his argument—that the war was about brute economic power and the allocation of political spoils—is a common theme among his fellows; so common indeed that it should lay to rest another misconception about the Lincoln haters: that they are romantics, pie-eyed with nostalgia for the lost agrarian South of moonbeams and magnolias. It's true that under the gruff exterior of many a Son there beats a romantic heart, but under that romantic heart you will find another, even gruffer interior. The Abephobes see themselves as hardheaded realists, proud to have shaken off the self-serving myths of American history. It is the rest of the country that has succumbed to sentimental delusions, specifically the syrupy legend of Father Abraham, kindly hero to the downtrodden, lover of freedom, and emancipator of the enslaved. "All the Father Abraham stuff—it's a fraud," Robert told me. "You know who's a big Lincoln buff? Mario Cuomo. All the left-wingers are. Tells you all you need to know."

The theme of fraudulence, of a comprehensive scam spanning decades, deluding even most contemporary Southerners, is the theme of *The Real Lincoln*, and Thomas DiLorenzo's clean, uncomplicated articulation of it has ensured his place at the head of what the Lincoln haters call "our movement." *The Real Lincoln* was one of the top-selling selections of the Conservative Book Club over the past ten years—which is more impressive than it sounds; this is one book club that knows how to move units. A professor at Loyola College in Maryland, DiLorenzo is an economist by training and a libertarian by conviction.

"I'd read a lot of economic history, of course, and I started to read a lot about Lincoln as sort of a hobby," he told me. "And it became clear to me how deeply Lincoln was involved in the Whig economic program of the early nineteenth century. The agenda was to centralize political and economic power—government subsidies for big business like the railroads and banks, tariffs for favored industries, what we call 'corporate welfare' today. It was really all Lincoln cared about. It's what he built his political career around. He was a railroad lawyer, a rich one. Certainly he wasn't interested in slavery. By his own admission, he didn't even make it an issue till 1854."

The pattern of DiLorenzo's awakening is common among the Lincoln haters. They all tell a similar story. Having inherited a vague but intensely admiring account of Lincoln in their youth, they were startled when they learned that some of it—at least—wasn't entirely accurate, and before long the whole edifice came tumbling down. The more DiLorenzo learned about Lincoln—and discovered, for example, that Lincoln was never an abolitionist, and that he expressed skepticism about civil rights for blacks, and that he had in fact advocated the colonization of freedmen to Central America—the firmer he grew in his belief that "there's this huge con job at the heart of our history."

"This man was not the saint I was taught about when I was going to public school in western Pennsylvania," he said. "And it started to dawn on me, the whole Whig platform, all these centralized policies that they hadn't been able to implement by democratic means in the first seventy years of our history—they were all implemented within the first six months of the war.

"And then, once the war began, it was about consolidating and using that power. Lincoln shut down hundreds of newspapers that dared to criticize him. He suspended habeas corpus. He had at least eighteen thousand Americans—the estimates vary—he had them thrown into jail on the flimsiest pretexts, or with no pretext at all. He clearly detested blacks and used slavery as a pretext to grab power. He was the exact opposite of what we've been taught."

DiLorenzo walked through the Marshall like a celebrity. In the ballroom and in the hallways, during breaks and over lunch, admirers formed queues to grab a word with him. But there was more at work than simple admiration. "One of the purposes of a conference like this," he told me, "is to explain how we got to where we are today." The audience was eager to learn about the past not for the past's sake, but to better understand what was happening to them, and to the country, right here and now. For a paid-up Lincoln despiser, history is a living thing. The pulses from the past still vibrate. The list of horribles rolling out from the 1860s to the present day is comprehensive: the income tax, affirmative action, urbanization and the death of agrarian communities, the erosion of local authority in the face of federal power, the dissolution of family ties, the twin eruptions of gigantism in Big Business and Big Government—these are for starters. Donald Livingston, a professor of philosophy at Emory University and a well-known scholar on the work of David Hume, gave a dazzling presentation tracing Lincoln's corrosive effects through our history. "Americans are morally deficient for never having considered the evil of launching the bloodiest war of the nineteenth century merely to preserve Northern political and economic domination of the continent," he said. "That failure has kept us from moral and political maturity."

Clyde Wilson, another star of the movement and a professor of history at the University of South Carolina, worked in an ad hominem mode. National myths, said Wilson, are a necessary part of history and its instruction. When Parson Weems published his fairy tale about George Washington and the cherry tree, he was illustrating a truth for the consumption of children—that Washington's life was motivated by a commitment to telling the truth. "But the Lincoln myth," Wilson said, "fails to make a solid connection with what really happened, to draw a connection between what he did and what his supporters say he did."

The real story of Lincoln's life, Wilson said, was "shabby and tawdry." The illegitimate son of a servant girl and a shiftless, no-account father whom he despised, Lincoln grew up to be a terrible father himself, spoiling his children and ignoring their mother. Some evidence—Mary Todd's accelerating mental deterioration, for example—suggested he might have given his wife syphilis. He had no intellectual interests other than winning legal cases and amassing personal wealth. He sought office primarily to reward political cronies and big business clients. Clearly he had a messiah complex, but he was a messiah with no purpose beyond his own aggrandizement; he told dirty jokes. When at last he died, one of his pallbearers bragged that no blacks or Jews were allowed at his funeral. By contrast, it's just a simple fact that at the funerals of the Confederacy's vice president, Alexander Stephens, and of the great Southern general Nathan Bedford Forrest, hundreds of blacks were welcomed. . . .

The ventilation in the ballroom was very poor. At lunchtime sandwiches of uncertain vintage were laid out for the guests in an adjoining meeting room, along with little packets of potato chips and lukewarm cans of soda pop. Politely as I could I turned aside Robert's invitation to join him for lunch and went out to get some air. Downtown was deserted. I walked several blocks past empty storefronts looking for someplace to eat. After a while I stumbled on an indoor food court, tucked next to the new convention center, recently opened on the outskirts of the old downtown.

That Saturday, I quickly discovered, the convention center was playing host to the annual meeting of the Virginia Association for Early Childhood Education. It's a teachers' union, and the members were noisily queuing up at Sbarro's Pizza, Subway, TCBY Yogurt, Taco Bell, Great Steak and Potato Company, KFC—America's great groaning board of starch, sugar, fat, and salt. Nearly all of them were women, and they formed a near-perfect racial mix, a demographer's dream, an ethnic rainbow, a gorgeous mosaic—whatever the going metaphor is. Everyone wore a name badge decorated with tiny handprints and silhouettes of somersaulting toddlers. Their lunch hour had followed a morning of breakout sessions, workshops, and seminars, with titles like "Banning Superhero Play: Fiddlesticks or Chopsticks" and "Being a

Guide by the Side, Not a Sage on the Stage." They looked very busy and very happy.

I got a sandwich from Subway and took a seat at one of the round metal tables. Normally I don't like crowds and noise but for the moment I didn't mind. Brilliant sunshine flooded into the food court through a skylight far overhead. Rainbow arcs of balloons had been set out, left to sway in the breeze from the air-conditioning vents, lending color to the commotion. The tables filled up quickly, and two women asked if they could join me. They told me they were "educators," which is, of course, the new word for "teachers." I said I was in Richmond for a conference on Abraham Lincoln and American history. They did their best to look interested.

"History!" one of them said. "Isn't that fascinating!"

Her friend nodded and chewed her slice of pizza thoughtfully. "History can be such a learning experience," she said.

We had a nice chat. It was only with some trouble that I forced myself to get up and walk back to the Marshall, and not merely because the sole of my sneaker was stuck in a puddle of coagulating Dr. Pepper.

I didn't want to go back because I was thinking, *Those guys say they don't like Lincoln, and they don't, but this is what they really hate, this right here. The country turned into something they don't like, and they think Lincoln's responsible, and they'll never forgive him for it.*

The unveiling of the new statue was set for April 5, a Saturday. I drove back down to Richmond the day before to meet up with David Leak, a Son who had attended the Lincoln conference at the Marshall. He had agreed to show me around town—"to see some of the sites that'll let you know what we're about," he said—and help me kill time before the ceremonies began Saturday morning.

Leak is in his late fifties, stout and balding, a banjo picker by trade. This sunny afternoon he was dressed casually, as he usually is, in baggy khakis, a purple polo shirt, and, both as a sporty touch and a shield from the sun, a wide-brimmed Panama hat. I met him outside the house he shares with his mother. He lives in what Richmonders call the Fan, a picturesque district of Victorian row houses, all red brick with white trim, set along wide boulevards that angle out from downtown and run westward for thirty blocks or more. Each house has a columned front porch and a small square of lawn edged in boxwood. The dogwood and azaleas were in full bloom.

I complimented him on the neighborhood.

"Charmin', isn't it?" he said. Leak is native to the capital, and his accent is deep and rich. "It's a wonder"—a *wondah*—"it's been preserved as well as it has. But Richmond is that way. To the naked eye a lot of things look like they'll never change."

The first stop on our tour was the Capitol grounds—notable for its statuary, just as the guidebooks say. The magnificent equestrian statue of Washington, where Lincoln may or may not have made an address to the freedmen, still towers over the lawn where it drops away toward the river. Leak nodded at it, then pointed me farther along the Capitol driveway to a statue of Stonewall Jackson, which sits in a prominent position—right next to a statue of his doctor.

I was saying, "They built a statue of Stonewall Jackson's doctor?" when Leak had me stop the car.

"You see old Stonewall standing there," he said. "Very impressive, isn't he? Well, here's the plan. They're gonna start on a renovation of this place real soon. Redo everything, make it good as new. However!" He raised a chubby finger. "There will be a shortage of toilet facilities for those visiting the Capitol. So honest to God, they've announced they're going to line the port-a-potties up right along here in front of this statue so no young innocent will have to be exposed to the horrible sight of Stonewall Jackson. Now whole busloads of schoolchildren will be able to tour their state Capitol and take a piss on the hero of Chancellorsville, all in the same day."

We drove back through the old downtown, past doorways heaped in trash and dim human figures huddled beneath blankets. "When I was a boy people would come from all over to shop here," Leak said. "Department stores, theaters, candy shops, haberdashers. Look at it now. Anyone who tries to stand up for tradition, for the past, when we do that, they call us 'alienated.' Well, yes, I guess I am alienated from this."

As we drove along, Leak quoted Tocqueville on the nature of "democratic consensus," Allen Tate on the character of the Southern imagination, and the art critic Robert Hughes on the value of representational, as opposed to abstract, art. Everything he said was interesting, but his observations were embedded in a long patter of complaint. I saw before too long that he was taking me on a grievance tour—perhaps the only way he could see his hometown, now that it had suffered so many indignities.

He told me he had been raised to revere history, but history, for him, had only taken on a political cast in the past fifteen years or so. In 1993, the city council unilaterally decided to place a statue of the tennis star Arthur Ashe, a Richmond native, on Monument Avenue, the miles-long boulevard dotted with memorial statues of Confederate heroes. Monument Avenue is Via Dolorosa for Southern nostalgists.

"It was the gratuitousness of it that bothered me," he said. "There was just no call for it. And then they tried to stop a mural of Robert E. Lee from going up down by the river. They were getting up some kind of tourist destination down there, a river walk, and Lee's was just one portrait in a gallery—a perfectly politically correct gallery of women, blacks, liberals, everyone else. You could have Frederick Douglass. Fine. They had Lincoln, of course. Got to have Lincoln. But not Lee. Oh no. Couldn't have Lee."

Leak took to writing letters to the editor, attended rallies, and eventually joined the Sons in their long-running guerrilla war with the city establishment. "The powers that control the city are like the powers that control the country: they cannot stand diversity," he said. "They say they love it, but really they cannot tolerate it. They want everyone to live like them, think like them, talk like them. They want everyone to honor *their* heroes, respect *their* values. Meanwhile they do everything they can to eliminate ours."

The city of his childhood had vanished. "The newspaper is run by Yankees. The businessmen are spineless. Cultural Marxists control all the major institutions. They're very cosmopolitan, these people. They have no sense of being rooted in a single place—to them Richmond is just this town they've moved to. They've been everywhere, and they're from nowhere."

He told me he'd recently seen a flyer from the city's Valentine Richmond History Center, sponsoring a "Lincoln Walk" in honor of the new statue.

"Here you've got the oldest, most revered museum in this city. They're just falling all over themselves to commemorate the great man's visit. They want the citizens of Richmond to follow in the footsteps of the American Caesar, to ooh and aah: Oh, he walked here! Oh, he stopped there! You ask: How can they honor a man who did everything in his power to destroy them? I'll tell you how. They've taught southerners to hate their history. All right. But after the history is gone, after their respect for their ancestors is gone, what's left? There's nothing to replace it with."

He pointed me down North Boulevard, another grand thoroughfare, past Battle Abbey, the bunkerlike headquarters of the United Daughters of the Confederacy. "You'd think they'd have some kind of Confederate flag flying, wouldn't you? You see a Confederate flag?"

I scanned the marble face of the building and its complicated foliage. I didn't see a flag.

"Look close. It's there."

I gave up.

"Drive around here," he said, and I pulled the car up at an odd angle where we could peer into a copse of trees—and sure enough, tucked behind a towering pine that almost precisely blocked it from the street was a Confederate battle flag, hanging limp from a pole trimmed with gold. "They moved the flagpole a while back," Leak said. "Had to get it out of public view! Can't expose the children! Even at the headquarters of the United Daughters of the Confederacy."

We drove farther down, past the Virginia Historical Society, where the building's original inscription, "Confederate Memorial Institute," has been covered over by a huge banner, and then through Hollywood Cemetery, where more than ten thousand Confederate soldiers are buried, and where, at Jefferson Davis's grave, the Sons were planning to hold a counterdemonstration against the Lincoln statue the next day. Leak said he wouldn't be at the counterdemonstration, but planned to be at Tredegar to protest the unveiling as it happened. "Got a bunch of signs being printed up at Kinko's even as we're standing here talking," he said.

On our way back to the Fan, we drove the length of Monument Avenue again, past Stuart, Lee, Jackson, and the other heroes, so Leak could show me the statue of Arthur Ashe. When the city council first approved the statue, a year after Ashe's death in 1993, civic groups from all over the city vied to have it placed in their neighborhoods. The council voted to place it on the avenue instead, notwithstanding, or rather because of, the odd juxtaposition—just a few hundred yards down the street from Jefferson Davis, who never in his life would have given a thought to Arthur Ashe or his ancestors, unless he'd been putting in a bid.

The city council's high-handed decision, and the energetic objections to it, made news around the world, drawing attention to Richmond as a place "where the Civil War was still being fought." With their marches and paid advertisements, the Sons campaigned loudly against the city fathers, in a prototype of the campaign they now waged against the Lincoln statue.

"Of course, we lost in the end," Leak said. "They won. They always do."

We looked up at the statue as cars circled by. Amid a clutch of crouching children, Ashe stands knobby-kneed. He holds both hands aloft, raising his racquet high in the air as though he's trying to keep it away from the brats at his feet. He's wearing a track suit.

The statue looked puny and absurd.

"It's a joke," Leak said.

"It makes the whole avenue seem like a postmodern installation," I agreed. *"Five Generals and a Tennis Player."*

In the car I said, "You have to admit Ashe is a great local hero. He deserves a statue, right?"

"That is an issue on which I have no strong views one way or the other," Leak said. "There are dozens of places where a thing like that would have been suitable. The important thing is, by putting the statue here, on the avenue, they realized they could trivialize the things we cherish and get away with it. They could rub our noses in it and nobody could be powerful enough to stop them. So of course it was just the beginning."

For our final stop, Leak had me pull over to the far lane of another traffic circle, in the center of which General Lee sat impossibly high and erect on his mount, Traveller. We got out and Leak removed his hat. "Robert E. Lee is of course the beau ideal of Southern manhood," he said, "a gentleman whose character was as close to perfection as Southerners have dared imagine."

I said, lamely, that Lee did indeed seem like a great man.

"You need to understand one thing about Robert E. Lee," Leak said. "And this one thing may help you understand other things. Lee inherited slaves from his wife's father. He freed them at once. Slavery was a sin against God, he said.

"And then—*then*—when his country, Virginia, was invaded by Yankees, he did not hesitate to take up arms to defend her. They can say what they want. But when this man took the field he was not fighting for slavery.

"When they brought the statue to Richmond, there were ceremonies to mark its progress as they pulled it through the streets. Grown men wept as it passed. *They wept.* It's not so hard to understand, is it? The people who paid for these beautiful statues, who built them and honored them and maintained them, they believed in something. You may like it, you may not like it—but they believed in it.

"What do people believe in now? Nothing. Commerce. Power. Money. Winning at whatever cost.

"When they put that statue in tomorrow, down at Tredegar, with the mayor and the businessmen there, and the editor of the newspaper and the governor probably, when they put in that glorious, expensive statue to Father Abraham, they will have won again, right? They always win. Fine. Winning is what they care about.

"But you think anyone's going to weep?"

The Richmond City Council had declared the next day "Lincoln in Richmond Day," and an hour after dawn the day was still dark, with slate-gray thunderheads rolling up from Petersburg in a line along the river. But the downpour never came. By late afternoon, when the shroud was tugged off the statue at the visitor center, the sun had splintered through and Tredegar was bathed in golden light. Hundreds of onlookers cheered, the bronze of the statue glowed, and the mayor and Mr. Kline and the Park Service people beamed.

Many of them had spent their morning at a "Lincoln in Richmond" symposium, held a couple of miles away at the headquarters of the Virginia Historical Society—the same building where, Leak had told me, a sign had been placed to cover up the word "Confederate." We met in a recent addition to the old building. It was built of polished marble and surrounded by audacious ferns and palmettos. Under an airy skylight a brunch table had been laid out, with clumps of grapes and heaps of strawberries, blueberry bagels, and muffins with satiny lemon centers—food that wouldn't be caught in the same room with the dubious sandwiches on offer at "Lincoln Reconsidered."

There were few signs of the haste with which the symposium had been thrown together. It was considered necessary as a rebuttal to the "Lincoln Reconsidered" conference. Like the Sons, the society had reached far beyond Richmond for its panel of Lincoln experts. They shared a pedigree common to the breed nowadays; indeed, it would have been difficult to bring together a panel of Lincoln experts more perfectly opposite to the group assembled by Brag Bowling and DiLorenzo. Harold Holzer, a specialist in Lincolniana from the Metropolitan Museum of Art, used to write speeches for Mario Cuomo. William Lee Miller, an ethics professor from the University of Virginia, was a speechwriter for Adlai Stevenson and later worked for Lyndon Johnson. The third panelist, Ronald C. White, was dean of the San Francisco Theological Seminary, which is a self-explanatory job title.

It's no surprise, then, that the Lincoln who emerged from their discussion was a cross between Adlai Stevenson and Mario Cuomo, if both had gone to the San Francisco Theological Seminary. Professor Miller noted how "unmoralistic" Lincoln was. The Great Emancipator was a specialist in self-criticism, a connoisseur of nuance, habitually thoughtful and introspective, much more severe in appraising his own shortcomings than those of anyone else. He never felt the need, despite constant provocation, to be "judgmental." White, for his part, said the Richmond statue was a great contemporary improvement on Daniel Chester French's heroic, awe-inspiring statue of Lincoln at the Lincoln Memorial. "We're in a new era," White said. "The new statue gives us a mild, contemplative Lincoln," in marked contrast to the Lincoln conceived by French, which stresses a "larger-than-life Lincoln" whose "triumphalism," so common in the early twentieth century, must strike contemporary Lincoln buffs as vulgar. "Today there's a different spirit, ready to identify with a gentler Lincoln—a Lincoln who could deal comfortably with ambiguity." From now on, he said, Tredegar and its healing Lincoln statue will create "a safe space for us to talk about those rifts that divide us."

Forget Stevenson and Cuomo. If Lincoln had been born 125 years later, he could have been Bill Moyers.

After the symposium I went down to Tredegar. Times do change: the "safe space" that White foresaw had once been known, more dangerously, as the "Mother Arsenal of the South." The old ironworks sits in a park on the banks of the James, at the foot of downtown, alongside a railroad trestle built long ago to carry numberless tons of ordnance from here to all points of the Confederacy. Trains still rumble by several times a day, hauling less spectacular cargo.

The site chosen for the statue sits in a little plaza outside one of the handful of mill buildings to have survived the foundry's shuttering in 1957. When I got there, a long row of protesters had already formed along the driveway leading to the iron gates of the parking lot. Cops were everywhere. Several of them, mounted on horseback, had ranged themselves around the hill above the visitor center. Half a dozen others manned a checkpoint at the gate. Everyone entering the park was required to empty bags and purses—pockets, too, in some cases. A printed sign read: "No Coolers, Glass, Signs, Flags or Banners."

I found Leak among the protesters, dressed festively in a top hat and a cutaway morning coat over his polo shirt and khakis. His signs showed the professional Kinko's touch: "No Honor for War Criminals" and "Jefferson Davis Was Our President." A friend next to him held another sign: "Your Hero Killed Five of My Ancestors." Behind us, a few of the Sons began singing "Dixie."

"And how was the love-in at the Historical Society?" Leak asked. "Did you learn about the greatness of the great man?"

"They think he was a wimp," I said.

Leak looked away, then back at me. "Jesus," he said. "Even I don't think he was a wimp."

A scuffle broke out at the gate. One of the Sons had tried to enter wearing a T-shirt bearing the Stars and Bars. "No flags," a cop said loudly.

"Just one more example of ethnic cleansing," the man said when he rejoined the other protesters. "They just want to remove the undesirable elements from the population." He saw my notepad and said, "Getting kicked around don't piss me off. We're used to it by now. What pisses me off is when they tell us we're supposed to like it."

I went up to the visitor center. A temporary platform had been set up for a surprisingly large group of speakers: Bob Kline, the park supervisor, several congressmen, the lieutenant governor, along with a quorum, probably, of state legislators. The mayor was at the microphone, commending his city on hosting the "the second coming of Abraham Lincoln." In midspeech he was drowned out by the sudden appearance of a small propeller plane, circling low overhead. It trailed a big banner: SIC SEMPER TYRANNIS—"Thus always to tyrants"—the motto of the Commonwealth of Virginia, and the words John Wilkes Booth sang out as he fell to the stage of Ford's Theatre, having put a bullet in Lincoln's brain.

I stood off to the side with a group of reporters from local television stations. Their cameramen milled about, looking bored.

"This is it?" one of them said. "Where's the action?"

Brag Bowling was at the edge of the crowd, on his best behavior. "For two months I'm getting e-mails," one of the reporters complained "'We're going to stop this thing by any means necessary!'; 'Prepare for the fireworks on April 5!' I guess they lost their nerve." He turned to his cameraman. "At least you got a shot of the prop plane, right?"

When the speeches were over, on toward dusk, the audience gathered around the plaza. The statue sat hunkered under a tarp. With a flourish, Mr. Kline and the park supervisor yanked the cover off.

"It's so small!" said a lady next to me. And it was—though life-sized, it looked smaller than life, diminutive almost, resting on the paving stones at ground level. Lincoln sits tilted forward on a bench with a faraway look in his eyes. Tad is next to him, looking up expectantly, presumably waiting for his father to say something. The effect is supposed to be contemplative, but really it looks as if son has caught dad puzzling through a senior moment. (*Conceived in liberty and dedicated to . . . dedicated to . . . damn! . . . dedicated to what?*") The bronze bench on which they sit extends on either side, leaving space for tourists to pose for pictures, and soon the statue was engulfed by the crowd, as everyone jostled to get close.

I joined Mr. Kline off to one side, where he stood with his partner, Martin Moran, the president of the U.S. Historical Society.

Mr. Kline was much moved. "Right at this moment the meaning of the statue is quite clear, don't you think?" he said, a catch in his voice. "It says, very simply, that we should love each other."

He fell silent, and Moran, who is much the more voluble of the two, began extolling the statue's significance.

"I've had historians tell me that this is the most important statue of Lincoln anywhere in the world," he said. "This is a day that will go down in history."

We stood watching the visitors elbowing one another, patting Lincoln's shoulders and hair, mugging for snapshots. The sun was sinking over the James to our back, and it gilded the statue in outline. I said something about how small the bronze figures looked.

"That was intentional," Moran said quickly. "Could we have got something larger, some huge icon sort of thing? You bet we could have. We could have done one and a half, double, triple life-size. We could have put it on a pedestal.

"And what would we have had then? A giant among the little people. Well, that wouldn't have been appropriate. We wanted Lincoln down here among the people, something more human, more approachable, something everyone could relate to."

As he spoke a mother tried to settle her three kids for a photograph. A little girl hopped into Lincoln's lap and pounded the crown of his head, while her brother knotted his little fingers around the statue's throat, and her sister, letting out a girlish "Eeeewwww," slipped her pinky into Lincoln's nose.

"And this," Moran said, "this is the Lincoln we've brought back to Richmond. People will come from all over to see it."

Tom DiLorenzo, oddly enough, had said something similar a few weeks before. Putting the statue in Richmond, he told me, reminded him of stories he'd heard about Russia in the 1980s, just before the collapse of the Soviet Union.

"People would walk by all the huge statues of Lenin every day," DiLorenzo said, "and the statues just reminded them of what a lie it all was. Those statues were erected by the Communists but they worked against the Communists, because they illustrated the lies the whole system was based on. The same thing'll happen with all the statues of Lincoln. In a few years, Americans are going to look at that statue down there at Tredegar, and they're going to wonder, 'What did this man really stand for?'"

2

BILLY HERNDON AND
THE INNER MR. L.

I f people decide to take Tom DiLorenzo's question seriously—
What does Lincoln stand for?—and then, having answered it, decide to make good on his prediction—*Let's tear down all the statues!*—they will face a discouraging task. Since 1865 hundreds of Lincoln monuments have been raised up, made from bronze, marble,
plaster, granite, fiberglass, limestone, even, as we'll see, a "polymer
blend." My favorite of them all sits half a continent away from Richmond, at the entrance to New Salem State Park, twenty miles outside
Lincoln's hometown of Springfield, Illinois.

On the Circuit, by Anna Hyatt Huntington, was installed in 1963, not
long before my family's first trip to the Lincoln shrines of Central Illinois. That year marks the end of the period when it was still common
to make heroic-sized depictions of Lincoln. Since Huntington, whether
owing to the expense or to the decline in craftsmanship or to changing
public attitudes and taste, Lincoln statuary has been cut down to size—
shrunk to less imposing dimensions and placed at eye level, as I saw in
Richmond. Here at the gate to New Salem, though, you can't help but

look up to him. Mrs. Huntington has put him atop a mountainous horse. The animal stands at ease but he's packed with coiled power—the musculature rolls and pulses under the bronze skin. And Lincoln, riding bareback, is even bigger. He studies a law book open in one palm, while his other hand loosely holds the reins. The horse has stopped to graze, but Lincoln seems not to notice.

Like all statues of Lincoln—like the Richmond statue too—*On the Circuit* is a kind of commentary. It tells us what the sculptor, and his audience, thought about the man they were honoring. At first look *On the Circuit* suggests Lincoln's gentleness: the horse dawdles but the master is too kind to prod him. The animal is so big it might have been a plow horse, busting the sod of Central Illinois. Instead it's been enlisted to carry a young lawyer on the legal circuit from county courthouse to county courthouse. The scene is rustic, but it holds the promise of something more—something beyond the hardscrabble life of physical labor that Lincoln was born into. And the way there, the way out, is through the book Lincoln holds in his hand. It absorbs him so completely he seems lost to the world that surrounds him, the world of trees and split-rail fences and plowed-up fields. Huntington used Lincoln to show the victory of the life of the mind over a life of grunt work, of brains over muscle, and she was showing, through the open law book, how the victory was won.

I was at New Salem because Richmond shook me up. I learned soon enough that I shouldn't be shocked that Lincoln was used as a proxy to score political points; this had been so from the moment Booth squeezed the trigger and made him a martyr. What threw me instead was the vehemence of the men who hated him and—just as surprising—the mildness of those who would defend him. In Richmond the scholars on both sides marshaled their arguments, flung facts here and there, and came up with one of two Lincolns: a racist, warmongering totalitarian, or a sentimental old poop—Mussolini, on the one hand, or Mister Rogers on the other. I didn't know enough to know what Lincoln really was, but I was relatively sure he was neither of those. And the more carefully I read the biographies, following footnotes and tracking sources, the dimmer he seemed; he faded behind scrims of scholarly interpretation and personal partiality. I was looking for firmer ground. I wanted to know what we know about Lincoln, and I wanted to know how we know it.

Anyone who asks such questions comes to New Salem sooner or later. It was to this prairie village on a bend in the Sangamon River—now reconstructed into a tourist destination by the state of Illinois—that Lincoln moved as a young man of twenty-two. It was here that he first ran for public office and formally studied the law and found a way to escape the yeoman's life. Just as important, for our purpose, it was here that he first made an impression on a young, excitable fellow named William Herndon, who furnished succeeding generations with a view of Abraham Lincoln that has never worn away.

Lincoln was twenty-three when Herndon, then fourteen, first laid eyes on him. Gawky and footloose, Lincoln had arrived in New Salem seemingly as a man without a past—"a piece of floating driftwood," as a friend later described him. "After a winter of deep snow, he had come down the river with the freshet; borne along by the swelling waters, and aimlessly floating about, he had accidentally lodged at New Salem."

But of course the young man did have a past; even if, ever after, he was cagey about its details and preferred to dismiss it with the phrase from a mawkish eighteenth-century poem: "the short and simple annals of the poor." Lincoln was born in a log cabin—really, he was—in 1809 in the remotest quarter of the American frontier, the wilderness of central Kentucky. Scholars differ—this is a phrase we will have to get used to—about the character of his father, Thomas, and next to nothing is known of his mother, Nancy Hanks Lincoln. Thomas and Nancy were both born in Virginia. Thomas was brought to Kentucky by his parents, but no one knows how Nancy got there; presumably she was an orphan girl, taken in by a Kentucky farmer named Richard

Berry. She and Thomas were married in 1806. A year later a daughter, Sarah, was born, followed by Abraham, and then another boy, Thomas, who died in infancy, though the dates of his birth and death are in contention.

Thomas was a hard-luck case. In Kentucky he moved his young family to a series of subsistence farms, but in each instance his claim fell victim to faulty land titles and he was forced to keep moving, supplementing a meager income with random work as a carpenter. At last, in 1816, he took the family across the Ohio River into Indiana, where the soil was richer and where land claims were guaranteed by the federal government. The Lincolns settled in the southernmost toe of the state, near a tributary of the Ohio called Pigeon Creek. Two years later an epidemic of a cow-borne disease, "the milk sick," claimed a quarter of the neighborhood's population, including Nancy Hanks Lincoln. According to some accounts her body was laid on the cabin's only table in the days after her death, while her husband, children, and neighbors came and went, preparing the funeral. Thomas and the nine-year-old boy dug her grave, and they cut the trees and hewed the wood for the box they buried her in.

Pioneer history, pieced together from the hard facts of births and deaths and land transactions recorded in court ledgers and family bibles, doesn't allow much room for sentiment. We know only that Thomas promptly went back to the old neighborhood in Kentucky to find a new wife. He returned with a widow, Sarah Bush Johnston, now Sarah Bush Johnston Lincoln. Lincoln's new mother brought children of her own, making a blended family, as we say nowadays, of at least eight, squeezed into the cabin on Pigeon Creek.

This period is a fertile source of Lincoln lore, thanks, as we'll see, to Herndon's efforts. The Indiana years are when we first hear of Lincoln's reputation as a bookish kid, borrowing from neighbors whatever volumes he could lay hands on, including law books; in Indiana he learned to wield an ax, becoming an accomplished rail splitter while simultaneously fixing his mind on ways to avoid a life of manual labor at all costs. To make ends meet Thomas sent his son to work wherever earnings could be paid in cash—on farms, at a nearby forge, on a river ferry—and the father was fastidious in collecting his son's wages when the boy returned home. Some recent biographers have speculated that Lincoln, bitter over the arrangement, learned to detest the "unrequited toil" that had its most virulent form in chattel slavery—"the same spirit," as he later put it, "that says, 'You work and toil and earn bread, and I'll eat it.'" Other biographers find the parallel far-fetched.

Lincoln's sister Sarah married a local boy in 1826. She died in childbirth about a year later, and the child along with her. Whether from grief, frustrated ambition, or general disposition, Thomas again grew restless. By 1830 Abraham had reached the age of majority and was free by law from his father's constraints, but he agreed to help Thomas move the extended family across the Wabash River into Illinois, and agreed again, when they arrived near present-day Decatur, to stay an extra year to fence and plow a new farm. In the spring of 1831, after a fabled "winter of the great snow," he was on his own at last. From then on he maintained only the most distant relations with his father—helping him out of financial jams occasionally but declining, for example, the usual custom of naming his firstborn son after him, as Thomas had named Abraham for his father. After the old man died, in 1851, his son never got around to buying a marker for his grave.

Scholars differ on how precisely Lincoln, the "piece of floating driftwood," happened to lodge up at New Salem. With a population that peaked at fewer than one hundred, it wasn't a boom town, exactly, but in the 1830s it had a fair chance of prospering if the Sangamon River had proved able to handle traffic from the newly invented steam boats. One such, the *Talisman* out of Cincinnati, made the attempt, and the young men of the village came out to greet it bearing axes to cut away any upstream foliage that impeded her progress. Lincoln was among them, and among the boys from the surrounding countryside who came to watch the spectacle was William Herndon.

He was cousin to two of Lincoln's New Salem friends, and they saw each other now and then over the next few years. Lincoln, with various partners, tried to make a go of running two general stores, then worked as a surveyor and as village postmaster after the stores "winked out." He hauled a flatboat of produce to New Orleans. It was only in public life that he found genuine success. When the local militia was called up to fight an Indian uprising led by a chief named Black Hawk, Lincoln's fellow soldiers elected him captain of the company. After mustering out he ran for the state legislature, gained admission to the bar, and, in 1837, moved up to the big town of Springfield (pop. 2,400). He took a room above a store where Herndon clerked, and the two men renewed their friendship.

"I became warmly attached to him soon after his removal to Springfield," Herndon later wrote. "There was something in his tall and angular frame, his ill-fitting garments, honest face, and lively humor that imprinted his individuality on my affection and regard. What impression I made on him I had no means of knowing till many years afterward. He was my senior by nine years, and I looked up to him, naturally enough, as my superior in everything—a thing I continued to do till the end of his days."

Lincoln called him "Billy." Herndon always called him "Mr. Lincoln."

In temperament they couldn't have been more different. Years later, after the two men had become law partners, a young man visited their office carrying an autograph book and came away with the perfect illustration of their respective characters.

In the book Lincoln wrote: "Today, Feb. 23, 1858, the owner honored me with the privilege of writing the first name in this book.— A. Lincoln."

Below Lincoln's name Herndon wrote, in a much larger hand: "The struggles of this age and succeeding ages for God and man—

Religion—Humanity and Liberty with all their complex and grand relations—may they triumph and conquer forever, is my ardent wish and most fervent Soul-prayer.—Wm H. Herndon. Feb. 23, 1858."

Herndon was jumpy and intellectually uninhibited, eccentric in manner and extravagant in speech, and vulnerable to fits of high moral passion. He called himself an Infidel in theology and a Free-Thinker in morals, and he eagerly consumed all the latest books on philosophy coming out of the Transcendentalists back east. Lincoln, though sociable and humorous and already well known as a storyteller, was far more self-contained; he read narrowly, mostly in newspapers and political tracts, and he showed no interest in the metaphysical speculations that so excited Herndon. Moreover, Herndon drank—episodically, it's true, but never less than heroically. Herndon himself later confessed that neither he "nor anyone else" ever knew why Lincoln took him as a partner. The firm of Lincoln & Herndon continued even after Lincoln, by then president-elect, moved to Washington sixteen years later.

How Lincoln advanced from his dim beginnings to the presidency was a story that Herndon himself was uniquely placed to tell. Lincoln's interest in politics showed itself early. Some accounts say he made his first political speech within days of arriving in Illinois; scholars differ. What's certain is that he hadn't been long in New Salem before he offered himself as a candidate for the state legislature, running as a member of the Whig party. He advocated tariffs, a strong national government dedicated to public works, and a vigorous expansion of market capitalism. The local paper printed his statement of candidacy. It is the first substantial bit of writing from his pen that survives, and to anyone inclined to find them it offers hints of what Herndon was later to call "the inner Mr. L."

In the concluding paragraph Lincoln wrote: "I have no other [ambition] so great as that of being truly esteemed of my fellow men, by rendering myself worthy of their esteem. . . . I am young and unknown to many of you. I was born and have ever remained in the most humble walks of life. I have no wealthy or popular relations to recommend me.

My case is thrown exclusively upon the independent voters of this county, and if elected they will have conferred a favor upon me for which I shall be unremitting in my labors to compensate. But if the good people in their wisdom shall see fit to keep me in the background, I have been too familiar with disappointments to be very much chagrined."

It's a remarkable statement from a twenty-three-year-old drifter. Herndon later wrote that the closing plea was carefully put together to appeal to the "chivalrous sentiments" of the men in Lincoln's district. Lincoln buffs find in it the characteristically Lincoln-like charm and dry humor, along with his deep self-awareness and a shrewd sensitivity to the impression he's making on his neighbors. Lincoln skeptics, on the other hand, see the first glimmers of a Uriah Heepish insincerity and a cool desire to manipulate voters by playing on their pity and class resentments. Scholars differ. But nobody doubts the political ambition it reveals, or the brass.

Lincoln was perfectly suited to frontier politics, where the campaigning often dissolved into hijinks tinged with a kind of cornpone demagoguery. Herndon later told the story of how Lincoln watched, with mounting agitation, a Democratic rival named Taylor attack Lincoln's Whigs for their "aristocratic pretensions." Lincoln sidled up to the speaker and ripped open Taylor's vest, revealing "a ruffled shirt front glittering with watch-chain, seals and other golden jewels." With his rival thus exposed, Lincoln took the stage.

"While Colonel Taylor was making these charges against the Whigs over the country," Lincoln said, "riding in fine carriages, wearing ruffled shirts, kid gloves, massive gold watch-chains with large gold-seals and flourishing a heavy gold-headed cane, I was a poor boy, hired on a flat boat at eight dollars a month, and had only one pair of breeches to my back, and they were buckskin." So tight were the buckskin breeches, Lincoln went on, "they left a blue streak around my legs that can be seen to this day. If you call this aristocracy, I plead guilty to the charge."

Lincoln lost his first bid for office in New Salem. But he offered himself at the next election and won, and within two years he ranked among the leaders of the Whig party in Illinois, winning reelection four times more. He was an active legislator. His first great project—persuading his colleagues to move the state capital to his new hometown of Spring-field—was a success. His next was a dismal failure. In 1836, the legislature backed $10 million in bonds to finance a staggeringly ambitious program of public works—highways, canals, and crisscrossing railroads to promote economic development. It was a rash move. A year later came the Panic of 1837, and the state government was saddled with interest payments amounting to more than eight times annual revenues. Scarcely any improvements were completed, though many speculators got rich.

Even Lincoln's friendliest biographers disagree about how much blame he can share for the fiasco, which burdened the state's finances for nearly fifty years. One, Paul Simon, says Lincoln's influence in favor of the measure was decisive; another, David Donald, says Lincoln "was a follower, not a leader." Whichever was the case, Herndon saw Lincoln's enthusiasm for the scheme as another sign of his ambition. One old friend told Herndon that Lincoln had told him he aspired to be "the DeWitt Clinton of Illinois," after the father of the greatest public works project of the time, the Erie Canal. It was a role for which he would have been ill-equipped. "He was endowed with none of the elements of a political economist," Herndon wrote. "He never had what some people call 'money sense.'"

Lincoln declined to run for reelection to the state legislature in 1842, hoping to be chosen by his party for a congressional seat instead. That same year he married Mary Todd, a wellborn woman from Lexington, Kentucky, whom he had met during her frequent visits to a married sister in Springfield. They were to have four children, all boys—Robert, Edward, Willie, and Tad—only one of whom, firstborn Robert, survived to adulthood. Mary was short, pretty, bright, and cultivated; she spoke French, followed politics, knew literature, and displayed elegant manners. Their courtship was long and erratic, and at one point Lincoln broke off their engagement. Nobody knows why, though everybody has felt free to guess.

The Lincolns' marriage, like your marriage and mine, was a mystery to everyone but the two people involved directly, and maybe to them too. This inconvenient fact hasn't kept biographers, buffs, and other kibitzers from theorizing about its true nature for one hundred and sixty years (and counting). Herndon was among the first kibitzers, and the most influential. He and Mary disliked each other, and his dark view of her, and of the Lincoln marriage, has worked to Mary's disadvantage ever since. But a few facts are undeniable. Their four children attest to some degree of intimacy, and husband and wife were often seen to treat each other with great tenderness. On the other hand . . . there are too many stories of domestic squabbles to discount. Maybe even more tellingly, long after any financial necessity should have pressed him into doing so, Lincoln chose to practice law by riding the circuit of county courthouses through Central Illinois, a grueling tour encompassing eight thousand square miles that kept him away from home for six months out of the year. Off the circuit he traveled constantly as well, giving speeches and tending to politics. Whether these absences suggest a tireless ambition or an unhappy home life—scholars differ.

Lincoln's initial play for a congressional seat failed. He redoubled his partisan efforts on behalf of the Whigs. He campaigned for other candidates and filled the columns of party-line newspapers with anonymous, satiric, and often scurrilous attacks on Democratic rivals. One of these was so successful that its target, James Shields, discovered Lincoln's authorship and challenged him to a duel. Lincoln chose the weapons—Shields, at five foot six, was known as a crack shot, so Lincoln, at six foot four, chose cavalry broad swords. Friends intervened before blood could be shed, and Lincoln rarely spoke of the episode, though an unlucky subordinate recalled making the mistake of mentioning it many years later to President Lincoln. "I do not deny it," Lincoln said, coloring. "But if you desire my friendship, you will never mention it again."

Finally, in 1846, party elders selected him to run for Congress, and he won. His two-year term in Washington was undistinguished. People have recalled it mostly for his vocal opposition to the Mexican War—which ever since has allowed opponents of any adventure in American foreign policy, from the Spanish-American War to the invasion of Iraq, to enlist him as a spiritual ally. Lincoln's antiwar stance played less well with his contemporaries. He declined to run for reelection when it became clear he would lose. But his candidate for president, the Whig Zachary Taylor, did win, and Lincoln lingered in Washington for several weeks after his own term was up. He used the time in the capital to file a patent for a riverboat flotation device—to this day he remains the only president to hold a patent—and he argued a case before the Supreme Court. And he was probably pursuing a patronage job with the new administration, as commissioner of the General Land Office.

How diligently did he seek the job? Did he really want it? Or was he merely trying to secure it for a political ally? This is, you won't be surprised to learn, a matter on which biographers differ. The evidence, drawn from later testimony and surviving correspondence, is ambiguous. It can support biographers who prefer not to portray Lincoln as a gnawingly ambitious, job-grubbing party hack, and it can support biographers, fewer in number, who don't mind portraying Lincoln that way at all. In any case, he didn't get the job—it went, in fact, to an applicant Lincoln had lobbied against—and at least one piece of correspondence suggests that his disappointment was severe. In this episode, however, Herndon saw, rather than ambition, further evidence of Lincoln's commitment to principle: "He was too scrupulous, and lacked too much the essentials of self-confidence and persistence, to be a successful suitor" for a mere patronage job.

Lincoln had little choice but to return to Springfield and to the practice of law. By all outward appearances his passion for a career in politics declined along with his influence among the Whigs in Washington. He took to the circuit, expanded his practice into appellate work, and in spare moments—there were lots of these on the circuit—taught himself logic and geometry by working his way through the six books of Euclid.

But something had happened, or was happening. All sympathetic biographers see the 1840s as a transforming period in Lincoln's life. Some locate the change early, in 1841 and 1842, with his marriage to Mary and the beginnings of worldly success; others place it at the end of the decade, when his political career seemed to have run its course and he was once again thrown back on his private resources. Whenever the biographers see it, they all see the same thing: a ripening in wisdom and seriousness—the end of the raucous and undisciplined party hack, and the emergence of . . . Lincoln.

The proof that some profound change had taken place, they all agree, comes with Lincoln's return to politics. "In 1854," Lincoln later wrote of himself, in a third-person autobiographical sketch, "his profession had almost superseded the thought of politics in his mind, when the repeal of the Missouri compromise aroused him as he had never been before."

For thirty-four years the Missouri Compromise had frozen the national government's official attitude toward slavery. Supplemented by other acts of Congress, the compromise had outlawed slavery throughout the territories stretching beyond Missouri all the way west to Oregon; slavery in the slave states, meanwhile, having been already established, remained untouchable, since the Constitution clearly didn't authorize Congress or the president to tamper with it. The status quo was thus tilted against slavery. Confined to the slave states, unable to spread itself outward, slavery would eventually wither and die, whether through its own economic illogic or, less likely, through some general advance in moral understanding among slave-owners themselves. The founders, Lincoln said, had "placed slavery in the course of ultimate extinction": a demise at once gradual, lawful, inevitable, and just.

What roused Lincoln in 1854 was the Kansas-Nebraska Act, a bill conceived by Senator Stephen A. Douglas, Illinois's leading politician and a rival of Lincoln's dating back to the days in New Salem. Douglas's act effectively shifted the government's position from an antislavery bias to official neutrality. Under a new principle of "popular sovereignty," it allowed each new territory, as it became a state and joined the Union, to decide for itself whether to permit slavery within its own borders. The possibility of westward expansion breathed new life into slavery and emboldened slaveholders. Their position was strengthened by the *Dred Scott* decision, in which the Supreme Court declared slaves to be constitutionally protected property beyond the reach of the national government. Together, *Dred Scott* and Kansas-Nebraska guaranteed the extension of slavery rather than its extinction. A new party of former Whigs, the Republicans, gathered in opposition to the new status quo. Lincoln and Herndon eagerly joined up.

Lincoln's political view of slavery, and his personal views on race, were not nearly so simple as most buffs would prefer. They don't fit into the historical categories we're used to dealing with: Lincoln was neither a supporter of slavery nor an abolitionist. He had never made much of an issue of slavery in his political career, as his detractors never fail to point out. His most notable public statement about slavery came in the state legislature, in 1837, when he and a colleague lodged a protest against a pro-slavery resolution that had condemned "the poison of abolition." Their protest read (again in the third person):

> They believe that the institution of slavery is founded on both injustice and bad policy; but that the promulgation of abolition doctrines tends rather to increase than to abate its evils.
>
> They believe that the Congress of the United States has no power, under the constitution, to interfere with the institution of slavery in the different States.

They believe that the Congress of the United States has the power, under the constitution, to abolish slavery in the District of Columbia; but that that power ought not to be exercised unless at the request of the people of said District.

Twenty years later, running for president, Lincoln reprinted this statement, saying that it still reflected his position "so far as it goes." He was against slavery, but he believed that the Constitution forbade Congress from banning it. And he thought that abolitionists, in their rush to eradicate slavery any way they could, undermined the democratic rule of law that was ultimately the surest hope for slavery's eventual and permanent eradication.

The complications continue, though, thanks in large part to Herndon, who was almost an abolitionist himself and hoped after Lincoln's death to shade the image of his old friend in that direction. Herndon made famous, for example, an anecdote that did much to mislead future generations about Lincoln's abhorrence of slavery—the same story that, a century later, soured my college friend on Lincoln and buffdom.

In Herndon's account, the young Lincoln, having delivered a flatboat full of goods to New Orleans, was wandering the city with his friends one morning when they happened on a slave auction in a public square.

"The whole thing was so revolting," wrote Herndon, "that Lincoln moved away from the scene with a deep feeling of 'unconquerable hate.' Bidding his companions follow him he said, 'By God, boys, let's get away from this. If ever I get chance to hit that thing [meaning slavery], I'll hit it hard.'"

Herndon said he had heard this story—so passionately told, so spookily prescient, so thoroughly implausible—from John Hanks, one of Lincoln's cousins, after Lincoln's death. Hanks told Herndon he had sailed the flatboat with Lincoln to New Orleans. Herndon, however, evidently failed to consider that third-person autobiographical sketch, quoted earlier, which Lincoln set down in 1860. In it Lincoln lingers over the flatboat trip but makes no mention of a slave auction. "Hanks," Lincoln wrote, "had not gone to New-Orleans, but having a family, and being likely to be detained from home longer than at first expected, had turned back from St. Louis."

If Lincoln's abhorrence had moved him to say, "I'll hit it hard," Hanks didn't hear it.

How deep was Lincoln's abhorrence anyway? Lincoln himself wrote about one of his early encounters with slavery, and he wrote about it twice. In 1855 Lincoln sent a letter to his friend Joshua Speed, a slaveholder, explaining his opposition to the Kansas-Nebraska Act by invoking his hatred of slavery.

"In 1841," he wrote, "you and I had together a tedious low-water trip, on a Steam Boat from Louisville to St. Louis. You may remember, as I well do, that from Louisville to the mouth of the Ohio there were, on board, ten or a dozen slaves, shackled together with irons. That sight was a continual torment to me."

On the evidence, though, the torment was purely retrospective. At the time of the trip, in 1841, Lincoln wrote a letter to Speed's half sister Mary.

"Nothing of interest happened during the passage . . ." Lincoln wrote. "A gentleman had purchased twelve negroes in different parts of Kentucky and was taking them to a farm in the South. They were chained six and six together . . . so that the negroes were strung together precisely like so many fish upon a trot-line. In this condition they were being separated forever from the scenes of their childhood, their friends, their fathers and mothers, and brothers and sisters, and many of them, from their wives and children, and going into perpetual slavery where the lash of the master is proverbially more ruthless and un-relenting than any other where; and yet amid all these distressing circumstances, as we would think them, they were the most cheerful and apparently happy creatures on board. One . . . played the fiddle almost continually; and the others danced, sung, cracked jokes, and played various games with cards from day to day."

There's no mention of a "continual torment" here—either Lincoln's or the slaves'.

Once slavery had become his party's defining issue, Lincoln publicly advocated several expedients that strike contemporary ears as coarse: "compensated emancipation" would have allowed the national government to buy slaves from slave-owners, and "voluntary colonization" would encourage the freedmen to resettle in land bought by the government in the American Southwest, Central America, or even Africa. Add to this murky record Lincoln's handful of recorded racist jokes and his more vehement comments on race—"I am not, nor ever have been in favor of bringing about in any way the social and political equality of the white and black races"—and you can imagine how historians have contested over the ambiguities and apparent contradictions, when they have acknowledged them at all. A biographer who wants to make Lincoln an abolitionist or a racial liberal either ignores them or tries to explain them away. Any skeptic hoping to discredit him can exploit them as evidence of cynicism, hypocrisy, and opportunism. After all, Lincoln's public opposition to the extension of slavery was a good career move. The roiling political currents of the late 1850s shot him out of retirement and into the Lincoln-Douglas debates in 1858, when he tried to unseat his great rival in a Senate race. Those debates brought him national fame, and his reputation was cemented eighteen months later with his Cooper Union address in New York. Carefully tended and nurtured, the fame led the Republicans to nominate him for president in 1860.

Lincoln won the election, of course, declaring again that as president he would have no authority to tamper with slavery in the slave states—insisting only that it be contained there, with the end in view that it would perish from suffocation. His victory split the country anyway, and within a month of his inauguration the garrison at Fort Sumter in South Carolina was under siege.

Before leaving Springfield, Lincoln came to say good-bye to Herndon in their office. The talk, Herndon later recalled, was meandering and nostalgic until Lincoln, after a pause, turned the conversation to the many lawyers who had counseled him over the years to drop Herndon as a law partner. Lincoln always refused because, he said, he believed in Herndon as a lawyer and as a friend, and he "would never desert" him. He motioned to the LINCOLN & HERNDON sign that hung outside the window. "Let it hang there undisturbed," Lincoln said, according to Herndon. "If I live I'm coming back sometime, and then we'll go right on practicing law as though nothing has happened."

They saw each other only once more, early the following year. Herndon traveled to Washington to ask Lincoln to award a patronage job to the brother of a woman he was courting. Lincoln gave him the job (and the woman gave Herndon her hand). During his stay Herndon saw the chaos of life in the White House, where Lincoln was importuned by favor seekers, protected by halfhearted guards, and undercut by rivalrous politicians and military men of dubious competence and loyalty.

All this was to get much worse. His Emancipation Proclamation, issued later that year, brought criticism from all sides, since it freed slaves only in rebellious states as a "military necessity" under the president's war powers; Lincoln continued to believe that the Constitution gave him no *civil* authority to free slaves anywhere else, specifically in border states that remained loyal to the Union. The proclamation's procedural modesty led to the charge, heard commonly today, that the thing freed no one at all, and that, in fact, the slaves were forced by Lincoln's timidity to free themselves.

Piled on top of the burdens of war were the burdens of his personal life. A month after Herndon's visit came the death of his favorite son, twelve-year-old Willie, after a painful illness. The behavior of his grieving wife grew increasingly erratic, veering close to scandal when she ran up bills she refused to pay or sought favors from unscrupulous flatterers, and when she opened the White House to an unbroken parade of clairvoyants, soothsayers, and other quacks.

Herndon left Lincoln and the White House with an emotional fare-well. Mrs. Lincoln, for her part, had declined to receive him. She some-times claimed to have clairvoyant powers herself, so maybe she divined, as her husband did not, that Herndon's role in Lincoln's story, and in her own, had only begun.

Herndon heard the news of the assassination with the rest of Spring-field, on the morning of April 15, 1865. "It is grievously sad," he wrote, "to think of—one so good—so kind—so loving—so honest—so manly & so *great,* taken by the bloody murderous hand."

He had long toyed with the idea of writing a biography of his part-ner, but for all his high spirits and generous nature Herndon was, at bottom, a feckless man, and for months he contented himself with being Springfield's foremost authority on Lincoln "as he really was." He was a celebrity overnight. Journalists and aspiring biographers queued up to see him, and he would talk as long as they cared to lis-ten; often longer.

But when he saw what these earliest chroniclers wrote with the tales and observations he had generously bestowed, he was horrified. The first articles and biographies were soupy and sentimental, containing errors of fact both large and small and, what was worse, errors of judg-ment, too: in none of them could Herndon discern the complicated man he had known. The biggest selling of the early biographies—one hun-dred thousand copies—was by a newspaper editor and Sunday school teacher named Josiah Holland. His view of Lincoln was soaked in folk-lore and Christian piety; presented with a real man of strong passions, relentless ambition, and ambivalent religious views, Holland had de-livered to his readers a prairie Saint Francis. Herndon thought Holland, who had spent an afternoon in the law offices interviewing him, just made it all up.

"[Holland] asked me many questions in relation to Mr. Lincoln," Herndon later wrote. "I answered all willingly and truthfully. He then asked me—'What about Mr. Lincoln's religion,' and to which I replied—'the less said the better.' He then made this expression—'O never mind, I'll fix that' with a kind of wink and nod.'"

Part of Herndon's resentment was mere pride: no one, he thought, quite appreciated Lincoln the way he did. He resolved to set the record straight by writing the true Lincoln biography—telling "the inner life of Mr. L.," as he put it. Quite apart from their long friendship, Herndon had great faith in his ability, which he thought verged on the mystical, to discern the motives of the inner Mr. L. It's a faith that nearly every buff, and scholar, has shared since.

Yet he also knew there were facts of Lincoln's life he didn't know. So Herndon began digging, and over the next two years he performed one of the greatest feats of research in American history; it is impossible to imagine the great body of Lincoln literature without it. Herndon traveled to the scenes of Lincoln's boyhood and young manhood, in Indiana and Illinois, and picked through the ruins of the cabins where the Lincolns had lived. He sought out the surviving countryfolk who had watched Lincoln grow up. He prodded their memories and painstakingly set down their recollections. If there were places he couldn't travel to or sources he couldn't reach, he activated his national network of fellow Republicans to find a local contact who could do the reporting for him. "Get *all* the facts," he instructed them more than once.

In September 1865, less than five months after Lincoln's death, he went to the farm where Lincoln's stepmother lived, forty miles from Springfield. It was the only interview the old woman ever gave—she died three months later—and an excerpt from Herndon's notes gives you a taste of his method, and of the indelibly human material he collected.

Friday—Old Mrs. Lincolns Home—8 m South of Charleston—Septr 8th 1865
  Mrs Thomas Lincoln Says—
Abe was about 9 yrs of age when I landed in Indiana—The country was wild—and desolate. Abe was a good boy; he didn't like physical

labor—was diligent for Knowledge—wished to Know & if pain & Labor would get it he was sure to get it. He was the best boy I ever saw. I can't remember dates nor names—am about 75 yrs of age. . . .

Abe read all the books he could lay his hands on—and when he came across a passage that Struck him he would write it down on boards if he had no paper and keep it there till he did get paper—then he would re-write it—look at it repeat it. . . .

He was here—after he was Elected President of the US. (Here the old lady stopped—turned around & cried—wiped her Eyes—and proceeded.) He never told me a lie in his life—never Evaded—never Equivocated never dodged—nor turned a Corner to avoid any chastisement or other responsibility. He was dutiful to me always he loved me truly I think. I had a son John was raised with Abe. Both were good boys, but I must Say that Abe was the best I ever Saw or Ever expect to see.

From Herndon's interviews grew the Lincoln that most Americans have come to know: the prairie boy bent on self-improvement, hungry for knowledge, kindly, humorous, upright, tireless, and loyal; the young shopkeeper and postmaster of New Salem; the rising citizen of the state capital, feeling his way through the complexities of law and politics; then the statesman; then the martyr.

But there was more. Herndon's informants told him of failed romances in Lincoln's early life; of his lack of religious piety; of psychological depressions leading to thoughts of suicide. The inner Lincoln, whose complexity Herndon prided himself on grasping, was even more complicated than he had guessed. Herndon's cache of notes and letters eventually grew to several thousand pages. He knew the value of what he had collected. In his rush to release it to the world he postponed writing a full biography and planned instead a series of lectures in Springfield. The first three, on the "character," "patriotism," and "statesmanship" of Lincoln, were great popular successes and soon published as pamphlets.

Then Herndon returned to his book and . . . and one thing led to another . . . and time passed . . . and his passion for the project cooled. Lethargy set in. He needed money. He grew disillusioned with the practice of law. He decided to try his hand at farming. The transition from city to rural life consumed more time than he expected, and the farm didn't pay as he hoped and . . . many years passed. In the meantime, Herndon sold access to the treasure trove of notes to a few other acquaintances who picked through it, extracting material for their own biographies.

One other factor may have spooked Herndon out of completing his biography. The reception to his fourth lecture in Springfield had alarmed him. A few old residents of New Salem had told Herndon the story of a star-crossed romance between young Lincoln and the daughter of a local tavern owner, Ann Rutledge, who had taken sick and died before they could be married, in 1835. Though Lincoln had never mentioned the affair to Herndon or, for that matter, to any other of his closest friends in Springfield, it did explain many aspects of Lincoln's character that Herndon found otherwise unaccountable: the great man's recurring melancholy, his fatalism, and above all his marriage, undertaken by default, to a woman that Herndon thought unworthy of him. Even better, the episode cast Lincoln's entire life with a patina of tragedy that appealed to Herndon's own fatalism and romantic nature.

When Herndon made this the subject of his next lecture, Springfield was scandalized. Friends loyal to the widow turned on him. The widow herself was deeply wounded. "This is the return for all my husband's kindness to that miserable man," Mary Lincoln wrote to a friend. "Out of pity he took him into his office, when he was almost a hopeless inebriate and . . . he was only a drudge in the first place."

As Herndon's fortunes and reputation declined he continued to receive journalists and historians, and one of them, a young Hoosier named Jesse Weik, finally persuaded him, in the early 1880s, to return to the biography. Herndon would furnish the research and the psychological insight, and Weik, a fine writer, would cast the narrative. After a struggle of several years the book was published in 1889, nearly a quarter of a century after Herndon had begun his researches. For Herndon, publication of a project so long in gestation proved a grave disappointment. With poor sales at first, it did nothing to reverse his financial difficulties. Yet it more than fulfilled his ambition in another respect. *Herndon's Lincoln,* as the book is now known, became the touchstone for all future attempts to understand Lincoln, as even the most fastidious modern historians acknowledge. It is "the essential book," as one Lincoln biographer, David Herbert Donald, put it; "the indispensable biography," in the words of another, Don Fehrenbacher.

These highly credentialed scholars praise the book understanding fully its flaws, which are impossible to ignore. But the first thing to say about *Herndon's Lincoln* is that it's an undeniably great book—one of the greatest American books of the nineteenth century. In its vivid depictions of frontier life, complete with neighborhood toughs, plucky frontier gals, unscrupulous river rats, and cracker-barrel pols, it rivals bits of *Life on the Mississippi* or even *Huck Finn*. Like Mark Twain, Herndon wanted to show a country coming of age. Civilization slowly advances, a wild culture is finally tamed, as hunters and farm boys move to the city and become merchants, lawyers, politicians, bankers—the earliest members of the "knowledge class."

The store where Lincoln first lived upon coming to Springfield, and where Herndon clerked, was a gathering place for the town's ambitious group of displaced frontier men. Herndon describes them gathered around the woodstove in the back room, arguing politics and current affairs and reciting poetry and drama. "The young men who congregated about the store formed a society for the encouragement of debates and literary efforts. . . . In that early day the young men had not the comforts of books and newspapers which are within reach of every boy now." The purpose was social, of course, but also self-improvement—the formation, to put it a little more grandly, of a civil society out of the roughest material of the prairie. In the rise of Lincoln the prairie lawyer and politician, Herndon shows us American democracy rising too.

This is just one of Herndon's grand themes, but the substance of the book, and the readerly pleasure, lie in its detail, culled from Herndon's tireless research and the firsthand testimony from Lincoln's friends. And here's where the problems begin.

Early in his research Herndon asked an acquaintance, George Spears, to set down his recollections of Lincoln, whom Spears had known from his earliest days in New Salem. In the end, to his great embarrassment, Spears produced no more than a few lines of reminiscence. "At that time [in New Salem]," he told Herndon by way of explanation, "I had no idea of his ever being president therefore I did not notice his course as close as I should of."

Few of Lincoln's contemporaries were so modest, or candid. Yet it wasn't until Albert Beveridge—the first biographer to apply modern standards of scholarship to Lincoln's life—sifted through Herndon's thousands of pages of research that the problems became obvious. Beveridge began his work in 1918, long after Herndon's death, and he never wavered in his high opinion of Herndon's reporting on what he, Herndon, had witnessed on his own. "I have gone into his credibility as if I were a lawyer trying a murder case," Beveridge wrote. "There is absolutely no doubt whatever about his entire truthfulness and trust-worthiness generally. When Herndon states a fact as a fact, you can depend upon it."

Yet Beveridge quickly discovered that the same could not be said for Herndon's hundreds of sources. John Hanks, who gave Herndon the vivid, unforgettable, and untrue account of young Abe in New Orleans, proved to be typical—not dishonest, necessarily, but eager to prove his intimacy with a great man, and beyond that victimized from the tricks played by an aging and faulty memory. The mass of Herndon's research, flavorsome and evocative as it is, was shot through with inconsistencies and contradictions, touching on the most elementary matters. A biographer could pick and choose, according to his own principles of selection, and piece together any number of different Lincolns.

Herndon's principles of selection were clear. First, he wanted to use his own memories, bolstered by his formidable powers of observation, to help us *see* Lincoln the man, down to the smallest detail—including, for example, Lincoln's habit of storing his more important business papers in his hat. And have you ever wondered how Lincoln ate an apple? Herndon's your guy: "He disdained the use of a knife to cut or pare it. Instead he would grasp it around the equatorial part, holding it thus until his thumb and forefinger almost met, sink his teeth into it, and then unlike the average person, begin eating at the blossom end. When he was done he had eaten his way over and through rather than around into it. I never saw an apple thus disposed of by any one else."

Beyond such homey recollections, Herndon never wavered in his view that Lincoln was a great man—indeed, "the greatest man ever to walk the earth." Yet he wanted Lincoln's greatness to be understood in a particular way. Holland and other biographers did too. They had portrayed Lincoln, for example, as an orthodox, indeed fervent, Christian. They cited friends who claimed to have seen him routinely brandish a New Testament, calling it "this rock on which I stand" and claiming it as the inspiration for his political views. Herndon, his partner of sixteen years, knew better. He was repelled by such testimony and sought evidence to refute it. Part of Herndon's mission was to let all pious Christians know that Lincoln wasn't like them; Lincoln was like *him*—a skeptic, perhaps even an infidel, at most a believer in impersonal providence rather than a redemptive and historical Christ. To Herndon it was inconceivable that a man as great as Lincoln could be content with the orthodoxies of any faith.

In the same way, Herndon refused the possibility that so great a man could have been content with a woman like Mrs. Lincoln, and the version of their wedding that he fashioned from his source material confirmed his view, in typically circular fashion. Mary, according to one of Herndon's informants, had carried on a flirtation with Stephen A.

Douglas into the early stages of her engagement with Lincoln. Lincoln, for his part, was so overwhelmed with uneasiness at the thought of a life with Mary, and so afflicted with love for the departed Ann Rutledge, that he failed to appear at their original wedding ceremony, on January 1, 1841, causing a scandal that rocked *tout le Springfield*. It was only Mary's ambition and hauteur that overcame her public humiliation; and when a repentant Lincoln came slinking back she snatched him up. Yet for each piece of testimony in support of this version of the Lincolns' wedding, there is an account that undermines it. And the public record, which Herndon didn't bother to check, gives it no support: county files show that no wedding license was issued to Lincoln for a wedding in January 1841. The story of the "fatal first of January," however, appeared in Lincoln books for the next sixty years.

In trying to reconstruct Lincoln's life, and particularly his inner life, any biographer has to take account of the contradictions and inconsistencies in the personal recollections. He has also to reckon with what isn't there. After the assassination, Lincoln's acquaintances, including those who had bitterly opposed him, imposed a strict self-censorship. His martyrdom, one journalist said at the time, "has made it impossible to speak the truth of Abraham Lincoln hereafter." Any anecdotes unflattering to the fallen hero went untold. The consequences for the historical record must have been profound, though most historians have declined to speculate about what's been lost. Even for Herndon—who vowed to show readers that Lincoln "was a man—not a God"—there were limits to how much of the inner Mr. L. he was willing to set down on paper.

Lincoln's humor, for example. Many Lincoln friends, from his childhood to his last years, mentioned his fondness for dirty jokes as an essential feature of his character, and of course Herndon knew of it, too. One contemporary biographer delicately calls Lincoln's taste "Rabelaisian." Like any good comic, Lincoln recycled his gags, and there must have been dozens of them. Yet scarcely a handful survive that can be attributed to him with any reliability.

One joke pops up in Herndon's material at least twice. It tells of the American patriot Ethan Allen traveling to England shortly after the Revolution. His English hosts, hoping to rile him, hung a picture of George Washington in their outhouse. Allen, after his first visit there, told them he thought this was a perfectly appropriate place for it. "Why, they asked [according to Herndon's uncensored notes]. For, said Mr. Allen, there is Nothing that will make an Englishman SHIT so quick as the Sight of Genl Washington." Another joke came from a young Springfield acquaintance, C. C. Brown, who told Herndon of meeting Lincoln the morning after Brown's wedding night. Lincoln asked Brown, "Why is a woman like a barrel?" Brown couldn't answer. "Well, said Lincoln—you have to raise the hoops before you put the head in."

No such stories appeared in *Herndon's Lincoln,* and even in Herndon's raw interviews and correspondence they're rare. It's not hard to guess why. An acquaintance of Herndon and Lincoln's once asked Herndon to write out and send along some of Lincoln's stories so he could use them in a speaking tour. (Lots of Lincoln's acquaintances went on the road, trying to cash in.) Herndon replied that he didn't know any that were fit for mixed company. Years later, however, he did send along a couple of Lincoln's jokes to Weik, and they finally saw public light when their correspondence was published after both men were dead.

Here's one, about a mother in southern Illinois who took an excessively showy pride in her young boy. She often commanded him to appear before visitors while she told them how charming and bright he was. The boy endured these sessions with growing resentment. One evening he went to bed early and was joined under the covers by the family cat. He had just nodded off when he heard his mother call from the next room. "'Tommy, come out here, the ladies & gentlemen very much want to see you.' Tommy grunted and rolled over, somewhat vexed at the calls and said sharply—'Mother, damn it—let me alone till I fuck this damned old she cat and get her with kitten.'"

Herndon told Weik he had once written out this story of Lincoln's in a little book and loaned it to another friend who, Herndon now worried, might publish it. "I can't get it back," he fretted. The apprehension was common among Lincoln's more respectable friends. In his definitive book on Lincoln's humor, the historian P. M. Zall notes that the reasons for the suppression had to do with commerce as much as taste. There were some things about Lincoln that the public simply didn't want to know.

Zall quotes a letter to Herndon from Leonard Swett, a political friend of Lincoln and a fellow circuit rider. Swett told Herndon he should never publicly allude to Lincoln's use of profanity or to the off-color stories, much less quote them in his book, which Swett, like Herndon, hoped would be the definitive portrait of their friend and hero. "The public does not want to hear them," Swett told Herndon. "If I should say Mr. Lincoln ever swore and you should publish it, the public would believe I lied about it. It would damage your book."

Swett didn't need to add that it would also damage both their reputations. So this innermost part, at least, of the inner Mr. L. went unreported.

Understanding the shortcomings of Herndon's book and source material, the great Lincoln biographer Beveridge tried to correct for them in his own work. Yet the first generation of historians who came after Beveridge—by the 1930s, they were calling themselves "scientific historians"—thought he was trying to do the impossible: Herndon's testimonies and interviews, the recorded memories of events long since past, and indeed Herndon himself were too unreliable for scientific historians even to tamper with. Efforts to get at "the inner Mr. L.," using such tools were bound to be fruitless. So the scientific historians sealed off the Herndon material as though it were a "toxic waste dump," as the writer Joshua Wolf Shenk put it. They forswore psychological speculation and took their raw material from the written, objective record: letters, diaries, ledgers, speeches, contemporaneous newspaper accounts . . . the repository of the public Lincoln.

Yet Herndon's influence had run too deep. His rich account of the "real Lincoln"—tortured, passionate, folksy—satisfied human curiosity in a way that the drier renderings of Lincoln's public life never could. With a nip here and a tuck there, Herndon's Lincoln became the Lincoln of the general culture. Movies (John Ford's *Young Mr. Lincoln*), plays (*Abe Lincoln in Illinois*) and popular biographies (Carl Sandburg's *Prairie Years*) were all shoots that sprung from the loam of *Herndon's Lincoln*. (Sandburg's shoot grew into a six-volume tree.) Academic fashions changed too. "Scientific history" declined in the 1960s and Herndon's reputation rose. A fascination with the lives of "ordinary people," rather than the "great men" of traditional accounts, led the new historians to discount the problems inherent in oral history. After all, the public record of historical events, bequeathed to us by the elites of their day, might be even more corrupted and self-interested than the recollections of less celebrated witnesses. Historians had long believed that they might be able to discern the nature of a private man by carefully examining his public acts. Herndon gave them license to turn this method on its head: they could explain public acts by examining the inner man.

Herndon-like psychological speculation led to a riot of Lincolns, an endless profusion of Abes; now, it seems, everyone has his own. L. Pierce Clark, an early psychohistorian, concluded his 570-page *Lincoln: Man and Myths* with a Freudian flourish: "The benignant attitude Lincoln took toward the weak and downtrodden, shown, for instance, in his making the abolition of slavery the slogan for continuing the struggle of the Civil War, was prompted not a little by the more than filial devotion he must have felt for his mother." (Imagine what Clark would have made of the cat joke!) Another seer-historian, William Petersen, in *Lincoln-Douglas: The Weather as Destiny,* tied Lincoln's behavior to the weather: the reason he performed so spectacularly in his debates with Douglas was that they were conducted in a sultry Illinois summer; when the temperature fell, so did Lincoln's spirits and performance. Yet another biographer attributed Lincoln's melancholia, his love of jokes, and his hatred of injustice to a kick in the head he'd received from a mule as a boy. Another historian, taking his cue from the school of "self-actualization" psychology, found in Lincoln's fear of "self-dissolution" the source of his fear of the dissolution of the Union in the Civil War.

Don E. Fehrenbacher, an astonished historian, actually read all these books and reported on them in an essay, "The Deep Reading of Lincoln." He pointed out that it was one thing for Herndon and Herndon's contemporaries to try to reconstitute Lincoln's inner life; they at least had the advantage of having known their patient. It's far more presumptuous today, when we can rely only on Herndon's written materials. And even Herndon acknowledged the greatest obstacle he faced: Lincoln himself. "Lincoln never poured out his soul to any mortal creature at anytime and on no subject," Herndon confessed. "He was the most secretive—reticent—shut-mouthed man that ever existed."

Yet you can't really blame contemporary historians. Nearly every biographer since Herndon has declared his intention, as Herndon did, to "get beyond the myth" of Lincoln, to do away with the "plaster saint," to prove he was "a man, not a God," to "humanize" him, to demystify the "icon." And when he sets about the task he finds Herndon's treasure trove waiting to be sacked, offering items to fit nearly every interpretation. And indeed the treasure trove of oral history has only expanded in recent years, as other nineteenth-century accounts and interviews have been discovered and admitted as evidence into the court of history.

Consider the case of young Billy Thompson as one final, small example of how the attempt to plumb the real Lincoln, drawn from long-ago reminiscence, can stymie even the most accomplished and reliable historians.

I was reading along one day in *Abraham Lincoln: Redeemer President*, one of the subtlest Lincoln biographies, published in 1999 by the historian Allen Guelzo. In passing, Guelzo makes the point that Lincoln was often personally aloof and chilly—a man preoccupied with abstractions who, in Herndon's words, "had no idea—no proper notion of particular men & women." To support this view, Guelzo quotes "Billy Thompson," who grew up in Lincoln's Springfield neighborhood. "[Lincoln] was not an observant man on the street; in fact he hardly ever saw us unless we spoke to him. He walked along with his hands behind him gazing upward and noticing nobody."

Interesting, I thought. An abstracted, impervious Lincoln, quite different from the usual picture of kindly old Abe!

Then, a week or so later, I was reading *The Inner World of Abraham Lincoln*, by the brilliant historian Michael Burlingame, who devotes a chapter to how kind and attentive old Abe was. I came across Billy Thompson again. In fact, it was the same quote, used to make the opposite point.

Burlingame omits the first sentence that Guelzo takes from Billy ("[Lincoln] was not an observant man . . . he hardly ever saw us unless we spoke to him"). Instead Burlingame begins the quote with the second sentence Guelzo uses: "He walked along with his hands behind him gazing upward and noticing nobody." Chilly Abe!

Yet then the quote continues: "But it was usual for all of the boys in the neighborhood to speak to him as we met him. He had endeared himself to all of us by reason of the interest he took in us. When one of us spoke to him as he was walking along in his absorbed manner he would stop and acknowledge the greeting pleasantly. If the boy was small Mr. Lincoln would often take him up in his arms and talk to him. If the boy was larger Mr. Lincoln would shake hands and talk with him."

Kindly old Abe!

The same quote, from the same source, in the hands of two careful historians, used to sketch contradictory pictures of Lincoln. And to top it off: Billy's testimony was published in 1916, more than a half century after Lincoln's death, in a book of testimonials compiled by a journalist, Walter B. Stevens, who is known to have falsified several of the entries, perhaps including Billy's.

Follow the footnotes in most Lincoln biographies and you'll find yourself slogging through a similar thicket sooner or later. The contradictions and inconsistencies—the murkiness of how we know what we know about Lincoln—can lead a sensitive soul into a kind of despair of postmodernism: the terrifying suspicion that, when it comes to Lincoln, there's no certain truth you can grab hold of. It's my good fortune not to be a sensitive soul, however, and besides, the suspicion turns out to be wrong. There are, to begin with, all the things that everyone agrees Lincoln did and wrote—the *Collected Works of Abraham Lincoln*, for instance, runs to eight volumes and contains two million of his undisputed words. So I resolved for the moment to abandon a quest for the inner Mr. L. and spend time instead in the places that are dedicated to preserving Lincoln the public man—the outer Mr. L. I went back to the museum that made me a buff.

3

THE PAST ISN'T WHAT
IT USED TO BE

C hicago is a good place to look for the outer Mr. L., and not
just because it was a town Lincoln knew well or because it's
the largest city in his home state of Illinois, where every
license plate is stamped "Land of . . ." Chicago grew with the Lincoln
legend and was, in part, a creature of it.

Lincoln died in 1865, and overnight his life story became a national
lodestar, thanks to writers such as Josiah Holland and even Herndon.
Six years later, in 1871, Chicago was leveled in a fire, forcing a plucky
and resourceful citizenry to conceive a city from nothing but cinders,
rubble, ambition, and credit. This new city gorged itself on all the en-
ergies of capitalism and entrepreneurial go-gettery that were unloosed
by the end of the Civil War, and which Lincoln himself was coming to
symbolize. The country that rose from the ashes of the war—reunited,
by law if not in fact, and dedicated, at least in theory, to the proposition that all men are created equal—was on its way to becoming the
country that Lincoln had foreseen: "whose leading object is to elevate
the condition of men—to lift artificial weights from all shoulders, to

clear the paths of laudable pursuit for all, to afford all an unfettered start and a fair chance, in the race of life."

The capitalism that roared out of the Civil War had its victims and dark consequences, of course, as today's students of history are unfailingly reminded. There was pitiless economic exploitation and concentrations of wealth so dense as to choke the promise of self-government. But even from the dark side came heroes—the great Chicagoan Jane Addams, for example, the social reformer, early feminist, gifted writer, and protobuff.

She was born well-to-do, the daughter of a small-town politician in northern Illinois. She moved to Chicago as a young woman and in 1889 founded Hull House, a settlement house raised up in the middle of the slums of the West Side, to serve the city's swelling population of poor immigrants. They flocked to her for schooling, food, clothes, companionship, and most of all for knowledge of the ways of their new country. In a word—a very old-fashioned word, though one of Addams's favorites—they came to Hull House to be "Americanized."

Hull House was sustained by donations from the city's rich folk, yet there came a time, not long after its reputation found a toehold, when the rich stopped giving. "I recall a time of great perplexity, in the summer of 1894," she later wrote, with typically gentle understatement. Workers at the Pullman railroad factory had struck. The city split. Addams's wealthy benefactors saw the strike as the provocation of anarchists, a premonitory rumble of the coming revolution; her clients, the laboring families of her neighborhood, saw it as a necessary remedy to their own mistreatment. Caught in the pincer, Addams insisted on remaining neutral. She was accused of a failure of nerve, though now her neutrality seems more an act of "integrity and courage," as a later biographer put it—born of her hope that Hull House might serve as a place of refuge in the class war. She wanted to stand for some principle larger than economic interest, narrowly conceived by either capital or labor. As the summer dragged on, though, her neutrality looked to be a fool's errand and she began to doubt herself. What she had built was in danger of crumbling away. In her "time of great perplexity" she decided she needed to see Lincoln.

He had been a political acquaintance of her father's, though she'd never met him, and together with her father he became the illuminating influence in her life. At Hull House, Lincoln was the exemplar of America's possibilities. His birthday was the second largest holiday of the year. At Christmas, "in spite of demands on my slender purse for candy and shoes," Addams instead gave each of the neighborhood boys a copy of Carl Schurz's *Appreciation of Abraham Lincoln*. (They must have been thrilled.) "I held up Lincoln for their admiration as the greatest American," she wrote later. From Lincoln she had learned many lessons, she told her critics and clients, but this one above all: to practice, in any dispute, "charity for both sides."

That summer of '94, strikers shut down the streetcar lines in solidarity with the Pullman workers. So she took off on foot to "see Lincoln," walking five miles through the dripping heat to the entrance of Lincoln Park on the city's north side. There, a few years earlier, Lincoln's only grandson, Abraham Lincoln II, had unveiled what is generally thought to be the greatest Lincoln statue of the nineteenth century, a towering figure by Augustus Saint-Gaudens, set in a little meadow by Lake Michigan.

"I walked the wearisome way," she wrote, "in order to look at and gain magnanimous counsel from the statue." She rested in the shade of the young trees. She read the lengthy excerpts carved in marble from Lincoln's works. Whatever it was she came for—inspiration, reassurance, instruction, balm of some kind—she found it, not just for herself, she later said, but for the warring city. "Never did a distracted town more sorely need the healing of 'with charity towards all' than did Chicago at that moment," she wrote, "or need the tolerance of the man who had won charity for those on both sides of 'an irrepressible conflict.'"

Addams lingered by the statue till the heat began to lift with the coming of twilight. Then she walked the five miles back to Hull House, determined to resist all pressure to make her do what she didn't want to do. Hull House survived and soon began to flourish again—nurtured by the image she carefully cultivated of herself, as a figure that spanned the chasm of class, unbought by either side but trustworthy to both. And for several more generations Hull House continued to make life tolerable for new arrivals, and to "Americanize" them, with Lincoln, as Addams knew him, serving as inspiration and guide.

More than a century later the shade trees are much bigger but the statue is still there, at the foot of Lincoln Park, in a glade along Lake Shore Drive, a stone's throw from Lake Michigan, across a lawn from the Chicago Historical Society. I stopped by to see it one spring day. It's set high on a plinth in a stone plaza ringed by a low marble bench— the bench where Addams had sat, perplexed. Lincoln has just risen from a chair, preparing to speak. His tousled head bows in reflection, his left hand grips a lapel in resolve. His shoulders are tossed back and his chest is thrust out, and one foot is placed slightly before the other, suggesting an unstoppable forward movement.

The effect is so powerful that it takes a while for you to notice that the downturned face bears little resemblance to the face of Lincoln's photographs. This one is too severe, the angles sharper, the eyebrows too pointed—menacing, almost. But there's something else in it too that softens the severity, a sort of world-weariness that seems almost kind. Lincoln's greatness, Saint-Gaudens believed, is a complicated business. It emerges from an odd blend of patience, sympathy, and iron will. Jane Addams, who had sympathy and will in larger amounts than most of her contemporaries, wasn't the first Chicagoan to seek out the Saint-Gaudens Lincoln for its restorative power, nor the last. For years this meadow by the lake served as a prime civic gathering point, the site of band concerts, speeches, protests, and patriotic celebrations. When royalty visited Chicago, this is where they came to lay a wreath.

I was on my way to meet Oscar Esche, who had a Lincoln statue of his own I wanted to see. I'd read about Esche and his statue in a wonderful book called *Never a City So Real,* by Alex Kotlowitz, about the difficulties immigrants face in Chicago these days, now that "Americanization," both the word and the ideal, seems so weirdly quaint—a phrase not just from another time but almost another language, a civic language that's as dead as Babylonian. Mr. Esche owns the Thai Little Home Café, in the city's Albany Park neighborhood. To get there you take Lincoln Avenue from where it starts at the southern tip of Lincoln Park, by the Saint-Gaudens Lincoln statue, and you drive north for several miles, past the Lincoln restaurant and the Lincoln National Bank and the Lincoln Life Insurance office, till you get to Lincoln Square, where you turn left, and pretty soon you're in polyglot Chicago. Mr. Esche's restaurant is on a stretch of Kedzie Avenue, tucked in among the Casablanca Hair Salon, the Arab Jewelry Outlet, a Super Mercado, Marbello's Bakery, Desayumos Burrito, and the storefront office of Al-Muhaseb Bookkeeping. And a Starbucks.

The Thai Little Home Café is a converted storefront, too. But inside it's neat and homey. Exuberant plants hang in the window and rise festively from urns on the floor. The walls are papered in travel posters from Asia, washed out by years of afternoon sun pouring through the plate glass. At two o'clock the place was supposed to be closing for the afternoon, but several customers, Asian and Anglo and Latin, lounged over coffee. Soft rock—a Norah Jones–type singer who might have been Nora Jones—purred from a CD player near the back by the bar.

A young woman came to greet me and I asked to see Oscar Esche, and she brought me to the back, where an elderly man sat with a woman of similar vintage at a table covered in ledger books and piles of silverware. The woman was rolling forks and knives in paper napkins for the evening rush.

Mr. Esche is tall and handsome, in his late seventies, I'd guess, with sharp features and large black Buddy Holly glasses. He looked at me and nodded. I told him I'd read about him in Kotlowitz's book.

"Oh, I'm just in there for two, three lines," he said, in uncertain English.

I said I was intrigued by what Kotlowitz had written about him and Abraham Lincoln, and would he mind telling me a little more?

He didn't say anything but turned instead to the old woman at the table. He spoke to her for a minute or two, in Thai. I heard him say the word "Lee-cone," and her face suddenly broke into a smile. She rose from her seat. She was very short, scarcely five feet, but commanding, with a wide, friendly face; humorous and shrewd. She extended a soft hand for me to shake. With Oscar, who was a foot taller than she but still very deferential, we went into an adjacent dining room. Their every move was a courtesy, to each other and to me. Oscar pulled out the chair for me, then for his wife, before he sat down.

Mr. Esche said, "We first hear of Mr. Lincoln"—Lee-cone—"when we move here from Thailand."

His wife spoke to him in Thai. He listened patiently, then turned to me.

"My wife says, we move here in 1973," he said. "We open the third Thai restaurant in Chicago."

She spoke again, in Thai, at some length, and at length he turned back to me.

"My wife sees the license plate on all the cars after we move here to Chicago. 'Land of Lincoln,' they say. She wonders, 'Who is this Lincoln?' So she gets a book from a friend to read about Lincoln."

She spoke again; he turned back to me again.

"She says, in our country it is our custom that we pay respect to the person who is in charge of the country. And here it is Lincoln's country. He's the head man in history. You see him everywhere. Everyone loves him.

"My wife reads the book, and we realize, we must go pay respects to this man. He is a very great man. He helps the poor. He tells everyone that they are equal, that no man is better than any other man. This is very important. Everyone is equal. Everyone have same right. This is what he says, and he makes sure the country is this way."

She spoke another paragraph.

"We went to Springfield," Mr. Esche said, after she'd finished. "We want to pay respects for Lincoln. We go to his grave site with our children. Very young then. We go to this temple"—I figured he meant Lincoln's tomb in the cemetery at Springfield—"and on the roof has a big, tall . . . I don't know the word . . ."

"Obelisk?" I said.

He looked at me a moment, then smiled and shrugged. "Okay," he said. "And we bring flowers, and when we are there, we sit, all the family, and we sit by his grave and we pray to him, to give him thanks for such a wonderful country. We just want to show thanks."

His wife seemed to follow his every word, nodding once in a while. She spoke again, and he listened carefully.

"This is the thing," he said at last. "All people, poor people and rich people, they are equal in their rights. This is what Lincoln teach. My wife hear this and she bought a—what?" He made a box with his long fingers. Neither could remember the word. In his frustration, he beckoned me to the bar. On it was an ivory reproduction of the Daniel Chester French sculpture of Lincoln, the one that sits in the Lincoln Memorial in Washington, D.C.

"Like this," he said.

Statue, I said.

"Yes, statue. We bought a statue, to show our respect, and we put this here, and ever since that time we have statue, our business never go down. Always the business goes up, never down, no matter what. Lincoln does this. And for many years, every year we do the same— drive in the car with the children, go down in morning, come back at night. We see his house and we see his grave and we pray and give thanks and we come home."

I asked about the Esches' children—when they were younger, did they learn about Lincoln in school? Mr. Esche translated the question to Mrs. Esche. She shrugged.

"We don't know," he said. "We make sure the children know what we tell them. We make sure they understand Lincoln and be grateful to him for our country and for letting us live here and bringing us this good life he make for us. We pass this down to them. They will pass it down too. The way we are brought up, we must look to him and respect him, every generation, old people, young people, everybody."

Beginning in 1976, the Esche family made their Springfield pilgrimage—that's the right word, isn't it?—in the spring. Now two of their three kids are married, one with children, and driving is getting to be a problem for Mr. Esche, especially at night. So he and Mrs. Esche haven't made the trip the past few years. But the children go every year, as they hope their children will when they have children of their own. "We must remember and respect," he said.

Mr. Esche showed me a plate of chicken satay behind the Lincoln statue. As a final form of commemoration, every morning he and his wife set out a meal for Lincoln in the restaurant, next to his statue.

"It's full meal—everything, entrée, dessert, appetizer, drink also," Mr. Esche said. "We change the meal every day, so it's always different. We serve him everything."

Mrs. Esche interrupted.

"Yes," Mr. Esche said. "Everything but no pork."

Oh?

"We do not want to be disrespectful."

I guess Mr. Esche saw my puzzled look.

"He is *Abraham* Lincoln, yes?" he said, with special emphasis. "Jewish people, they don't eat pork."

When a Thai restaurant owner in an Arab neighborhood builds a Buddhist shrine to a Jewish president, my interest is piqued—of course—but of all the interesting things Mr. Esche had to say, I was struck by something he told me as he walked me to the door—that his children had been to the history museum when they were younger, but now there wasn't much to see about Mr. Lincoln. By history museum I assumed he meant the Chicago Historical Society.

The historical society, or CHS as it has more recently called itself,* was for most of the past century the premier Lincoln museum in the country. Before a series of renovations the building itself was a solid and stately thing, columned and balustraded, built of red brick in the Georgian style. It stood back from Clark Street by the little meadow where the Saint-Gaudens Lincoln stands, with the lake rising and falling just beyond. Visitors passed Lincoln on the way from the parking lot. From his plinth on high he looked down with that unnerving look, fierce and kindly all at once. The historical society was a temple for buffs—and a place of enchantment for me as a kid, as it was for anyone with a taste for the long-ago.

The temple no longer exists, in fact or in spirit, but the memory of visiting it is hard to shake. Through the giant doors and into the entrance hall you were met with a thrill—the visual equivalent of a trumpet fanfare. The stockade from the old Fort Dearborn, the 1812 settlement that eventually grew into Chicago, had been reassembled in a foyer. A fort indoors! It seemed an act of magic, a physical eruption from a distant age into our own. Fort Dearborn's inhabitants had been massacred by a band of Potawatomi during the War of 1812. A massive bronze statue commemorating the battle was placed in front of the reconstructed stockade. It showed a friendly Potawatomi rescuing a pioneer woman from a much less friendly, tomahawk-wielding Potawatomi, while at their feet a crumpled soldier gasps his last breath. Directly from your first steps into the museum, then, the tone was set: history was something extraordinary, full of drama, heroism, savagery, high emotions, and only the passing of the years had managed to tame it, so we could come to stand safe in a marble foyer adjacent to Lincoln Park, imagining its terror and wonders.

The heart-stopping tableau was put together in the early 1930s, too late for the society's great benefactor and original buff, Charles Gunther. But it would have been to his taste. Not long after coming to

* It has since changed its name again, to the Chicago History Museum.

America from Bavaria, in the 1840s, Gunther settled in Chicago and started making candy. He may not have invented caramel, as he sometimes claimed, but he did manage to mass-market it into popularity, and the stuff became the gooey center of his formidable fortune. In middle age he began a second career as a collector of antiquities, which he housed on the second floor of his candy store downtown. He placed a heavy emphasis on the lurid and the sensational, much to his customers' satisfaction. His standards in collectibles were less exacting than his standards in chewables, and some of his first buys brought him international fame, as either collector or chump: He bought the skin of the serpent that tempted Eve in the Garden of Eden, for example, and later an Egyptian mummy who in happier times had been the lady who fished Moses from the bulrushes.

When his collection outgrew the candy store, Gunther traveled to Richmond and bought the dilapidated Libby Prison, the same hellhole before which Lincoln had allegedly wept during his visit to the Confederate capital. It was huge: an acre of rusticated brick, piled four stories high. Gunther had the building dismantled and its pieces trained to Chicago, where he rebuilt it on Wabash Avenue and stocked it with his stuff. It opened to swollen crowds—one hundred thousand visitors in the first three months. Tourists could visit the Libby Prison galleries and stay at the Libby Prison Hotel. They could dine at the Libby Prison Restaurant, on the same cobblestones where thousands of Union soldiers had starved to death only thirty years before. (And you thought Baby Boomers invented irony.) Later Gunther had similar designs on at least one of the Great Pyramids, thinking it might look good on the Chicago lakefront. He made what he thought was a generous offer, but the Egyptians were unwilling to sell.

Their reluctance must have puzzled Gunther, for he embodied the heedless, blustering commercial mentality that gave Chicago its peculiar character: Everything and everyone has a price. This is an invaluable trait in a collector as in a businessman, and it is often accompanied by a deep sentimentality, which Gunther soon attached to both Lincoln and George Washington. Lincoln items were objects of special veneration. Like Jane Addams—like Mr. Esche, too, I assume—Gunther saw in Lincoln the strength, idealism, and general goodness of his adopted country, and in displaying the leavings of the great man's life he hoped to make him live for his fellow immigrants. The museum was part showmanship, part edification—half P. T. Barnum, half Horace Mann. The Libby Prison infirmary became the Lincoln Room. In advertisements the collection of Lincoln artifacts was described simply as "*The* Exhibit—There Is But One." And the stuff was impressive indeed: Abe's cane and combs, Mary's hairbrushes, the carriage the couple used in Washington, letters their young children wrote to friends. The exhibits were also accented with a crowd-pleasing semi-ghoulishness: wisps of clotted hair snipped from Lincoln's head wound, Mary's mourning jewelry, and most of the furniture from the room in the boardinghouse near Ford's Theatre where Lincoln died. The deathbed was displayed with a bloodstained sheet still stretched across it and a crusted pillow resting at its headboard.

After his death in 1920, in accordance with his will, Gunther's estate sold his collection to the Chicago Historical Society at a tenth of its market value. By then the artifacts had grown beyond Lincoln and Washington to include the table on which Lee and Grant had signed the surrender at Appomattox, the deed to the Louisiana Purchase, Benedict Arnold's battlefield pass, and much else beyond price (plus the serpent skin and Moses' stepmom).

The historical society was the perfect steward for such wonderful goods. Not only had Gunther been a director and member, but so had Robert Todd Lincoln, and Abraham himself, in 1860, had accepted the society's first honorary membership. In 1864 President Lincoln gave his handwritten draft of the Emancipation Proclamation to the society—a gift whose long-term significance Lincoln understood better than anyone. So honored were the society's directors that in 1868 they built a magnificent, state-of-the-art repository for it on the city's north side, advertised as invulnerable to any disaster from the hand of man or God, "the perfect fireproof structure." It burned to a cinder three years later, and the handwritten proclamation went up with it.

By 1923, when it received the Gunther collection, the society had recovered and established itself as a Lincoln shrine second only to the recently opened Lincoln Memorial in the nation's capital. Though much more earnest than Gunther—more Mann than Barnum—the society's curator embraced Gunther's Lincoln stuff as "the greatest American-ization force that can be assembled." And that's how the society treated it—in a city flooded with new arrivals from Europe and Asia and the rural South, Lincoln would evangelize Americanism. The beautiful Georgian headquarters was built in 1932 near the Saint-Gaudens statue to make the collection more accessible. In the Civil War Room, battle flags flew over dummies dressed in gray and blue uniforms and armed with every conceivable weapon from the nineteenth century. Artists from the Works Project Administration designed twenty Lincoln di-oramas depicting moments from his life, and these became the narra-tive anchor around which the collection was arranged. They appeared as little windows of light along the walls of a room painted black as pitch. When you peered into one you might see a thumb-sized Lincoln signing the Proclamation, as a dramatization of his strength and wis-dom; or Lincoln in his New Salem store, as evidence of his enterprise and his common origins; or Lincoln accepting, with head bowed, the news of his nomination in the parlor of his Springfield home, as a sign of his humility. A kid could last an hour or more among the dioramas. My favorite was a young Abe rescuing a dog as he crossed the frozen Wabash River into Illinois—showing his kindness and fellow feeling.

The dioramas traced the tragic arc from poverty to political success to martyrdom, ending in a final flourish of patriotism. The message came through without a lot of cumbersome description or scholarly second-guessing. I can testify to their power. The effect was all the more indelible because the designers had taken care to include in the scenes tiny versions of artifacts that were on display in the Lincoln Gallery only a few yards away. There were Lincoln's house slippers and eyeglasses, his umbrella and shawl, and pages from Tom Lincoln's family bible and little Abe's sum book. The Lincoln carriage stood on a riser on the hardwood floor, near the family's piano and the very same table upon which Lincoln signed the Emancipation Proclamation. In a corner was a life-size re-creation of the Springfield parlor, just like the one in the diorama, filled with furniture from Lincoln's home. Incredibly—the insouciance of the curators is unimaginable in hindsight—visitors in the 1930s and '40s could sit on the Lincolns' divan and have tea, chatting with docents dressed in the society's collection of Mary Todd's dresses; on special occasions visitors could even wear the very dresses themselves. Later, a reproduction of the Lincoln birth cabin from Hodgenville, Kentucky was installed. In the tour's final tableau, all that had gone before came to an end in a re-creation of that small back bedroom in the Peterson boardinghouse, with the furniture Gunther had bought. Empty chairs ringed the empty bed. Hymns quietly played.

The Civil War and Lincoln Galleries remained intact for more than two generations. But both disappeared years ago, which is what I had supposed Mr. Esche was alluding to. Behind the displays, it turned out, the historical society was undergoing changes that traced an unhappy arc of its own, and Lincoln was the most prominent casualty.

I called to make an appointment to see Russell Lewis, a veteran curator who had recently been named the society's temporary director. From the outside the entrance to the building itself was unrecognizable, having undergone several extensive renovations since the 1970s. Inside, the stockade was gone; so was the "massacre statue." The stockade was in storage, dismantled. The statue had become an object of ridicule and protest from political activists in the seventies and eighties, so the society had offloaded it to the Chicago Park District, which grudgingly displayed it in a park on the South side for a few years before retiring it to an old car barn. Once so hushed and stately, the lobby was now all skylights and polished wood and exposed steel beams painted white. To the contemporary eye the refurbished look, compared with the old, must have come as a great relief, as if a chrysalis had popped open in a burst of color and light.

The exhibit space was about to shut down for yet another renovation. Waiting at the security desk for Lewis's secretary to fetch me, I watched workmen take down what had been the CHS's last blockbuster exhibition, "Teen Chicago." It was a good example, I learned, of the new post-Lincoln CHS and its approach to history. The exhibit had been curated by teenagers for teenagers—and was, therefore, colorful and noisy and not terribly well organized, like teenagers. The brightly painted walls undulated through the space in endless curves, and from every direction video screens jumped with images of young people partying, clowning, and complaining. You got an impression of constant motion and, before too long, seasickness. The artifacts were culled from the everyday: skateboards, report cards, old album covers and eight-track tapes, yearbooks and fan magazines, posters and pillow covers. One display re-created a 1950s soda fountain, another a teen bedroom from the 1970s. CHS officials had told the local newspapers that "Teen Chicago" was a way of "reaching out" to an "underserved constituency," offering them "an exploration of what it means to be a teenager in Chicago." Schools had bused kids in by the class full, on the premise that Chicago teens needed to go to a museum to see what it means to be them.

Lewis's secretary came out to the lobby and led me from the new building, with the skylights and exposed beams, into what remained of the old. Walls had been put up in long corridors to create office space. She told me that this is where the exhibitions had once stood, but it was impossible for me to place what had been where. Down one corridor we came to Russell Lewis's office. Out his window you could see the Saint-Gaudens Lincoln, the hand tugging the lapel, the hawklike nose, those severe eyebrows. Beyond the trees the ice-blue lake rose and fell.

Lewis has a broad, smooth face of the kind you often see in Chicago, where the brutal winters force the human organism to grow an emergency layer of insulation just beneath the epidermis, stretching the skin taut as a birthday balloon. In a broad striped shirt and polka-dot tie, he presented the very picture of a Baby Boom establishmentarian. His hair is thin now and combed back, but the picture on the ID badge that dangled from a lanyard around his neck showed a much younger man with long hair tucked behind the ears and coming down in fistfuls to his shoulders. He wasn't long out of graduate school when he went to work for the CHS in 1982. There he joined a new generation of curators and administrators who were already well on their way to changing the institution—and its view of the society's first honorary member.

Lewis had pegged me for a buff, or at least someone with buffian sympathies. "Our relationship to Lincoln has always been very important to us," he said. "Let me stress that. His relationship to Chicago was important to him. As best as we can make out, he visited this city fourteen times between 1848 and 1860. The founders of the society were friends of his. So, sure, he means a lot to us." Just a few years ago, he said, the society had paid $800,000 for a presidential order, signed by Lincoln, that instructed his secretary of state to affix the seal of the United States to the Emancipation Proclamation. "That's an expensive piece of paper. It's a sign of a continuing relationship we have with him. But yes, as times change, the nature of the relationship has changed too."

The society's original exhibits, he said, showed a mythic Lincoln— "Lincoln as a moral force, savior of the Union, the man who freed the slaves. We had a Lincoln gallery, right where we're sitting now. There were a lot of objects, a lot of biography. Lincoln was venerated. Back over here, in this general area"—he pointed out toward the hallway— "we had a reproduction of the bedroom where he died. People would stand at the railing and look at the deathbed and they'd press a button and a somber voice would recite an account of what happened that night. And then it played the 'Battle Hymn of the Republic.' And people would cry. They would weep."

He sat back, with what I thought was a can-you-believe-it look. But I did believe it. I saw it happen. I cried too.

"Since then," he went on, "we've been less interested in the myth or the icon, more interested in a Lincoln that's much more human—a man placed very much in the context of his time. And it's a much more powerful story."

The old Lincoln Gallery came down in the late 1980s. The dioramas were mothballed, likewise the birthplace cabin, the dresses, most of the personal effects. A new exhibit was conceived, the culmination of a long reconsideration of how the historical society should approach history. The story of that reconsideration, Russell told me, was best recounted by a young historian named Catherine Lewis (no relation) in *The Changing Face of Public History,* which had been published as a kind of authorized biography of the Chicago Historical Society.

It's revealing in a way few authorized biographies are, but it's not easy to read. A trained professor, Ms. Lewis tends toward sentences like: "Change is a set of interventions that disrupt categories of knowledge and the current power structure." I suppose the academic clichés are appropriate, since what happened to CHS in the 1980s had its origin in academia. As new ideas and intellectual fashions reshaped the approach to Lincoln biography, they trickled down from the ivory tower to less rarefied institutions like museums. Most of these ideas were intended to strike a blow against the power structure that had excluded what Catherine Lewis called "ordinary people" from the presentation of history. By dwelling on dramatic events and on the relatively small number of (usually) men who shaped them—Lincoln, for example—traditional historians and curators mislead their audience, according to the new academic view. The falsified past needed to be replaced for political reasons, too: it had been used as an instrument for that very same power structure to maintain its privileges and keep ordinary people out.

This was the same "new history" or "social history" that led to the restoration of Herndon's reputation and the revival of interest in the personal testimonies he had collected. Before long the idea was so widely accepted by academic historians that it seemed not so much an approach to be argued over as a shared, self-evident premise—a piece of dogma. Traditionalists who defended the old "great man theory of history" took to mocking the new attitude as "political correctness." But traditionalists were badly outnumbered. PC publicly established itself as the house worldview of CHS in 1987, when most local and national history organizations were celebrating the bicentennial of the U.S. Constitution. As Catherine Lewis explains, with evident distaste, in many communities "bicentennial programs were generating patriotism and an appreciation of the American way of life," acting as "an assimilative tool or a reminder of the superiority of the American system."

The Chicago Historical Society was having none of that. Instead, to mark the bicentennial, it mounted a permanent exhibition about the Revolutionary era called "We the People," which took a more detached view of the matter. The nation's founding was presented as a series of "struggles between rich and poor, landed and landless, enslaved and free." In this way a period "dominated by sacred symbols and godlike figures" could be "demystified." Previous CHS exhibits on the American Revolution, the curators noted, had referred to ordinary Americans as, among other things, "Americans," "patriots," and "an aroused citizenry"— loaded terms that suggested a single, national identity on whose behalf the "patriots" waged war against old King George. "We the People" took pains to group ordinary Americans according to skin color, sex, or economic class. Displays were built around everyday items like farm equipment, kitchen implements, and carpenter's tools. These had no special associations with any godlike figures and no claim to special interest, which is why they were suddenly of special interest to the new historians. The society had long showcased beautiful pitchers and crockery, for example, because they were beautiful, "the skillful creations of colonial craftsmen." Now they were displayed for other reasons: "They became evidence that household items were highly politicized."

Thus did CHS take sides in the contest between—quoting an academic admirer—"the protagonists of a new history which is multicultural and democratic in its inspiration and emphasized the history of everyday life; and the self-styled traditionalists who demand restoration of the nation to the center of the curriculum and a history which turns on great events and great men."

In the new history Lincoln's reputation could only suffer, since it was designed to discount the very possibility of "greatness," and indeed a number of new historians offered debunkings that would have thrummed the heartstrings of Tom DiLorenzo and his neo-Confederate colleagues. Yet at CHS Lincoln was not so much slandered or insulted as simply pushed to the background. The exhibit that rose in place of the Lincoln Gallery was called "A House Divided: America in the Age of Lincoln." Like "We the People," the new exhibit was "thematic," meaning that it had less to do with the actions of individuals than with the movement of masses of people. The text was written by one of the pioneers of the new history, Eric Foner, who had complained that "the old Lincoln Gallery was sort of a church." Foner's exhibits, by contrast, were more like an illustrated text in econometrics. They offered the visitor a wealth of data about transportation systems, technological advances in agriculture, and the migration of ethnic groups, with a special emphasis on marginalized "constituencies," in the CHS terminology. In the displays there was again a relentless emphasis on the everyday: surveyor maps, bank ledgers, sewing kits, spittoons, sheet music, textile punch cards, rakes and hoes, nails and lathes, the stuff of ordinary life. History enthusiasts are partial to such stuff—I'm a sucker for it myself—but it doesn't arouse great excitement in the average visitor, the not-terribly-interested weekenders who have dragged the kids out of bed for a bit of educational uplift.

Yet the new history had a marketing angle, too. The curators believed that the new thematic exhibits would bring in a whole new generation of museumgoers—precisely those who were not terribly interested in history. "A good exhibit makes people see themselves," as one CHS official put it. "People come to places where they see themselves." Therefore an emphasis on ordinary people could mean big box office. The logic may have been superficially sound, but it was also condescending. It presumed that ordinary people suffer from an extraordinary lack of imagination—that no ordinary person will respond to information unless it concerns people just like him. This would certainly narrow the appeal of someone like Lincoln, who, in addition to being extraordinary, as even his revilers agree, was white, midwestern, heterosexual, male, poor for most of his life, and, at the end of it, dead. What if a woman who's white and lesbian and northeastern and alive comes to the museum? Or a live black rich guy from the Southwest, or a breathing Hispanic homosexual from Alaska? By the curatorial logic of new history, such people should have no interest in Lincoln, not sharing with him the proper income level, melanin count, genital profile, sexual proclivity, or ontological status.

There were, of course, some old-timers who objected to the museum's shift in "A House Divided." "Some people said there was a lack of balance," Russell Lewis told me. "The Civil War people wanted more ammo, more swords, more guns—they always do. The Lincoln people wanted more Lincoln. But we had to let people know that we were committed to change and to doing and seeing things in new ways."

I think he wanted to tell me it could have been worse. Even with "A House Divided," he said, there had been criticism from the more radical of the new historians. "Some of them really wanted to undercut, really attack, the myth of the Great Emancipator," Lewis said. "Because I think the consensus view was developing that, in fact, Lincoln's role had been more marginal than we'd thought and that the slaves freed themselves. These scholars made a very strong case that we had to respect.

"But eventually we had to put our foot down," Russell said. "I had to say, 'Look: We're an Illinois institution. This is the Land of Lincoln, after all. We have to give the guy *some* credit.'"

As it happened, however, the marketing logic was faulty. With the arrival of the new history at CHS, box office plunged. For decades museum attendance had held steady, even as other forms of entertainment proliferated, from radio to movies to TV. In 1990, as the social historians did their work, 207,000 visited the historical society. Fifteen years later, the number had fallen by 25 percent.

You can make a long list of where the new historians went wrong. For starters, they were wrong that the traditional approach to history, which they did away with, was "elitist" rather than "populist," as Catherine Lewis puts it. Her book reproduces pictures of the Chicago Historical Society's founding fathers, old guys in high collars and walrus mustaches. They may have been WASPy and clubby, but they were public-spirited and largehearted. And as their charter said, they were committed "to the general diffusion of historical information." They thought anyone, rich or poor, powerful or powerless, could be improved by learning, that everyone could share in the refined pleasures of historical knowledge. That's why they built the beautiful building in the park and the stockade and the dioramas. They were egalitarians in the truest sense. And they didn't pander.

Where the new historians most obviously went astray, though, was in thinking that their new approach would have wide appeal. Whatever its ideological and methodological merits, new history is boring. The marketing premise was precisely wrong: people don't want to come to museums to see themselves. Ordinary people are surrounded by ordinary people; we run into each other wherever we go, constantly, as hour chases hour, day in, day out. When we take the trouble to strap our ordinary kids into our ordinary car and drive someplace to show them something, we want to make sure it's something or someone extraordinary—something with guns and pretty dresses. Something like a civil war, and someone like Lincoln.

The continuing decline in attendance forced the renovation that Russell and I picked our way through as he walked me to the door. "A House Divided" was dismantled several years ago and it will not be reinstalled; Lincoln himself doesn't figure large in future plans, which are, in any case, unformed. It's possible there may yet be another Lincoln Gallery, Russell said: "At some point in the future, maybe after the Lincoln bicentennial in 2009." Until then, the dioramas and much of the Lincoln collection will remain underground, literally, stored in an old bomb shelter on a farm forty miles northwest of Chicago.

And even if, at some distant date, a Lincoln Gallery were reinstalled, he said, "I'm afraid the dioramas aren't going to be included." Not enough space.

I'm sure Russell could see my disappointment, and as he walked me back to the entrance he did his best to console a mossback buff from another age. "A lot of the attention on Lincoln will turn to Springfield from now on," he said. He asked if I'd been downstate to the state capital, to where a lavish new Lincoln museum was being built. I told him I hoped to go there the next day.

"Good," he said. "You need to see it. A lot of what places like the historical society used to do, in terms of Lincoln, will shift down there."

I headed back to my car for the drive to Springfield. I walked back behind the building through the little meadow, by Jane Addams's bench, beneath the downcast gaze of Lincoln. He looked slightly pissed.

4

THE KINGMAKER'S WIFE,
THE EMOTIONAL ENGINEER,
AND THE TRIUMPH OF FUN

T hough I wouldn't have mentioned it to Russell Lewis, I had the
thought when I left the Chicago Historical Society and headed
for Springfield that I was leaving something vaguely geriat-
ric and out of date. The new historians had complained about how
stuffy the old CHS was, with its starchy veneration of dead "heroes."
But it's hard to imagine, in the latter part of the first decade of the
twenty-first century, anything quite as stuffy as the political correctness that has the curators still in its thrall. It seems so schoolmarmy, so
purse-lipped and bitter . . . so ten years ago. I know that committed
conservatives still get huffy about PC, and that left-wingers, particularly in education and especially in higher education, still do their best
to initiate the younger generations into its sacraments. It's also true that
some PC preoccupations, such as those with skin color and sexual identity, are now absorbed into the conventional views of every polite person. But most Americans seem to have moved on to other things. Once

thought of as the vanguard of the future, the schoolmarms of PC are being left behind, hands fidgeting, faces tightening, looking clueless and forlorn.

For here in the Land of Lincoln what has vanquished PC, what has delivered Our Man from its bitter clutches, is the most irresistible force in America: Fun.

A recent and unexpected eruption of fun, in the form of a mint-new Abraham Lincoln Presidential Library and Museum (ALPLM), is what drew me to Springfield. The town has never been known as a mecca of merrymaking. Lincoln was twenty-nine when he moved to Spring-field, and the next twenty-four years he was a dutiful civic booster. As a state legislator he successfully maneuvered to have the state capital relocated here, and the old Capitol building where he served still stands in a rectangle of lawn in the center of downtown. Yet he always had a wry, Lincoln-like ambivalence about his hometown. He used to tell a story about the man who came to Springfield to give a series of lectures and was told he would have to ask permission from the secretary of state.

"What are your lectures about?" asked the official.

"They're about the Second Coming of the Lord," said the man.

"Don't waste your time," the secretary of state said. "If the Lord's seen Springfield once He ain't comin' back."

The ambivalence ran in the other direction as well. As soon as the wire brought word from Washington of Lincoln's death, the city fathers managed to control their grief long enough to make a cool assessment of the commercial possibilities. For the site of his final resting place they chose a prime piece of real estate—the spot where today's new state Capitol stands, as it happens—because it was easily visible from the intersection of two railroad lines. A sufficiently grand monument glimpsed from a train window, they reasoned, and showcased with appropriate signage, might tempt passengers to make an overnight stop. They offered the property free of charge to Mary Lincoln for her husband's burial. Offended, she threatened to bury him in Chicago instead. She got her choice of a quiet cemetery north of Springfield, near picnic grounds where she and her husband had once courted.

Still, the locals jealously guarded their claims. One reason that Lincoln scholarship remained for so long the work of amateurs and hobbyists is the state government's iron grip on much of his physical legacy. The state's Lincoln holdings have included, at one time or another, his house and furniture, his carriage, many of his clothes and personal effects, and a vast quantity of his papers. All were controlled by patronage workers with immaculate political credentials but no scholarly training or curiosity. The tradition continues. If anything, Illinois's famously corrupt politics—two of the last four governors have been indicted for abusing public office—are more dismal than ever. A professor who specializes in Lincoln once complained to me about the impossibility of placing his graduate students in historians' jobs at the state library or the Illinois Historic Preservation Agency, the two bureaucracies that hold sway in Lincoln affairs. "These are good scholars who would kill for those positions," he said. "But the jobs always went to party hacks."

There are exceptions—the current state historian, Tom Schwartz, and the first director of the new library and museum, Richard Norton Smith, are both widely admired—but if you spend much time among buffs in the Land of Lincoln you hear complaints about an entity that has come simply to be called "Springfield." The word, darkly whispered, refers not so much to the place as to a faceless, politicized bureaucratic blob that engulfs Lincoln activities in the state capital. It's a term of derision, used like this: "Do you know why a new edition of the *Collected Works of Abraham Lincoln* hasn't been done in fifty years? It's Springfield"; or, "There will never be another great traveling exhibit of Lincoln artifacts—Springfield won't let it happen." The bad feeling may be justified, but it carries as well an echo of the class resentment and regional snobbery that Lincoln himself endured as a politician eager to make a national reputation. Coming from nowhere, he was presumed, by competitors back east, to be a nobody, until he proved himself otherwise. Among some scholars and buffs, a kind of astonishment prevails about Lincoln's origins: How could someone so grand come from somewhere so tacky? Why couldn't he have come from the Upper East Side?

So you can sympathize with Springfield. But it really is a clapped-out old burg, the kind of place where the tourist brochures list the VFW Hall in directories of recommended restaurants ("Cuisine: American"). The downtown is given over to empty lots and vacant storefronts and dying linden trees still gasping from last year's misbegotten attempt at urban beautification. Lincoln haunts the place, of course, an ineffaceable presence. For years tourists would line up to take their pictures at one of the town's impressive assortment of Lincoln bronzes; there's another tribute every few blocks, it seems. The state Capitol building alone boasts four of these, and outside of town, beneath the obelisk where Lincoln lies buried, is an unequaled collection of Lincoln statuary. These are stern images, for the most part—grim though not quite forbidding, a mixture of kindness and resolution, like the Saint-Gaudens in Lincoln Park.

And then suddenly, in 2005, they seemed out of date too. The statue where tourists flock nowadays, fanny packs bobbing and cameras in hand, isn't technically a statue at all. It stands in the "Museum Plaza," as it's called, of the new museum (which has been dubbed, unromantically, the ALPLM). The plaza is indoors, a soaring space paneled in polished wood and ringed in skylights. This Lincoln is life-sized, as all newly made Lincolns are, and he's posed with his family, wife Mary and sons Robert, Tad, and Willie, looking just as they looked on the day they left Springfield for good. (Edward, the second son, had died in 1850.) This is a homey Lincoln—Lincoln the family man. He is dressed in real clothes—black frock coat, square-toed boots—and underneath he is made of rubber.

Rubber is the layman's term. Technically, he's a "polymer blend," a sculpted slab of blubbery foam coated in fiberglass and covered with a silicone skin that's been tinted to a ruddy hue. His hair is a mixture of human and synthetic hair. Sometimes, as the families crowd around him in Museum Plaza, it's hard to get close enough to get a good look at him, but when you do you notice that his face, like that of the Saint-Gaudens Lincoln, isn't a precise, painstaking re-creation of the face you see in photographs; like that other Lincoln, it has been reconfigured by the artist to suit his own purposes. The nose is a millimeter too long and the lower lip a trifle too pendulous. The eyes are brighter but less humorous. Each feature has been exaggerated to a degree that's just barely perceptible, for a cartoonish effect.

But it's a face you've seen before, and if you're among the 98 percent of Americans who have ever spent a day in Orlando, Florida, or Anaheim, California, you might suddenly remember where. Springfield's new-generation Lincoln, standing with wife and kids in the Museum Plaza, is a dead ringer for the President Lincoln in Walt Disney's Hall of Presidents.

This odd revelation spreads as you move along through the museum. An impression of Disney—maybe a Disney *aesthetic* is the better way to say it—pops up everywhere. Beyond the Lincoln family, to your left, is a life-size mock-up of Lincoln's boyhood cabin in Indiana, against an idyllic woodland backdrop that might have been lifted from Disney's *Pocahontas*. Perched on a rail fence is a young silicone Abe, looking just like *Aladdin*. Inside the cabin a goofy figure from *Pirates of the Caribbean* snores comically. Farther on you walk through a horrifying slave auction, with figures plucked from *Song of the South*. Later, Mary Lincoln reappears, as plump and apple-cheeked as the fairy Flora in *Cinderella*. Suddenly we come upon a corridor where the walls are set at disorienting angles and whispers rise creepily from hidden speakers—as spooky as the Haunted Mansion. In another corridor we walk a gauntlet of nightmarish images flashing from either wall, meant to depict the political pressures impinging on Lincoln as he considered freeing the slaves; but the nightmare recalls the ghosts that hector poor Ichabod Crane in Sleepy Hollow . . .

Cute and chilling and sad and chipper—and fun!—and never, not for a moment, more realistic than an animated movie. Unless a visitor was prepared for it, he might be stunned to find such a style throughout the most important Lincoln tribute to be built in eighty years. And if the visitor was a buff, he'd think: "There's got to be a reason for this."

The story of how Lincoln entered the era of fun begins in 1981, and it begins with Julie Cellini—the woman whose perseverance was the one indispensable element in the creation of the ALPLM. "It's amazing what you can accomplish," she likes to say, in a staccato, unsmiling delivery, "when you don't care how many people you annoy."

Most people cannot afford to live by such an axiom. Mrs. Cellini is not one of those people. She's a striking woman, tall and angular as a fashion model, favoring scarves and brooches and designer ensembles. She came to Springfield fresh from college to work as a reporter on the local paper. Covering politics in the late 1960s, she met a young city councilman named William Cellini. "Springfield has always been a city of young men on the make," she told me over lunch one day. "Guys come here to get their card punched. Always have. Lincoln was one of them. And I married one."

She had invited me to meet her at the Sangamo Club, a members-only dining spot favored by pols and lobbyists, two blocks from the state Capitol. Beefy men wearing wide pastel ties and tasseled loafers squeezed around the tables, drinking iced tea and nibbling unhappily at salads (even in Springfield, the lobbying life isn't what it used to be). Now and then one of them would walk by our table and pay their respects to Mrs. Cellini—always with the same semaphore: a wink, a grin, and that finger-extended popgun gesture that political people, above all others, rely on as a gesture of goodwill. And always Mrs. Cellini would nod and say, "Good to see you."

From the start of their marriage, Mrs. Cellini said, she and her husband dreamed big. "We had the career all charted out," she said. "We were going to go into politics in a big way. He was going to be governor. Then our son was born, and he had some disabilities and we realized that we were going to need lots of money for special treatments and so forth. So my husband decided to give up politics and make money."

Within a decade Cellini had built a fortune by "turning state government into a cottage industry," as one Chicago newspaper put it. He started a construction firm that specialized in government-subsidized housing for senior citizens and office buildings that could be leased back to the state. He helped secure state-subsidized loans for the President Abraham Lincoln Hotel, a "luxury hotel" he built in downtown Springfield. When the state legalized gambling on riverboats, it sold him the first license—an $85,000 investment that led to a company later valued at $500 million. At the same time he became the most powerful lobbyist in Illinois, nominally a Republican but one who crossed the aisle with ease, earning a reputation as a confidant of governors of both parties.

Mrs. Cellini said, "Bill thought, 'Okay, if I can't be a king, I'll be a kingmaker.'"

Having left her job as a reporter, Mrs. Cellini found herself with lots of spare time. She began volunteering, at a very high level. She'd always had an interest in state history in general and Lincoln in particular, so in 1981 the governor appointed her a trustee of the Illinois State Historical Library. The library's collection of Lincolniana—47,000 letters and manuscripts, 2,000 artifacts, making a collection bigger than the Lincoln holdings of the National Archives, the National Park Service, and the Smithsonian Institution combined—was housed underground, in a renovated parking garage dug below the old state Capitol building. Even by state government standards—even by *Illinois* state government standards—the facility was a sty, unventilated and poorly maintained. Stacks of dusty boxes teetered in the hallways, leaves gathered in drifts by the exit doors, exotic fungi sprouted in the corners. "It was awful," she said. "Filthy. And then— *then* I saw the collection."

Jim Hickey, the state historian, took her for a tour through the stacks. "I couldn't believe the state of Illinois owned this stuff," she said. "There was Mary Todd Lincoln's wedding dress, their marriage certificate, Tad's toy cannon—I had no idea. Then Jim hands me a pair of white gloves. I say, 'What do I need these for?' He says, 'I'm about to hand you the Gettysburg Address.' And there it was, right in my hands! There are five of these in the whole world, and I'm holding one. I said, 'Jim, everybody needs to see this. We need to open this stuff up.'"

Mrs. Cellini wasn't the only one to sense the need for a new library. Scholars had been protesting the building's shortcomings for years. But Mrs. Cellini had connections far beyond any scholar's reach, along with the energy and ambition to prod the government to do . . . something. The original idea was to build a new, climate-controlled library to protect the Lincoln collection; adjacent to it would be a Lincoln Heritage Center, to display the library's treasures to the public. Yet when the legislature, as a kind of down payment on the new facility, allocated $75,000 for a new case to display the Gettysburg Address, Mrs. Cellini got permission to use the money to develop preliminary drawings for a much grander facility—a place built not merely to serve Lincoln lovers who were coming to Springfield but to attract tourists to Springfield who might not otherwise have come.

Like many small midwestern cities, Springfield continued to decline in the boom years of the eighties and nineties. Hollowed out by a depressed farm economy, a juiceless state budget, and a flatlining tourist trade, the city proved resistant to every scheme of urban renewal— neither tax breaks nor enterprise zones, neither pedestrian malls nor interest-free loans could lure business to the abandoned buildings downtown. Among the casualties was the President Abraham Lincoln Hotel, which never generated sufficient funds even for Cellini and his partners to repay interest on the $40 million in state-financed debt. "We needed something that would convince visitors that Springfield was really a two-day destination, an overnight stop," one tourism official, Nicky Stratton, told me. It was the same lament that moved the city fathers to try and plant Lincoln's body by the train tracks in 1865, and the same reasoning. Overnight visitors stay in hotels, spend money in bookstores and gift shops, buy meals in restaurants—and real meals, too, dinners and breakfasts, not just the chips-and-soda fare of day-trippers and brown-bagging bureaucrats. "Heads on beds" became the catchphrase for Springfield's revival. And Lincoln was what would lure them to their pillows. Springfield would make Lincoln pay.

Politics in Springfield is still, as it was in Lincoln's day, the preserve of powerful men. Yet their wives, unlike wives from an earlier era, weren't content with coffee klatches and bridge parties; they founded well-financed nonprofit groups and sat on boards of directors. From their ranks Mrs. Cellini assembled a powerful team of boosters. She brought Pat Daniels, the wife of the speaker of the Illinois House, onto the board of the Illinois Historic Preservation Agency. After seeing the drawings and plans that Mrs. Cellini had commissioned, Mrs. Daniels convinced her husband to break a legislative logjam and support the library and museum.

Later, Mrs. Cellini cornered the governor's wife at a cocktail party. "I'm in," said the state's first lady, without a moment's thought.

"She went to her husband that night," Mrs. Cellini told me. "The next morning I get a call: 'Come over and let's talk.'" Eventually, the governor arranged for state funding that would have seemed unimaginable only a few years before, when the library and heritage center were conceived as a $10 million project. When it was finished in 2005, the museum and library cost more than $150 million.

Yet the main question was still unanswered: What would the new Lincoln project be, aside from large and expensive and delightful enough to bring tourists in to stay awhile? With her committee Mrs. Cellini traveled the country, fact-finding. "We had an amazing concept—library and museum together. And we had the best guy in the world: Lincoln. What we needed were the best storytellers to do justice to both the concept and the guy." The Springfielders visited all thirteen of the nation's presidential libraries, as well as every "cultural heritage" site they could think of, from Disney World and Knott's Berry Farm to Graceland and the Gene Autry museum.

The best storytellers in the world, Mrs. Cellini concluded, were Walt Disney's.

Through her political contacts she arranged for Disney "imagineers," as the theme park designers are called, to come to Springfield. They scouted the sites, drew preliminary sketches, and made economic projections for heads on beds. She kept Disney's involvement with Lincoln "under the radar," as she put it. Even then she knew the sensitivities that might be riled by mixing the world's glitziest entertainment company with American history's most revered personage. Only a few years before, Disney's plan for a historical theme park in rural Virginia, outside the Washington Beltway, had been canceled, at great expense to Disney, after appalled historians joined in a nationwide protest—a kind of scholarly upchuck. "We simply could not have sold this project—to anybody, politicians, Lincoln people, scholars—if it had been a quote-unquote Disney project," she said. "People in the scholarly community were already referring to 'the D word,' as though Disney was something horrible and unmentionable."

When at last the state put its Lincoln contract out for bid, half a dozen museum-design companies entered the competition. Disney imagineers had their own recommendation: BRC Imagination Arts, headed by a former Disney employee named Bob Rogers. Yet most insiders in the museum business assumed the job would be awarded to the New York firm of Ralph Appelbaum Associates, which had recently won praise for its understated, almost unbearably moving Holocaust Museum in Washington, D.C. Mrs. Cellini and her committee were unimpressed. "Ralph Appelbaum was hot stuff," she said. "He was sure he'd get the job. So he sent a third-stringer to give the presentation. He had very mundane drawings. He just taped them to the walls. No energy. No excitement."

Bob Rogers from BRC, by contrast, showed up with a multimedia presentation, a collection of props, and a full complement of writers and artists. He won the contract.

If Springfield couldn't get Disney to put heads on beds, it would get the next best thing.

In a squat office building in Burbank, California, next to an off-ramp of the Ventura Freeway, at the edge of a vast, gray neighborhood of low-rise warehouses and light industry, sits the international headquarters of the next best thing, the magical world of BRC Imagination Arts. BRC—the acronym stands for Bob Rogers Company—is just a mile or two down the road from the international headquarters of Walt Disney Company. I parked in the gated parking lot and went through heavy glass doors that a guard pulled shut behind me. The tinted windows dimmed the sunlight and the rumble of the freeway faded into a pleasant hum. An astonishingly beautiful receptionist rose dreamlike from behind a desk. She asked my name and offered me a seat. She brought me a fresh copy of *Variety* to read while I waited. Hollywood! I struggled to orient myself among the rubber plants.

"Bob Rogers is a genius," Mrs. Cellini had told me. "And in this Lincoln project, he is *the* genius." The walls of his offices in Burbank are hung with faded posters of the first generation of rides from Disneyland: Pirates of the Caribbean, Twenty Thousand Leagues Under the Sea, and the Matterhorn Bobsleds, each showing cute kids in various stages of cute excitement or even cuter mirth. It was at Disneyland that Bob got his start in show business, working as a juggler and magician with an equally young and ambitious Steve Martin. He made a series of short films, two of which earned Academy Award nominations. "I wanted to be Steven Spielberg," he told me once. "Unfortunately, that job was taken."

Instead, in 1981, he started BRC, which today employs more than a hundred animators, set designers, writers, makeup specialists, car-

penters, and electricians to dream up and build exhibits for Knott's
Berry Farm, Epcot Center, Universal Studios, the Kennedy Space
Center, the Museum of Texas History, the Henry Ford museum, and
dozens of other clients. Bob and BRC move effortlessly between the
world of theme parks and the world of museums.

"There's not a big difference between the two anymore," he said.
"The two worlds are coming together, and we've positioned ourselves
right where they intersect."

Bob is a colossus in his field—his firm is booked years in advance,
and he himself makes more than a million dollars a year, just in salary—
because he foresaw the consequences of a profound sociological trend:
for years unprecedented amounts of money had been poured into grade
schools and high schools that still managed to turn out large numbers
of graduates who scarcely knew anything. Study upon study had shown
this to be so, but when Bob entered the museum-design business, American museums hadn't yet caught on. They were designed for an audience
that was dying off. Traditional exhibits were text oriented, Bob saw, "covered in clouds of words" printed on wall plaques. They "buried dead stuff
in glass boxes and lined the boxes up in dull, empty rooms."

Bob says things like this as if by rote. But he means them too. Bob
understood that today's audiences have no patience for inert glass boxes;
they get antsy in empty rooms. They lack the knowledge to make sense
of artifacts, and they don't have the patience for explanatory text. Weaned
on TV and sozzled by video games, today's audiences are subverbal. They
require constant stimulation. This is particularly true of young people,
Bob said, and in designing the Lincoln museum he wanted to reach young
people above all—nine- and ten-year-olds, up to thirteen- and fourteen-
year-olds. Exhibits therefore had to draw in the visitor, rather than just
passing along information. The museum had to be fun.

"Weren't you ever worried about dumbing Lincoln down?" I said,
after he'd offered me a seat in his office.

Bob sat back in his chair and looked at me for several seconds in
silence.

"I mean," I said, fidgeting, "worried just a little bit?"

With appropriate modifications—he's much taller, of course, with darker hair—Bob could pass for Doc, *primus inter pares* of Snow White's Seven Dwarfs; he has the same cleft chin and rounded cheeks, the same domed forehead, the same chronic problem of glasses slipping down his nose. Slowly now he pushed them upward.

"I don't understand that 'dumbing down,'" he said. He uncapped a felt-tip pen and drew a big X on a piece of paper in front of him. I was to discover that Bob doodled and diagrammed constantly. "Listen. You can do a lot worse than aim at today's seventh-grader. Seventh-graders are damn smart these days. They are the toughest crowd there is. To speak to them is not dumbing down. It's scary how smart they are. The way they process information in a digital age—it's incredible, beyond anything you or I can do."

Notwithstanding this intelligence—this dazzling capacity for processing information—Bob felt the way to reach these young savants was "through the heart." A heart appeared on the piece of paper. "Get their heart and their heads will follow," he said. "You lead with the emotions rather than the intellect. And remember, it's not just any old emotion—the emotion they feel is the one *we* want them to feel. With Lincoln, we are hooking them into a specific cascade of emotions. Then, if they want to follow up, they can find the intellectual part, read a wall plaque or buy a book or whatever." He called this strategy "emotional engineering"—a way of insinuating knowledge into people who, on their own, would have no interest in it.

"That's the first thing, emotion over intellect. The second is, you do the visual rather than the verbal. You'll notice, when you experience this museum, every scene plays totally visual. The communication comes through what you see. Example: You know what a great movie is? A great movie is when you can see it on an airplane without buying the headset, and you still get about seventy percent of what's going on. Without hearing a word. That's what we've done with Lincoln."

And it was a point of pride to Bob that the information he conveyed about Lincoln would be absolutely unimpeachable—"One hundred percent scholarly accurate."

"We were totally committed to the idea that we wouldn't do anything that wasn't true," he said. "We would never sacrifice accuracy for storytelling. We were going to charm the socks off your seventh-grader. Yet we weren't going to totally offend the scholar. Every date would be correct, every figure would be correct down to their eye color, the clothes would be true to the period, the hair. Everything."

So Bob's first step on the Lincoln project was to invite an assortment of Lincoln scholars to a series of "brainstorming sessions" in Springfield. By now the Lincoln world was buzzing with word of the new library and museum. Scholars and buffs knew that the ALPLM, backed by a staggering bankroll, would "define Lincoln for the next generation," as one of them put it. Most leapt at the chance to shape the outcome. Mrs. Cellini and members of her team sat in as well, along with a handful of grade-school teachers, who had been invited to represent their own constituency, the museum's target audience.

Over the course of the next year, for two or three days every six weeks or so, the scholars gathered in a conference room on the second floor of one of Springfield's many abandoned office buildings, with a wall-sized plate glass window overlooking the old statehouse square. The conference tables were covered in butcher paper, and a box of crayons was placed at each setting. "We wanted to loosen them up, get them in touch with that inner child," Bob said. "The crayons were a way of getting down to that." The scholars were encouraged to scribble and doodle at will. "Some really took to it right away," Bob said. "Others, it took a while. These were old geezers, after all."

Some of the geezers were taken aback by the New Age accessories. Yet by now even old geezers have learned that contemporary customs will require them to act like children more often than they'd like, as a means of "breaking down barriers" and "facilitating dialogue"— loosening up. A team of BRC staffers ran them through a series of team-building exercises. One exercise was called "Entry Points." Scholars were asked to dig deep into their childhoods and visualize the occasion when they first became enamored with the study of history, and then, of course, to share their experiences with their colleagues. Now and then, Bob said, the sessions grew quite emotional, as the scholars dredged up long-forgotten memories. For another exercise, the staffers emptied the tourist brochure racks at local hotels and brought the brochures to the workshop. "This is your competition," the staffers explained, passing around touts for waterslides, amusement parks, and adventure camps. "See if you can beat it." Gripping their crayons the scholars designed brochures of their own.

They loosened up. Ideas caromed around the conference room like Ping-Pong balls. The participants were briefly taken, for example, with the thought of a Lincoln roller coaster. "Lincoln had a lot of highs and lows in his life," Bob said. "He was bipolar, right?" At the peak of the roller coaster, riders might see Lincoln telling funny stories; at the low points they might see him looking gloomily out the window of his White House office, with wounded soldiers in the distance. "Back and forth, up and down, from war casualties to jokes," Bob said. "We brainstormed it." But the idea was soon discarded. "Too *out there*," said Bob.

After a year of sessions BRC had a rough "story line" for the museum—a plan for the sequence of exhibit rooms dramatizing Lincoln's life. Though genuine artifacts would be scattered here and there, these wouldn't be ordinary exhibits. They would constitute an "immersive visitor experience." From the first, *immersive* was a crucial word for the museum's boosters, replacing *interactive* as the reigning cliché. Immersive is interactive, only more so—interactive squared. If your target audience is a school boy who arrives at the museum having only moments before detached himself from the ear buds of his iPod and stashed the Game Boy in his backpack, you had better offer him an immersive experience quick, before he nods off from lack of stimulation. For the curator, the intractable problem of the era is distraction, the inability of museumgoers to attend to their surroundings. And total immersion, emotionally engineered, is the answer: exhibits that overpower you, displays you walk through and participate in, filled with music and sounds to alter your mood, lit in ways to startle or soothe, studded with objects you can reach out and fondle. It is the same principle that says the surest way to get someone wet is to drown him.

A few weeks after meeting Bob, shortly before the museum's dedication ceremony, I got a chance to see what he and BRC had done with Lincoln. Already boosters were comparing the museum to the opening of the Lincoln Memorial in 1922. Except the ALPLM would be even better. "You go to the Lincoln Memorial, you get an icon," Smith, the museum director, told reporters. "You get a statue. Here you get the man."

Certainly no institution since the Memorial had generated such publicity for Lincoln—the *New York Times* had been following its progress at every stage, and *Time* magazine was about to feature the museum for a cover story that summer—and certainly nothing in the Lincoln world had ever cost so much. Of the final expenditure of $150 million, nearly $60 million went to Bob Rogers and BRC.

Tom Schwartz, the state historian, showed me around the museum. Tom had been among Bob's team of experts. Like Bob, he wanted to impress upon visitors the museum's fastidious commitment to historical accuracy. The participation of the scholars and the designers' deference to them was, boosters reasoned, the best rebuttal to charges of "Disneyfying," or trivializing, Lincoln.

Carpenters and electricians bustled about the Museum Plaza, making final adjustments. Tom pointed out the trees that tower above Lincoln's boyhood cabin. They were made of Plexiglas and fashioned from plaster molds of real trees found in first-growth midwestern forests—"just like those Lincoln would have known," Tom said. BRC artists had even painted singe marks on the paper leaves that hung from the limbs above the cabin's fake chimney. At the other end of the plaza, opposite the cabin, stood a three-quarter-size replica of the south portico of the White House. A crowd of historical mannequins was gathered there, including Sojourner Truth and Frederick Douglass, both visitors to the executive mansion during Lincoln's day. The two originally had been paired alongside each other. But when one killjoy historian pointed out that Douglass and Truth had never visited the White House *together*, curators dutifully separated them by several feet, for the sake of verisimilitude. Douglass, by the way, looks just like Powhatan, Pocahontas's father.

Bob and the scholars had decided to divide Lincoln's life into two "journeys"—a word heavy with emotional connotations nowadays, since the journeys being described are not Lincoln's movements from place to place but his own "process of personal growth." Before entering Journey One, Tom said, visitors are encouraged to attend an orientation video called *Lincoln's Eyes*, in a theater just off Museum Plaza. The theater is tricked out in red velour, as tastelessly overdone as if the Victorians of Lincoln's time had done it themselves.

In *Lincoln's Eyes*, the curtain rises to show an actor standing before an enormous screen, and on either side of the proscenium other screens light up, flashing ever-changing images from Lincoln's life. They fade to gray, then light up again, then fade, only to light up again with more colorful images. Some multimedia effect or another is never more than a few moments away. When rains drench the prairie, a cool breeze emerges from hidden vents. The narrator mentions that young Abe was once kicked by a mule, and suddenly the seats jump with a deafening thud. The Civil War begins and the side walls open up and cannon barrels dart out, belching sparks and real smoke rings toward the audience. Seats quake with every blast.

Actors playing Lincoln's contemporaries appear in pore-penetrating close-ups, alternately excoriating him, praising him, getting mushy and sentimental or steely-eyed and cynical. On one screen Lincoln appears with a halo; on the opposite screen he grows devil horns. Then, says the narrator, after Lincoln was shot (BANG!) "he became a legend, and we've never seen him clearly since." The implication is that here you'll be able to see him clearly at last. Even better, the narrator says: "You may even see a little of yourself in Lincoln's eyes."

The exit doors swung open and Tom led me into Journey One, through the boyhood cabin to the slave auction just beyond it, to the years in New Salem, where we walked through Lincoln's general store as he courts Ann Rutledge, into the living room of a friend's house where we find him courting plump fairy Mary on a horsehair divan. Tad and Willie (Wendy's brothers from *Peter Pan*!) toss ink bottles and raise general hell in their father's law office. Journey Two likewise emphasizes Lincoln's home life and personal traumas. The first room displays a semicircle of fancy dresses worn by Mary and by the grande dames of Washington society who condescended to her. In the White House cabinet room, dummies dressed as Lincoln's advisers react histrionically—some with arms upraised, others with head in hand—as he reads them the Emancipation Proclamation. In a darkened bedroom, we see Abe and Mary standing helpless as their Willie lies in his deathbed. We then pass through a "Hall of Sorrows," where Mary sits in mourning, and into the White House kitchen, getting a glimpse of the life led by Lincoln's servants.

"From here to the end," Tom said as we emerged from the kitchen, "it's sort of a race to the finish. Of necessity we've had to compress a great many events into a limited space." Most of the compressed events have to do with the Civil War, represented in several extravagant murals and a roomful of touch screens. After a mock-up of Ford's Theatre, Journey Two closes in a huge, candle-lit chamber where Lincoln's coffin rests in a cloud of white lilies. Music plays everywhere and always—great orchestral washes of sound, as in a Disney romance, then quieting to Olde Tyme zither and fiddle tunes, like the sound track from a Ken Burns documentary. Bob had designed the journeys so that the tone would shift abruptly from room to room, to "reset the senses" of visitors every couple of minutes, lest they grow bored. The museum is the narcoleptic's cure.

On our way out, passing through Museum Plaza, we ran into Bob with a phalanx of assistants in train. They were dressed in identical blue sport shirts with the BRC logo stitched on the breast pocket. They'd been doing a final walk-through before the Grand Opening. They carried clipboards. Bob seemed to be breathing quickly. "We need to talk," he said to Tom. "Right now."

"Fine," said Tom.

"I need you to stand in these rooms with me," Bob said, "and I need to tell you why this doesn't need to be changed. I need to take you through these things, one by one. I will show you why this is just fine the way it is. It is really time to do the final clampdown. It is time for this to stop."

It turned out that Richard Norton Smith, Tom's boss and the museum's director, had been busily writing more wall text and posting it in the exhibits. Smith was a master publicist and an enthusiastic booster of the museum, but on certain questions—such as how much wall text should be available to visitors with an old-fashioned taste for information and words—he seemed very conventional, very traditional.

"Hey, the man's the director," Bob said that night with a shrug, when we met for dinner. "Whatever he wants, right? He wants more plaque copy, he gets more plaque copy. Sure. Fine."

He had calmed down considerably. In fact he seemed almost chipper, for he had just solved a problem that had been bedeviling him for weeks. Test visitors—those lucky folk given sneak previews of the museum, so that their reactions could be monitored by BRC—had been leaving Willie's bedroom and turning toward the emergency exit instead of turning left, toward the "Hall of Sorrows."

Bob took a sheet of paper from his notebook and began drawing. "People are phototropic," he said. "They walk toward the light. And they walk toward colorful things. They're like crows. They like shiny, colorful things. So if you don't want them to go *there*, you don't give them shiny things to see over *here*."

He sketched a square and then pathways inside it. "If you're standing over *here*, I'm going to put the only interesting thing you can look at *here*. That turns you in this direction. Then another visual draws you here. So you walk toward it, and as you pass this corner—hey, look!— another interesting thing! And you walk toward that. So you're constantly being turned and then pulled forward in the direction I want you to go."

The emergency exit, however, was shiny and colorful, drawing people away from the intended path. So he tried painting the walls a darker color. That helped. Yet some unruly visitors were still turning the wrong way. Finally he dimmed the exit lamp—"We're still consistent with fire code," he assured me—and hit on the right combination of darkened wall and dimmed light. That afternoon all the visitors had turned the right way. "Now," he said, dropping his pen and examining a breaded loop of calamari, "you can set anybody down anywhere in that museum, and they'll move in the right direction. No signs. No traffic cops."

He asked me how I'd liked *Lincoln's Eyes*, and I told him I was surprised at the range of views expressed about Lincoln. He'd been called a racist, a war criminal . . .

"Damn straight," he said, with evident pride. "We're not in the business of shoving anything down anybody's throats. After six years of living with Abraham Lincoln, I can give him to you any way you want, cold or hot, jazz or classical. I can give you scandalous Lincoln, conservative Lincoln, liberal Lincoln, racist Lincoln, Lincoln over easy or Lincoln scrambled."

After a sip of bubbly water, he said, "You know who's going to be pleasantly surprised by this museum? Neo-Confederates. Oh, they won't like that we still make Lincoln out to be a quote-unquote hero. But they're going to hear things they agree with. Lincoln is called a fraud. We hear John Wilkes Booth call Lincoln an aggressor, and they're going to go, 'Damn straight!' We say Lincoln did things that were unconstitutional. We say the Emancipation Proclamation was unconstitutional. The Yankees really did do bad things in the South. And we never go back and refute those points."

He said he and the historians also strained to include newer, revisionist views on slavery. "There's a new interpretation in black history that says Lincoln was not the Great Emancipator—blacks freed other blacks, not Lincoln. And we don't contradict that at all. We actually make the case a little bit. We have a black abolitionist saying the Emancipation Proclamation was the quote slick and empty trick of a cynical politician unquote. And this guy is angry. And we never contradict him either."

Bob said there had been instances where he and the scholars hadn't always seen eye to eye—the Emancipation Proclamation Room, for example, the immersive exhibit where Lincoln is shown reading the proclamation to his cabinet. The moment was first depicted in 1864, two years after the event, in a staged, formal painting by Francis Carpenter. In Carpenter's rendering, the cabinet members are posed stiffly around a table. It's an idealized version of a scene that the painter, his audience, and the subjects themselves knew was fraught with significance for the country's future—and it's exactly what Bob wanted to get away from.

"Some of our scholars said, Let's just do the Carpenter painting. Very dignified. Everybody's looking very important—and very Victorian and artificial and false. We said, 'Bo-ring!'" The scene Bob and his designers conceived bears no resemblance to Carpenter's version. The silicone Lincoln stands dejected, looking the downside of bipolar, and the cabinet members are arrayed in various attitudes of outrage or distress. "Right away," Bob said, "you walk in, and you think, 'Uh-oh. I've been in this meeting. This room is giving him shit. These guys are not buying it.'

"They're not standing there with their hands in their shirts in some gallant pose. They look like they've been there awhile. The place is a mess—papers everywhere. Their hair's a mess. And you can read everyone's mind. And everybody's got a different spin. One guy's going, 'Oh shiiiiiit.' Another guy's got a map, I think it's whatsisname, Blair"—Montgomery Blair, Lincoln's postmaster general—"he's pointing to Kentucky, he's going 'You'll lose Kentucky! You lose Kentucky, you split the country in half!' One guy's thinking, 'Jesus Christ, he's already written this thing and I wasn't consulted? What am I doing with this guy?' It's so real, you can almost smell the body odor.

"And here's the thing: it's completely one hundred percent historically accurate. Oh, maybe we pushed it a little in terms of the dramatic moment. But the point is, today we tend to look back, we think Emancipation Proclamation, it's a no-brainer, right? Free the slaves? Well, duh. *Hello?* Of course we'd free the slaves! Who wouldn't? It's unanimous. A no-brainer.

"This scene says: Huh-uh. No way. Not a slam-dunk. At all. Lincoln's North was just as racist as the South. Very powerful stuff. And you're going, 'Whoa. This is stuff my seventh-grade teacher never taught me.'"

Other changes were made to protect particular political sensitivities—in a kind of yuppie version of political correctness.

"Think," he said to me. "Did you see a gun anywhere in the museum? Not a picture of a gun, but a real gun? Huh-uh." And of course he was right. Even John Wilkes Booth, seen approaching Lincoln's box at Ford's Theatre, conceals his derringer behind his cape; even the Lincoln cabin, out there in the wilderness, doesn't have a gun. I was surprised. I remembered old black-and-white photographs of the Chicago Historical Society, from the 1930s, showing groups of immigrant boys from the West Side huddled over display cases—glass boxes—and gazing at row after row of Henry repeating rifles. They seemed enthralled.

"But boys love guns!" I said to Bob.

"No," he said. "We made a conscious decision that we did not want to glorify war, and we did not want to glorify the mechanics of war."

Fake cannon could burst from the walls and belch pretend smoke rings and simulated sparks. But no one would see a real gun that might have been touched by a real soldier. Bob is anti-gun.

He is also, needless to say, anti-Confederate battle flag, and the stars and bars are nowhere to be seen; ditto the word "nigger," he said. It's never used in the museum, despite its ubiquity at the time. "We could have used both, the n-word and the flag, but both are very volatile," he said. "We couldn't control what the reaction would be— and if you can't predict the audience reaction, well, you don't want to be in that situation. Bad emotional engineering."

He likewise stretched history to include more female figures in the exhibits, where they play a much more prominent role than they did in real life. "It was a constant battle to make this thing interesting to women," he said. "The Civil War was sort of a guys' time, you know? That's why we have an entire room devoted to dresses. That's why we show the White House kitchen. That's why we have Ann Rutledge. Every time we could, we brought in a lady."

I asked Bob about the last room in Journey Two, the one that shows Lincoln lying in state in Springfield after the two-week trip from Washington on the funeral train.

"Did you notice, in the exhibit, his casket is closed?" Bob asked. He gave me a conspiratorial look. "In 1865, Lincoln's casket was open.

"The client said, 'Can we do an open casket? It's the historically accurate thing.' We said, Okay, sure. Whatever you want. But, uh, you guys understand this was before refrigeration, right? This body's been traveling by train, through the heat, taken off the train in ten different cities, put on display, put back on the train, with hundreds of thousands of people filing past it, exhaling, sneezing, whatever. We said, 'Are you getting the picture?' This body was not well treated. In fact, sometime between Erie, Pennsylvania, and Chicago, they opened up the casket and they saw the body had turned dark purple. True—it's documented. They tried to fix it with makeup. He looked like a black man in white face. His beard had continued to grow. His fingernails were still growing.

"We say, You want that, we'll do a helluva job. We'll do him all in white, then smear the dark coloring all over him. The Great Emancipator in blackface, you see the irony!" Bob cackled. "Hey, he's going to look a little dried out. His eyes are going to be a little sunken. We can do the makeup just so you see the discoloration right around the mouth . . . They shouted no! 'Close the casket!' We said, 'Wait! It's not historically correct!' They said, 'Close the casket!'"

It was late, by midwestern standards, and the restaurant had emptied out. The waitress hovered. Bob paid the bill. Outside the streets had been closed off in anticipation of the dedication ceremony the next day.

"I'll give you one final example," he said. "Lincoln's law office."

The museum is heavily weighted toward depictions of Lincoln's family—on the assumption that this will be appealing to families of tourists. That's why they devoted an exhibit room to the Lincoln boys raising hell in their father's law office.

"We got the scene from Herndon, and we're true to his account—up to a point," Bob said. "What Herndon really says is, when he walked in the office once, he caught one of the boys pissing on the hot stove in the middle of the room. So I asked the people in Springfield, 'Hey, can we do this? It's true to history!' I begged 'em. I said, 'We can do it tastefully. We'll have the kid's back to the visitor, we get recirculating water going so you see the piss spraying out, we use colored water, we get a fogger so we see the steam rising from the hot stove, you hear the *sssssss*, we get an aromascape so you can smell it.' Jesus! How great would that be!"

He cackled again.

Would you have really done that? I said.

"Hell yes, I'd do it! You want to get kids interested in history— that's what we're about, right? That's the whole point of the museum. Learn about Lincoln? Then use toilet humor! They'll go wild, they'll love it!"

We walked half a block not saying anything. I could see Lincoln's law office, now renovated into a tourist spot, down on the corner.

"Hell yes!" Bob said again. "But they said no. They said"—he lowered his voice to a huffy tone—"'Kids get enough toilet humor these days.' So I'm like, Fine. Okay. You're the boss.

"But God, it would have been beautiful. And one hundred percent historically accurate."

When I got back to my hotel, I took out the diagrams Bob had drawn at dinner. I looked at the big square with the pathways in it, showing the ideal flow of visitors through the museum hallways. The flow was represented with bold, commanding arrows, the people with little dots. It looked like a maze with mice scurrying through.

Bob's design was intended to manipulate people, of course. That's what he'd been hired to do, and he did it better than anybody. But to what end? I was back to an old question. Among all our many presidents and historical figures, why care so much about Abraham Lincoln? What does he stand for? You could spend hours in the museum without finding an answer. "It's all emotional," Bob had said, as though giving me a hint. And there's no mistaking when you walk through the museum, you're meant to feel sympathy for Lincoln, even feel sorry for him. Pulled from room to room, you're asked to be touched by his humble beginnings (but many of our presidents were born poor). You feel terrible because his son dies an agonizing death (but many presidents watched helpless as their children died). We ache because he was reviled (most presidents were reviled by someone) and because he had an inexplicable marriage (Hello, Mr. and Mrs. Clinton). It's not a Lincoln that Jane Addams would walk five miles to see, or a Lincoln that would inspire Mr. Esche if he ever returns to Springfield. In the end what you come up with is that he's interesting because a lot of people over the past 150 years have been interested in him. He's been hated and loved, pondered and studied, honored and mourned so intensely for so long that it doesn't seem to matter why. He's reached the zenith of American celebrity. He's famous for being famous.

As keynote speaker for the museum's dedication ceremony, Mrs. Cellini and other Springfielders had hoped to enlist Oprah. Over the previous few years, as the project gestated, they had even invited Oprah's mysteriously long-standing boyfriend, Stedman Graham, to host an occasional preliminary event, as a way of gaining influence with Her Eminence. But it didn't work out. They were forced to lower expectations. The president of the United States was invited instead.

Local television stations broadcast the first pictures of Air Force One as it angled down from a blue sky onto the runway at Springfield's Abraham Lincoln International Airport. The city shone that morning; I'd never seen it look better. The streetlights downtown had been replaced and new curbs and sidewalks installed. The Boys Club had volunteered to drape colorful fabric on the cyclone fencing around empty lots. Murals covered abandoned storefronts. Thirty new trees, according to the local paper, had been plopped into new planters. An expensive pigeon-extermination program had been concluded in triumph. The President Abraham Lincoln Hotel was booked solid.

The motorcade snaked up to the museum entrance, and Richard Norton Smith escorted the presidential party on a lightning tour. The president and first lady, like any family that finds itself in Museum Plaza, got their picture taken with Lincoln and his silicone family. Then the president emerged into the brilliant sunshine and climbed the dais to deliver a beautifully written speech. The crowd spilled down the side streets in every direction.

"I am honored to be here to dedicate a great institution honoring such a great American," the president said. "Lincoln embodied the democratic ideal—that leadership and even genius are found among the people themselves, and sometimes in the most unlikely places." He said,

"Lincoln has taken on the elements of myth. And in this case, the myth is true." He said, "In the character and convictions of this one man, we see all that America hopes to be." And he said, "Every generation strives to define the lessons of Abraham Lincoln in its own way."

That's the nub, I thought. Defining the "lessons of Lincoln" is what the ALPLM has done for our generation. We're just not sure what the lessons are.

Bob avoided the dedication ceremonies—"the glorification of the uninvolved," he called it. But Mrs. Cellini was seemingly everywhere. Later she told me her nine-year-old nephew had been to see the museum.

And?

"Loved it," she said. "Absolutely loved it. He said, 'It's great! So much fun! I didn't have to read anything!' And I thought, 'Yeah, kid, you get it.' But of course he gets it. He's nine years old."

5

THE MAGIC OF STUFF

One evening I was at the presidential library after hours, waiting for Tom Schwartz, the Illinois state historian, in the reception area outside his office. Like most government agencies, the place had been more or less deserted since 5:01 p.m. Tom had offered to walk me out, past the security desk, after he finished a few phone calls.

So there I am minding my own business when I notice a large blue cardboard folder teetering on top of a stack of books on the receptionist's desk. A Post-it note was stuck to the cover. Scribbled on the note were the words "Gettysburg Address."

I figured it was a file of papers and clippings related to the most famous speech in the history of Western civilization—what else could it be?—and when Tom emerged I pointed to the folder. "I hope that's not important," I said.

Tom's shoulders fell and his eyes half closed. "Oh," he said, sounding weary. "This—obviously—was supposed to go back to the vault. I don't know who left it here."

I said, "You mean?"

He gave me a sidelong look. "Okay, you get a special treat this evening." Embarrassed, and with the utmost reluctance, he untied the black string that held the folder together and lifted it open and there it was. Thanks to the near criminal neglect of some time-serving patronage flunky in the state historian's office, combined with my own nosiness, I got to hold a copy of the Gettysburg Address, written in Lincoln's hand.

I couldn't have said at the time what it felt like. There are only five of them in the world, after all. The handwritten address that belongs to the state of Illinois is today the centerpiece in the museum's Treasures Gallery. One of the unfortunate quirks of the ALPLM is that what began as a $10 million Heritage Center, designed to show off the state's collection of Lincoln documents and artifacts, ballooned by bureaucratic and entrepreneurial huffing and puffing into a $150 million presidential-museum-and-library that does not, in the end, show much of the state's collection of Lincoln documents and artifacts. Sprinkled throughout Bob's exhibits are the Lincolns' house key and the name plate from their front door, a few splendid handwritten papers and various paraphernalia from political campaigns, but these are swallowed up in the carefully designed immersive experience.

The Treasures Gallery is reserved for the state's most prized possessions. Visitors come to it at the end of Journey Two. It's a dimly lit circular room modeled, I was told, after the crown jewels chamber in the Tower of London. The allusion is altogether fitting. For a certain kind of American, for a buff, *these* are the crown jewels—the totems of a nation that is ruled by ordinary men rather than by divinely anointed kings. In place of silver orbs and glinting scepters are Lincoln's briefcase and glasses, his notebooks and pens, the rarest printings of his canonical speeches. In the innermost room is the state's Holy Trinity of Lincoln artifacts. Against the dark they glow in little pools of light: the handwritten Gettysburg Address, a signed copy of the Emancipation Proclamation, and one of three Lincoln stovepipe hats known to survive, this one made of beaverskin. On the brim of the hat, two small ovals have been worn away by the impress of Lincoln's index and middle fingers, from where he tipped it to passersby or held it steady against the wind on blowy days.

I've stood in the Treasures Gallery for an hour at a time, watching the visitors. They had been pulled along effortlessly through the immersive galleries by Bob's unerring visual cues. But here they lingered and gazed, their downturned faces still and steady in the reflected light, as though at last they'd come upon something substantial that might carry over the reality of the man: a book or a pen or a hat. Even the twenty-first-century museum, even immersive experiences—*even fun*—can't kill the transcendent magic of stuff. This is where much of the Lincoln legacy survives, and in the unlikeliest stuff, too, as Lincoln collectors can show you.

Now here's something you don't see every day: a larger-than-life statue of Lincoln, except this time he's in motion, a man of action; he strides purposefully; his beardless jaw is set in steely resolve; his frock coat billows at his sides; and just beyond him lies a panoramic view of distant hot tubs and tennis courts nestled between hedgerows, of pastel mansions sprawling among groves of eucalyptus and pine. This is Abraham Lincoln come to Beverly—*Hills*, that is: swimming pools, movie stars . . . all the show-offy glamour of Lotus Land spread out in the valley behind him, like sequins sprinkled on folds of green velvet. The giant statue is placed on the edge of the bluff with his back turned to paradise, as he strides to the rear entrance of the house where Louise Taper lives.

"Isn't he great?" said Louise, who was showing me around. "He's so strong and confident looking." Louise's house is the largest house I've ever been in that wasn't once owned by royalty, yet even so she told me she had recently moved into it because her earlier house, which was down there in Beverly Hills somewhere, got too big for her. This new one sits on the topmost ridge above the city, in a neighborhood so exclusive my rental-car map showed the local streets dead-ending before they reached this far into the Hills. Louise's private secretary had given me directions. I'd found it only after making multiple wrong turns and confronting several unwelcoming security guards who popped up like Whac-A-Moles from the palmettos. Louise's house is part of a gated compound, and the gated compound is set deep into a larger gated community, which is itself surrounded by an outer perimeter of fences and more gates. Louise has excellent reasons for wanting to be secure. She owns the most spectacular collection of Lincolniana still in private hands. Her house is her Treasures Gallery.

She was still unpacking from the move, and as she led me inside to the living room we had to pick our way around upended boxes and half-empty crates. A manservant brought us tea and wafer-thin cookies on a bone china set. Louise is too formidable, and too rich, for anyone ever to have worked up the nerve to ask her her age, but she's surely pushing sixty, though her hair is raven black and ironed perfectly straight in the Vidal Sassoon style once favored by caged go-go dancers on *Hullabaloo*. Her face is completely unlined and her eyes, ringed in black liner, are startlingly large. Her taste in clothes is youthful too, running to dimple-tight jeans and form-fitting sweaters. When I first met her she'd been a widow for three years. Her husband Barry, a full-time philanthropist, was the son of the real estate developer Mark Taper, who built the city of Lakewood, California, and several others, after World War II. If you knew where to look you could see Lakewood out the back windows, far to the south past Beverly Hills, over Abe's right shoulder.

She was divorced with two children when she married Barry in 1985. "I think he liked me because he was meeting all these fluffy women who weren't interested in anything except having lunch," she said. "And here I was, interested in *something*." Her Lincoln fixation predated her marriage to Barry by fifteen years at least. It was a romance, too. "I was at home with two small kids, and one day I picked up *Love Is Eternal*, by Irving Stone." She flicked a painted fingernail toward me. "You have to read this book," she said.

*   *   *

There was a time, through the late forties to the mid-sixties, when millions of people read Irving Stone. Rivals in the book-writing business compared him to a mint. He tippy-tap-tapped on his typewriter and sheets of thousand-dollar bills rolled off the paten. He specialized in the biographical novel, juiced up by a florid title like *Lust for Life* (the story of Vincent van Gogh) or *The Agony and the Ecstasy* (Michelangelo), with the emphasis on the lust and the ecstasy. His subspecialty was famous marriages of American history—John and Abigail Adams, Andrew and Rachel Jackson, and, in *Love Is Eternal*, Abraham and Mary Lincoln.

I had already worked my way through *Love Is Eternal*. It opens with two sisters, Mary and Ann Todd, making snippy comments to each other about the size of their respective bosoms, which signals to the discerning reader that Stone is working a genre that nowadays we call chick lit. Like all chick lit *Love Is Eternal* is idealized, but it's also bracing in its author's audacity. Stone's main technique for enlivening historical figures is to make them screamingly, improbably sensual. As you'd expect, Mary and Ann are vying for beaus, and Mary's search leads her to the prairie town of Springfield, where she meets an awkward—but sinewy!—young lawyer named Abe. Their romance quickens at a picnic, when Abe bests the other fellows in a contest of muscle by lifting two heavy axes straight out in front of him:

> For Mary it was an exhibition of strength such as she had never seen; through the thin white shirt and the heavier material of his trousers she could see the powerful muscles and the indestructible male strength of him as he stood there almost like the oak tree under which he was accomplishing his feat, his legs and arms sturdy branches on a long, lean and incredibly virile trunk. . . .
> She felt faint, turned away.

Stone had a quaint respect for his historical characters—enough to prevent him, thank God, from writing sex scenes. But in *Love Is*

Eternal there's never much doubt about why they called Abe "The Rail-splitter."

Nowadays, of course, it's easy, indeed almost obligatory, to make fun of historical potboilers like Stone's for their impertinence, but there was ambition in them, too; a middle-brow earnestness and a desire to educate his readers showed through the cheesiness. *Love Is Eternal* lifts Abraham and Mary out from behind the impenetrable barrier of those dour-visaged daguerreotypes and pumps them up with color and life, however implausibly. Reading it as a young housewife, Louise was enthralled and inspired.

She read everything about Lincoln she could get hold of, and her researches led her before long to a rare-book dealer in Beverly Hills who specialized in Lincoln books and manuscripts. Under his direction she read more and more, digging into out-of-print books that she'd scout other dealers to find. The dealer offered her a job part-time, and in lieu of cash she asked to be paid in books and manuscripts. From the dealer she learned all about provenance—the paper trail of letters, testimonials, and affidavits that certifies whether an artifact is genuine. She learned how to study Lincoln signatures for telltale marks of authenticity, and she came to know the relative value of books, though now she admits to a certain lack of discrimination in her wants.

"I'd go to every book fair and go from stall to stall and I'd say, 'Do you have anything about Lincoln?' and, oh God, I just started buying. I'd walk out with ten, fifteen Lincoln books. You just catch this . . . this fever. That's what it is—it's a fever, a Lincoln fever. And I caught it."

She divorced in the early 1970s. This being Los Angeles, a friend in the movie business suggested she meet the producer David Wolper, who was making a six-part TV movie on Lincoln, and this being Louise, she instantly got a job as the film company's researcher. Movie people are so startled to meet someone who owns a book that they immediately assume you're an egghead. "I'd wheel my little book cart around the back lot at Paramount like the library lady." Her taste for homey anecdotes about Lincoln the family man perfectly suited the needs of the scriptwriters. "I told them that Tad and Willie had goats in the White House. They loved that—'Get us the names of the goats!' They wanted lots of action, and when Lincoln's president, let's face it, there isn't much, not in the White House anyway. Then I remembered. There was a fire in the White House one time, and Lincoln ran out to the stables and saved all the horses. Did you know about that?"

I said I didn't.

"He did—he saved the horses. I'd bought back issues of the *Lincoln Herald* and I read about it in that. Well, they loved that idea. So they had Hal Holbrook, who played Lincoln, racing around the White House lawn and the fire's raging, and he's jumping hedges with his long legs and rescuing people and horses—very dramatic."

Her greatest moment came offscreen, however, when she was sent to Springfield to scout locations with the movie's art director. Where a more jaundiced eye might see a small, decrepit midwestern city slowly dissolving back into the prairie from which it had once been carved, Louise saw a land of enchantment, glowing with Lincoln; years later, with Barry, she even bought a condominium there, making her the only Beverly Hills grande dame ever to have a pied-à-terre in downtown Springfield, Illinois. More important, on that first visit she met Jim Hickey, Tom Schwartz's predecessor as state historian and the man who, years later, first showed Julie Cellini through the archives. At the time Hickey served informally as the impresario of the Lincoln market—books, manuscripts, and personal artifacts all seemed to pass under Hickey's gaze when sellers sought buyers and vice versa. "We became great buddies," she said. He taught her how a world-class collection might be assembled—knowledge that wasn't much use to her until she fell in love with Barry.

"I'd say to my husband, 'You know, I don't really want that purse for my birthday. But you know there is this, um, book I'd really like to have—or this or that, a mourning silk from Lincoln's funeral, some artifact, whatever. And he said, 'I'll back you in whatever you want to do,' and for the next twenty years we just went crazy. Berserk. I mean, I really went to town."

*   *   *

Some collectors have come to think of the market in Lincoln collectibles in terms of epochs: there's pre-Louise and there's post-Louise. Beginning in the mid-1980s, the price of Lincoln pieces rose far beyond the price for comparable items associated with other American historical personages like Thomas Jefferson or George Washington. Lincoln had always been the most popular collectible anyway; only Napoleon has drawn as much interest. But Louise's entry in the field transformed it, as she competed with one or two other deep-pocketed collectors— Malcolm Forbes of *Forbes* magazine and even, for a time, the Texas billionaire Ross Perot.

Prices leaped. Items that might have sold for under a thousand dollars —President Lincoln's signature on a mundane bureaucratic directive— now sell for five thousand dollars or more, putting them beyond the reach of most hobbyists, while items of singular historical value—a significant letter in Lincoln's own hand or a personal artifact—which might once have fit the acquisitions budget of a museum or some other institution, can now be bid upon by only the very wealthiest private patrons. That Lincoln beaverskin hat in the Treasure Gallery at Springfield, to cite one instance: it's on loan from Louise. Even with its $150 million budget, the ALPLM could never have afforded to buy it for itself.

Like all great collectors, Louise in time became a collector of collections. She might buy the entire holdings of one seller just to lay hands on the single object she most desired. Buffs cherish "Wide-awake torches," for example—the lighted plumes carried by Lincoln supporters (called Wide-awakes) during vast rallies in the 1860 presidential campaign. But Louise wanted only the rarest of them, a torch adorned with an eagle medallion; very few of these have survived. "I told this collector, I want the one with the eagle. He said no, you've got to buy them all. He had fifteen torches! I bought them all. What am I going to do with fifteen torches? But I did get the eagle."

There was always a principle controlling her purchases, she told me, a thought-out plan beyond the urge to splurge. "I always knew just what

I wanted," she said. "I wanted the personal Lincoln, I wanted the un-usual Lincoln, I wanted the family Lincoln. And I wanted every phase of his life, from the very earliest to his death. Well, that's not quite right. At first I didn't want to get into the assassination. I just didn't want to see him dead, you know? The whole death part—I just didn't like to think of him that way. I was so gung ho on his *life*. And now, of course, I have the largest collection of assassination artifacts there is, I suppose." She popped up from the couch and adjusted her sweater. "Here," she said. "Come see."

She led me into the breakfast room off the kitchen, where her secre-tary and two friends sat at a table covered in tissue and boxes. "I'm loan-ing fifty-odd things to Springfield for an assassination exhibition," she said. Louise's son-in-law, a professional curator, was cataloging them before packing and sending them. Stuff was everywhere. "This is Mary's mourning veil," Louise said, opening a flat box and pulling back the tissue. A handbill from Ford's Theatre advertised *Our American Cousin,* the play the Lincolns went to see that evening. There were commemorative badges and mourning ribbons, a cutaway chunk of the coat Lincoln wore that night, a scarf John Wilkes Booth gave to a lover not long before the murder. "See the 'L'?" she said, fingering a black bit of jewelry. "Lincoln's cuff link. Monogrammed. He wore it the night he was shot."

She said she began collecting assassination material almost as an afterthought, during a foray into Booth collecting. Usually, Louise's husband attended auctions with her, she said. He served as a kind of bumper on her wildest sprees. But sometimes not. She told me about one auction in Chicago that offered assassination relics: the papers of the man who embalmed Lincoln's body, passes issued to the public to view Lincoln as he lay in state. Her husband came with her, but he ducked out to go shopping before the auction began, leaving her to bid alone.

"I'm sitting there and the auction starts, and I'm a wreck," she said.

At the table her friends looked up from their cataloging.

"I'm sitting there and I don't know how high to go, I don't know how much money I can spend—nothing like that. Barry's gone, he's stuck in traffic. So, well, I just start bidding. Seriously. They go through the lot numbers, and when they got to a lot I wanted, I just sat there with my paddle up. I never put it down. I just had to have the lot. I guess I intimidated other people, because their paddles started to fall, and mine's raised the whole time. But I had to have it." She shook her head, as if still unsure how it happened. "I think maybe I overpaid."

Like a fever. A Lincoln fever.

"I've got some hair here, too, somewhere," she said, casting about.

"Lincoln's hair?" I said.

"Mm-hmm," she said. "And Willie's. Oh wait. Here. This will blow you away." She reached down to fetch something from a box on the floor. It was a pair of white gloves, brittle with age. "Lincoln carried these to Ford's Theatre. See here?" she said, pointing to a stain.

"Blood?" I said.

Louise's eyes were even wider than usual. "Blood," she said.

Tastes in Lincoln stuff differ. Not everyone goes for the hair.

"I don't know why," said Dan Weinberg. "Hair just doesn't cut it for me. It seems so . . . so Catholic. Like something in a reliquary." Weinberg runs the Abraham Lincoln Bookshop in Chicago. I went to see him not long after I visited Louise. The bookshop has been a haunt of buffs since the 1930s. Weinberg bought it from its founder in the early 1990s, and as owner he immediately became the premier dealer in Lincoln collectibles and memorabilia. Every Lincoln collector makes a pilgrimage to see Weinberg sooner or later and to browse his handsome space just west of the city's magnificent mile. We were standing among tall cherry bookcases packed with first editions.

"There's so much hair around, for one thing," Weinberg said. "The Chicago Historical Society has fistfuls of the stuff. Now if every bit of hair that somebody said was cut from Lincoln actually came from

Lincoln's head, the man would have looked like Telly Savalas at his autopsy. Collecting hair was a memorial thing for these Victorians. Even if it wasn't genuine. Nowadays the provenance is a nightmare. Unless it's attached to a letter from someone who was actually there, actually in the room at the Petersen house or with the body when they brought it back to the White House, it's going to be very difficult to place such an item with any confidence.

"But people do go for it. I just don't get it myself," he said again. "I don't go, 'Oooo, wow, Lincoln's hair!'"

He paused and arched his eyebrows.

"Now, blood! Blood's a different story."

He showed me a framed patch of fabric with a rust-colored stain. It was grouped with other grim mementos of the assassination—a playbill like Louise's from Ford's Theatre, a mourning ribbon.

"I have been fortunate enough to have two samples of blood pass through here, absolutely authentic. I'll tell you, though, I don't think this particular one here is Lincoln's," Weinberg said, tapping the glass. "I think it's Rathbone's."

Oddly, considering his head wound, Lincoln bled relatively little in the box at Ford's Theatre. But attending the Lincolns that night were a military officer and his fiancée—Clara Harris and Henry Rathbone. Major Rathbone grappled with Booth after the shot was fired and the assassin sliced him along the arm with a long knife, nicking an artery. Unlike Lincoln, the major bled like Russian royalty.

The box was awash in blood but not much of it was Lincoln's, and this terrible fact has constituted a blow to generations of collectors and buffs, not to mention ghouls. There have been a few compensations. Not long after Booth had made his getaway out the rear door of the theater, the actress who starred in the play that night, Laura Keene, made her way up to the box where Lincoln lay. A drama queen by profession, she proved to be one offstage as well. She asked the doctors who gathered around the stricken president whether she might not comfort him by cradling his head in her lap. There was no medical necessity for elevating his head, and, as the author James Swanson points out in his history of the assassination, *Manhunt*, it certainly couldn't have made Lincoln himself any more comfortable. But nobody had the nerve to tell her no—she was the Barbra Streisand of her day. So she lifted the bowed head onto her skirt, where it trickled obligingly.

Scraps of Keene's dress made its way into the marketplace over the following decades, though precisely how, and in what quantities, are matters of dispute. A year after the assassination Keene visited Springfield and presented one such bloody swatch to the city fathers, as a token of her affection. It's still in the hands of the state library. When one purported Keene scrap, suffused with Lincoln blood, made its way to Weinberg, he was able to travel to Springfield to compare it with theirs. "I held it up," he said proudly, "and the line of the bloodstain on ours aligned perfectly with theirs." You can't get much better provenance than that.

After he was removed from Ford's Theatre to the Petersen house across the street, Lincoln continued to bleed as doctors "irrigated the wound." The room where they laid him was rented by a young soldier named Willie Clark, who comes down to us through history as a rough mixture of practicality and idealism. In a letter to his sister, written four days after Lincoln's death, he describes the excitement of his new celebrity and mentions casually that he's still sleeping on the same mattress and coverlet the president had died on. (Young men can sleep anywhere.) But Clark was still sufficiently aware of the historical moment to think ahead.

"Enclosed," he wrote his sister, "you will find a piece of lace Mrs. Lincoln wore on her head during the evening and was dropped by her while entering my room to see her dying husband; it is worth keeping for its historical value." As for himself: "I have a lock of Mr. Lincoln's hair, which I have had neatly framed; also a piece of linen with a portion of his brain." Lucky boy! But superintending such treasures kept Willie Clark on his toes: "Hundreds daily call at the house to gain admission to my room," he wrote. "Everybody has a great desire to obtain some memento, so that whoever comes in has to be closely watched for fear they will steal something."

Many succeeded, apparently. For years bits of stained linen have been passed around, duly cradled and revered, and often sold as samples of the martyr's essence. Some of these supposedly came from the cloths that were draped over the blood-soaked pillow, for reasons of delicacy, whenever Mrs. Lincoln entered the room to see her husband. By one account, Mr. Petersen, who was out of town when Lincoln was brought to his house, returned in horror to find the place littered with mustard patches and soiled sheets. In his anger he chucked them out the window, where mourners and entrepreneurs were waiting with open arms. Lincoln's autopsy was attended by innumerable doctors, politicians, aides, and domestics, and many claimed to have been given scraps of fabric or locks of hair. Lincoln had been dead brief hours, and already collecting had begun in earnest.

But, as Weinberg said, the trail of provenance from those distant rooms and alleyways to today's market has been hopelessly obscured by the intervening years. As a consequence, the process of supply and demand in blood and hair is a jumble of sham and contention; no one knows what a fair price might be for any claimed fragment of the great man's physical remains. Weinberg told me that DNA testing could clear up the confusion once and for all. Yet no one has yet had the nerve to try to extract a full, testable strand of genetic material from an undisputed Lincoln sample, such as those owned by Louise or the Chicago Historical Society.

"It's kind of a game of chicken," Weinberg said. "Nobody wants to be the first to do it. You'd need a pretty big sample to get a full strand, which means you'd probably have to destroy the sample to get the DNA." Indeed, the historical society has convened a conference of bioethicists to ponder the questions of taste and propriety raised by DNA testing on historical figures. But so far, among those lucky (or unlucky) owners of blood and hair, the standoff, and the uncertainty, remain.

*   *   *

Back in the house above Beverly Hills, surrounded by stuff he had owned and touched and bled upon, I asked Louise what it was about Lincoln that inspired her. It was a question I asked her several times as I got to know her, and I was always struck by her response.

"He was just an amazing man," she would say. "To do what he did, with so little education, keeping the country from splitting up, it's just amazing. And he was so intelligent."

She seemed much more inclined to show rather than tell, as though by handling the stuff I might figure out her answer for myself.

"Follow me," she said. We left the dining room and went into another living room. A glass case was filled with china. "Most of these are from the White House," she said, pointing to full place settings of the china that Mary and Abraham designed for their official use. "Some of it's from the house in Springfield, which is harder to find." There was silverware too. "And that's the chamber pot he used in the White House," she said.

"You own Abraham Lincoln's chamber pot," I said.

Louise thought for a moment, as though the weight of this extraordinary fact were just sinking in.

"Yeah," she said finally. "Yeah, I do."

I followed her into her library, which was as big as the second living room. She apologized for the mess. I jammed my foot against a piece of furniture disassembled on the floor. "Are you okay?" she said when I winced. "I'm so sorry. That's a daybed. We're still putting it together. Thomas Lincoln made it." I hopped backward, away from the treasure, and steadied myself against a hutch cabinet. "He made that hutch cabinet too," she said.

As she picked out things to show me—Lincoln's plaster life mask, the clock that hung in the Lincoln & Herndon law office, Mathew Brady's box camera—she told me how the collection set her apart from her neighbors.

"I'm not like a lot of women in Beverly Hills," she said. "I don't do lunch. I don't go to parties so much. I don't like to sit around and gossip. That's what women do here. I don't. They say, 'Come to lunch!' I say, 'I'm busy!' They say, 'Busy? What do you do?' I say, 'I collect Lincoln.' And they laugh at me! They—laugh—at—me. They actually laugh at me, in my face. They say, 'Oh, what do you have—a five-dollar bill? A bunch of pennies?' They can't even imagine."

So she has found a hospitable home in what she calls "Lincolnworld."

"This takes up my whole life," she said. "I have a lot of collector friends, and they're all men. I like to be with people who appreciate all this. I'm in every phase of Lincolnworld. I'm on the board of the Abraham Lincoln Association. I'm a trustee at Lincoln College. I'm on the board of the Abraham Lincoln Foundation; I help choose the Lincoln Prize for books every year. I'm a commissioner on the Abraham Lincoln Bicentennial Commission. I travel, I speak. And you know what? Everyone's very nice to me. Lincoln people fight with each other sometimes, they can be very nasty, but they're all very nice to me. I get along with all of them."

"Why is that?" I asked.

"Because," she said, sweeping her hand in front of her, "I've got the stuff!"

While we were talking, Louise's secretary had shimmered unnoticed into the room and opened a hidden safe. A thick plated door stood open. The safe was big enough to walk around in.

"And now you can see the really good stuff," Louise said.

She led me into the safe. "When I got on the board for the Lincoln Prize, I started to notice something. All these scholars started swarming around me, because every year I'm one of the judges for the best Lincoln book—$50,000, a lot of money for a scholar. And they're suddenly all over me. But I noticed: you never see them writing, 'I love Abraham Lincoln. He was a great guy, very intelligent, a great president, he held the country together.' Never. It's always got to be controversial. Controversial sells. 'He was gay! They had the worst marriage! He and Mary couldn't stand each other!' I mean, come on! Oh look. There are those Wide-awake torches." They were leaning back in the corner like a bunch of garden tools. "I was wondering where they were."

Suddenly she was sitting cross-legged on the floor, opening file drawers. "You want to see the sum book page, don't you?"

In her safe Louise had what collectors agree is—with the possible exception of the handwritten copies of the Gettysburg Address—the greatest piece of Lincolniana: a page from a schoolbook Lincoln kept when he was fifteen years old, the earliest piece of him that survives. When Herndon, doing his research, went to interview Lincoln's step-mother in September 1865, the old lady gave him the book as a token of affection. Plus, she might have been senile.

Louise handed me a frame that held the first page of the book. It was covered in handwritten long-division exercises—and doggerel, which she read to me.

> Abraham Lincoln is my name
> And with my pen I wrote the same
> I wrote in both hast and speed
> And left it here for fools to read

"I love the human stuff," she said. "I love the humor, the children. Tad used to bother the soldiers around the White House. He asked them to shoe his horse. They said, nah, go ask your father. So Tad went away and came back with a card that says, 'Shoe Tad's horse for him. A. Lincoln.'"

I told her I'd seen pictures of the card.

"Here it is," she said.

She pulled open more drawers. "Sometimes I'll just come in here and leaf through things," she said. "You forget what you have. Last year this curator at Christie's was describing something to me—I can't re-member what—and I thought he was trying to get me to buy it, and I said, 'Well, that sounds interesting.' And he said, 'Louise, you already own it.' I said, 'Oops!'"

I'd heard that her collecting had slowed down quite a bit. She said that was true. "There's still stuff out there to buy, but not much that I'm interested in," she said. "Back in the eighties and early nineties, when I was buying heavily, people realized they could make a lot of money. So if they had anything to sell, they sold it then. I bought so widely, it's difficult to find things now. Oh, look at this." She unfolded a length of felt to reveal a pair of Lincoln's reading glasses. A slender box held his monogrammed billfold. Letters and his legal briefs, vol-ume after volume, were shelved in binders and cataloged by date.

Louise showed these to me matter-of-factly, hurriedly almost, but when she arrived at the items having to do with Mary she took her time. In recent years Louise's Stone-induced fascination with Lincoln has evolved, maybe inevitably and by now almost exclusively, into a fasci-nation with his wife.

"These are such personal things," she said. "Everything I try to buy now is so personal." She had the Christmas gift—a bound album of keepsakes—that Mary gave to Tad in 1867, two years after his father's death. From another drawer she brought out—well, Mary's drawers: a full set of fluffy undergarments; her sleeping bonnet also, soft and intimate. She showed me Mary's "sewing pin safe," a cloth wallet that opened up to reveal multiple likenesses of Abraham woven in silk. "You can see how much she loved him, can't you?" she said.

"It's why I get so exasperated with the scholars," she said. "They don't seem to even try to understand her. People hated her because she didn't fit the mold. Her father raised her to be the way she was. When the room divided up after dinner and the women went to one room and the men went to the other, she went with the men to talk politics. She wasn't just going to be one of the girls. She was very intelligent, and Lincoln loved that about her.

"They say she beat him!" Louise said suddenly. "Where? Where do they get that? Show me the document! Show me where it says that! They're all men who will tell you she was a shrew. She wasn't. They'll tell you she was crazy. She wasn't.

"Well, let me tell you what I've learned doing this: It's just not true. They loved each other. He loved to buy her things. He loved it that she had excellent taste and appreciated beautiful things and that she wasn't just some other society girl. And he was proud of her for that. They loved each other, they cherished each other. When these people say that—they don't see what I see right here."

Cross-legged on the floor, surrounded by stuff, she unrolled the pin safe again, exposing the likenesses that Mary had told her seamstresses to sew of her husband, years after his death. "It's obvious," Louise said. "The passion that was between them, it's all right here. When you collect things, you can feel it."

Can you really? I don't mean the passion necessarily. But can you imbibe some essence of the venerated man and honored woman by holding the things they held, the clothes they wore, the sheet of foolscap that received the ink from their pens as they pressed upon it the words they thought up? This kind of veneration does sound very Catholic Churchy, as Weinberg says, or at least very mystical, and Lincoln wasn't a Catholic and not really a mystic, either. But there's mysticism at the heart of most Lincoln collecting, from what I can tell—a connection between the collector and the collected that crosses space and time and infuses bits of matter with its opposite. This is a question on which the church is due some deference, since it has been in the collecting business longer than anyone, and as an institution that holds elaborate and complicated views about nearly everything it makes useful distinctions among different kinds of relics, or what the buffs, using secular lingo, call collectibles.

Relics of the First Class, in the church's view, are parts of a saint's body. Bones, fingernails, and teeth have been especially popular with saint collectors, while blood and hair, as we've seen, are the big draws for Lincoln buffs, though the market for these, as we've also seen, is highly unreliable and confused. No one, so far as I know, has tried to buy or sell the tibia or molars of Abraham Lincoln. The bit of brain that Willie Clark was so happy to own has vanished; it now belongs to the ages and not to some creepy collector with access to eBay. It's true that in the government's National Museum of Health and Medicine in Washington, D.C., bits of Lincoln's skull, gathered after the extraction of Booth's bullet, are preserved in a glass case under the watchful eye of security guards, but don't try to make them an offer.

Relics of the Second Class are objects "sanctified," as the church puts it, by close contact with saints—items they wore, regularly used, or were otherwise connected to them in an intimate way. Louise's mansion in Beverly Hills is thus a regular reliquary for Second Class Lincoln relics, from the billfold to the sum book page to the document binders to—assuming a passionate marriage—Mary's undergarments. The old Lincoln exhibits at the CHS made up a reliquary too, and so does the Treasures Gallery in Springfield. You see the power of Second Class relics in the faces of the people as they pause before the beaverskin top hat or the handwritten Gettysburg Address. And as for Third Class relics, says the church, these are objects that have come in extended contact with relics of the first or second class.

Unfortunately, this is where the church's guidance ends—no further classes are identified. Yet with Lincoln collectibles, this is where most of the action begins.

Here we move into a realm where worlds collide—where the vaporous inscrutability of mysticism meets the iron laws of supply and demand. The craving for Lincoln stuff is intense and unyielding, and has been for 150 years, from one generation to the next; most estimates put the number of active, relatively serious collectors of Lincolniana at fifteen thousand or more. Lincoln's attraction for collectors is partly a testament to the vastness of the man himself—to the numberless roles he's played in history, to the endless facets disclosed by even the quickest survey of his life. No matter what your hobby is, Lincoln will likely pop up sooner or later. If you're interested in politics, war, civil rights, literature, economics, the law, religion, romance, human psychology, celebrity, or the infinite application of the graphic arts, then your interest will likely bring you into contact with Lincoln the politician, the commander in chief, the emancipator, the writer, the rhetorician, the free marketer, the lawyer, the martyr, the husband of Mary, the manic depressive, and the most celebrated and most graphically depicted man in American history.

Yet what happens when demand far outstrips the supply of good Lincoln stuff—the supply, that is, of relics of the Second or Third class? Few really singular Lincoln documents reach the market anymore, and artifacts with ironclad provenance, things we know for sure he wore or touched, are rarer still. Their rarity has priced them beyond the wherewithal of everyone but Louise and a handful of other collectors. In response, the market in Lincoln collectibles has performed one of those tricks that markets sometimes do: under the pressures of escalating demand and fixed supply, it has expanded the definition of "good Lincoln stuff" to include stuff that doesn't, to most people, look so good at all—relics of the Forty-eighth Class, or the Ninety-second Class, and beyond.

The supply is now limitless. You'll never scrape the bottom of this barrel. For a century marketers have thought they could catch the consumer's eye by putting Lincoln's name or face on the package; and the gambit still works. If your interest in, say, politics or literature has led you to an interest in Lincoln, and if you have a hankering to make your interest tangible—if you have the itch to be a collector—then you can lay hands on Lincoln stamps, handbills, photographs, playing cards, campaign buttons and ribbons, books, folk art, sheet music, glassware, advertising posters, pamphlets and monographs, food containers, tobacco pouches and pipes, porcelain, bubble gum cards, liquor bottles, cigar boxes, soap tins and boxes, cartoons, funeral items, ashtrays, matchbook covers . . . *matchbook covers.* Maybe you can't afford Abraham Lincoln's chamber pot. But you can afford a matchbook cover from the Lincoln Life Insurance Company circa 1950, which you can buy, according to the book *Collecting Lincoln,* for a mere six dollars. If that's your thing.

Talking to Lincoln collectors I came to think of Lincoln as a great sun surrounded by a solar system of numberless collectibles, turning in ever wider orbits around him, spinning out farther and farther yet still picking up enough of the original radiance to capture some buff's interest. Because the interest is inexhaustible, the radiance is inexhaustible as well.

Two more examples: many catalogs published to advertise the sale of Lincoln items are now themselves collectors items, trading for hundreds and sometimes thousands of dollars—which means, in typical postmodern funhouse fashion, we have collectors collecting catalogs of collectibles rather than collectibles themselves, a bit like a gourmand gnawing at the menu instead of the dinner. Even more amazing, collectors who can't afford a Lincoln signature, and even some who can, have begun trading in forged Lincoln signatures—fakes, acknowledged and advertised as such, yet still somehow carrying (in the eyes of the willing collector) an ion of the original radiance. Bogus Lincoln letters can sell for thousands of dollars apiece, if they can be traced to one or another of a half dozen legendary forgers who flourished in the early twentieth century. Entire collections now rest on the flimflam produced by Eugene Field II, Charles Weisberg, Joseph Cosey, and other departed con artists.

Has the mojo of celebrity ever extended so far? We are in the furthest reaches of the Lincoln solar system, past Neptune, past Uranus—which is what I would feel like if I paid thousands of dollars for a forgery on purpose. Lincoln collectors will disagree. "You just have to make sure it's a real forgery—a real Weisberg or Cosey," a Lincoln collector once cautioned me. "The market's so hot now we're seeing a lot of fakes."

*   *   *

"Oh sure," Frank J. Williams said, "I've got a couple. Forgeries are part of the Lincoln story. They help round out the collections."

Numbering, by his own estimate, 22,000 items, the Frank and Virginia Williams Collection of Lincolniana is generally regarded as the largest in private hands; sometimes it seems as if there's no type of Lincolniana that Frank doesn't have a couple specimens of, at least. Statuary, for instance. What strikes you about the Lincoln statuary in Frank's office isn't the quality, which varies, but the quantity, which is huge. Frank's office is very large itself—it is, in fact, a judge's chambers, for Frank is chief justice of the Supreme Court of the state of Rhode Island—and the statues are everywhere, of every size, busts and full figure both. They line the walls, perch on window ledges, peek out from bookcases, and stand stoutly in corners, as if they've been posted as pickets around the perimeter of a bivouac under siege.

Frank took me around the room, pausing before treasures of various kinds. From a bookshelf he brought down a few volumes of the ten-volume edition of the Lincoln biography by Lincoln's secretaries, Nicolay and Hay. This edition was specially printed by the authors for selected recipients, and in its pages Frank had tipped more prizes: letters from Hay and Robert Todd Lincoln, and a couple of documents and slips of paper in Lincoln's own hand. Gingerly he opened an 1845 edition of the Revised Statutes of Illinois to the title page, where the owner—William Herndon, of the law offices of Lincoln & Herndon— had penciled in his name. He showed me a copy of the Emancipation Proclamation bound in leather and velvet with a small brass plate tacked to the cover: "Presented to Abraham Lincoln in 1864 with gratitude from the Freed Colored People of Shreveport."

"So it's not just a copy of the Emancipation, you read me?" Frank said. He is a large and emphatic man, with a head that seems to have been carved from oak, and his baritone crowds out all other sounds in a room, with each syllable carrying the inflections of his native state:

lawr for law, *collectah* for collector, *heya* for here. "It's who this copy is from that makes it precious. The Freedmen! All right? Think of how Lincoln must have treasured it. That's why I treasure it. That's the collector's art. For example, here . . . " He directed my attention to a framed note on a wall. I recognized it as a military commission signed by Lincoln. Thousands of such commissions survive.

"But look closer," Frank insisted, placing his face to the frame. "This is a commission to James Shields. Eh? You know the name?" Shields was the Illinois politico with whom the future president nearly fought a duel in 1842. "Now, twenty years later, Lincoln is giving his rival a commission into the armed services to fight for his country. For the Union! You see the meaning of this. It's about forgiveness, isn't it? It's about putting jealousies and rivalries behind you for the greater good. It's about overcoming pettiness! This is Lincoln's greatness, right here, on one piece of paper."

We were high up in the Rhode Island courts building, with the office towers of Providence rising just beyond the point where the Woonasquatucket and Moshassuck rivers meet. We paused for a moment to admire the view before he invited me to sit by the fireplace, under an engraving of Carpenter's *First Reading of the Emancipation Proclamation*. Among a row of Lincoln busts on the mantel was a judge's gavel chiseled from a tree at Lincoln's birthplace. "Lincoln is never far away from me," Frank said, as he eased his bulk into a Windsor chair. Here in his chambers, getting away from Lincoln would be an impossibility, physically, but Frank meant it spiritually. "I couldn't have got through what I've gotten through without Lincoln inspiring me and showing me the way. Of course not!"

The governor of Rhode Island appointed Frank chief—and that's what most people call him, simply "Chief"—in 2001. From the start, his tenure has been a maelstrom of criticism and conflict. Some of the trouble, he acknowledges, is owing to his own personality, which he calls "dynamic," and the rest to the difficulty of the tasks he set for himself. Rhode Island's politics rivals Illinois's for shadiness and self-dealing; ethical difficulties had driven two of the last three chiefs from the bench. Frank offered himself as a reformer. He immediately went to war with the governor and the legislature over control of the judiciary budget and other questions of judicial independence. He tried to discipline his department's bureaucracy and modernize its computer systems, and he embarked on an ambitious construction program to build new courthouses in underserved regions of the state. By now a river of bad blood—a Moshassuck of bad blood, a Woonasquatucket of bad blood—separated him from the other powers in the state, the media included.

Wise-ass newspaper columnists took to calling the Chief "Frontpage Frank." They scored him for printing and distributing, at state expense, monographs of his speeches lavishly adorned with color photographs of himself, often surrounded by delighted schoolchildren. They drew particular pleasure from his personal Web site, www.frankjwilliams.com. On the site the Chief was described—apparently by himself—as a "staunch patriot who for more than twenty years has been widely acknowledged as the foremost leader of America's Lincoln fraternity, the large, nationwide community of Lincoln historians, students, and enthusiasts." The Web site posted a form for people to ask the Chief—a "gifted speaker" —to address the next meeting of their business or civic organization, with fees left to negotiation. He posted pictures of his dogs. A "noted pastry chef," he posted his favorite recipes, including one that relied on Duncan Hines cake mix and lemon-flavored Jell-O. Oh, how the columnists loved that.

On at least one matter, however, there was no exaggeration. For many reasons, including the size of his Lincoln collection, the chief really is a potentate in the Land of Lincoln, even if, like Napoleon, he crowned himself.

Acquiring stature and repute is easier to do in the Lincoln fraternity than in many other places. There are so many points of entry, for one thing. If you're a Washington buff or a Madison maven, if you're an Adams aficionado or have a jones for Jefferson, you will find at most one or two gatherings of fellow buffs around the country where you can make contacts, exhibit your talents, and establish your expertise. The Land of Lincoln, by contrast, bristles with possibilities. There are Lincoln groups and roundtables in Boston and Washington, Chicago and Los Angeles, Philadelphia, Seattle, Milwaukee, Topeka, Wilmington, Indianapolis, and Fort Wayne . . . All you need to break in are lots of get-up-and-go and a minimal amount of guile.

An old Lincoln hand, a historian by trade and a cynic by inclination, once told me how it's done.

"The best way to move up in the Lincoln world is to give a lot of speeches," he said. "It can be the same speech over and over again if you want—you just have to give it to a lot of different groups. And you're in luck, because there are so many places where people are willing to sit still for a talk about Lincoln. Expectations are low. The field is wide open. You can always find somebody to talk to, and they'll always be appreciative.

"So you start by offering yourself as a luncheon speaker at some Lincoln roundtable. Then you move on to the next group, and you offer yourself as a dinner speaker—after all, you're already a veteran luncheon speaker. And now that you've spoken to their dinner, you might offer to serve on their board. They'll say yes. Trust me, they'll say yes. And after you're on their board for a while, you might want to run for president. Chances are you'll run unopposed. Pretty soon, you're a figure in the Lincoln community—you're a veteran speaker and you've served on the board and you're president of the Lincoln Roundtable of Somewhere or Other. You write an op-ed for the local paper when Lincoln's birthday comes around. You prepare quotes for the next time the paper does a Lincoln story and a reporter calls you for an interview. People defer to you. They defer to you because you're president of the roundtable and you've given speeches, both luncheon and dinner, and you're quoted in the newspaper, and you've published an op-ed.

"There. Mission accomplished. You're officially a Lincoln expert.

"Please understand me," the old hand said. "This makes no sense. You cannot become recognized as a Washington expert this way, or a Jefferson expert. There is no other field of American history where this could take place. But in the Lincoln world it's been happening from the very beginning."

What the old hand was sketching for me, I guessed, was a sly caricature of the Chief's rise as a Lincoln figure, and coming from the old hand, a certified scholar, it carried a whiff of the professional resentment that I'd seen elsewhere among Lincoln historians. With no academic training beyond his law degree, the Chief might be seen by professors as a dilettante or worse. Still, he could just as easily be seen as I prefer to see him, and as he prefers to see himself—an exemplar of the amateur tradition, a long and honorable line that has kept the Lincoln field blessedly free of the guild mentality that can make academic history seem the dreary province of pedants and bullies.

"Here," the Chief said in his chambers, when we were settled before the fireplace. He chucked me a copy of his résumé. The résumé was fifty-one pages long—a majestic thing. In addition to the usual items like birthdate (1940) and education (Boston University College of Law) its bulk was taken up with a list of "Frank J. Williams Selected Publications, Conferences, and Speaking Engagements."

"And here—I had my assistant prepare a little packet of material for you." He pointed to a table where a stack of photocopied speeches, magazines, and brochures had been placed. The stack was a foot high. "You'll want to take those with you, I'm sure," he said.

"These are a lot of speaking engagements," I said, fluttering through the résumé.

"It's a partial list," he cautioned me. "We're looking at, what, six hundred, six hundred fifty, speaking engagements here but this is just over the last ten years or less. I've given thousands and thousands and thousands of talks. I joined the Lincoln group of Boston when I was still in college, and I began by giving little reports on this or that little bit of Lincoln research—just to get practice and get over my nerves. I had nerves then, huh? Nerves! I'd get nervous! Not anymore." He grinned. "Then I built up to my first real talk: 'Abraham Lincoln's Visit to Providence.'" By the mid-seventies he was president of the Boston Lincoln group and he was speaking constantly. "Everywhere," he said. "Schools, rotary clubs, historical societies—there are so many groups out there. I'll talk on Lincoln the lawyer, Lincoln and the constitution, and of course I'll talk about the collections, with illustrations."

He usually uses the plural when he talks about his collection of Lincoln stuff. "I got started early," he said. As a boy in the public schools of Cranston, outside Providence, he sat where the alphabetical order placed him, in the back of the class; his grandfather had changed the family name, Guglielmo, to Williams years earlier. Right above his school desk was the portrait of Lincoln that once hung in every American classroom. "I'd look at that portrait and I was fascinated with that face. I wanted to know more about that man. I could see something there, an affinity, do you know what I mean?

"My mother would give me lunch money every day, twenty-five cents. I'd skip lunch and save the money, and then I'd hop a bus to Providence and go down to the used bookstores. The bus driver knew what I was doing. He wouldn't charge me. Good guy. I'd go to the used-book stores and buy whatever I could get my hands on—good books about Lincoln, terrible books, it didn't matter, whatever I could afford. I wanted the books not just to read but to have. I felt it very early—this proprietary sense about him.

"I became a lawyer because of him. I saw there was a symmetry between our situations, because of our upbringings. My grandparents had come over from Italy and started a landscaping business and my father took it up. So summers I worked in it too. Like Lincoln, I worked with my hands. It's a good business, landscaping, but . . . I decided I'd be a lawyer instead. Lincoln had the same reaction."

He continued to buy books during a stint in the army, mailing volumes back to his mother in Providence, where boxes of them accumulated in her basement. He met his wife, a Texan, while stationed in Germany, and she augmented his collection with interests of her own. "She was always interested in ephemera. You know that word, 'ephemera'? Gimcracks and gewgaws, we call them. Tchotchkes."

By the time he graduated law school he had more than a thousand Lincoln books, along with a swelling assortment of gewgaws. Despite collecting and speaking and traveling through Lincolnworld in every spare moment, he built a flourishing law practice over twenty-five years—"exactly the same number of years Lincoln practiced law. Then we went into public service. He went into politics, but I didn't have the fire in the belly for politics. Too many compromises. Too many give-ups. You know? I went on the bench."

As we spoke, the chambers was a hive of activity, phones chirping, doors opening and closing as clerks and secretaries darted in and out, shuffling papers and asking quick questions. Conversation with the Chief is a headlong rush, though susceptible to quick reversals of direction. Moods cross his large, open face like weather on a radar map, from blinding sunshine and sparkling eyes when he thinks of what pleases him ("Lincoln's an inspiration, the gentleness, you understand, the kindness . . . ") to sudden, ferocious typhoons that sweep through, upending entire trailer parks and leaving dozens dead. At the mention of becoming chief justice he rose from his chair and paced the length of the chambers. His hands and gaze were never far from some representation of Lincoln.

"The abuse Mr. Lincoln took—the thought of that kept me going, I will tell you. He was president of a divided United States, I've been the chief justice of a divided state. When I fought for judicial independence, when I fought for a new courthouse, when I fought to convert our computer system from Wang—you know they don't even make Wang anymore? That's how old it was—when I beat off the naysayers, when I withstood the envy from people who were envious of my success and my drive—because that's what it was, envy, jealousy, clearly—I would sit here and I would see Lincoln and I'd say, 'He could survive for the sake of the whole country, I can do it for one state.' I understood the loneliness. And it was from him that I learned to survive, I can tell you that!"

A secretary came in to announce the arrival of a reporter from the local paper, here to do a scheduled interview. The Chief makes good copy and, despite the rough treatment, he welcomes reporters, who are just as eager to come see him. They treat his Lincoln obsession with the condescension that is a hallmark of the journalist's trade. The reporter was writing a story on a new program to hire interpreters for the immigrants who wind up in Rhode Island's courts.

While they talked I leafed through the Chief's résumé. One reason for its impressive length, I saw, was repetition. Several of his speeches are listed as publications, and several publications are listed twice or three times, appearing in one section of the résumé and then reappearing in another. The Chief often describes himself as author of a dozen books, for instance, but in fact he's sole author of one book, a collection of previously published articles called *Judging Lincoln*. He's cowritten three other books, two of which are brief enough to be considered pamphlets. The balance are books on which he's credited as coeditor.

When the reporter was done with the interview she turned off her recorder and put away her pen and pad and folded her hands in her lap. The serious business now over, she cocked her head and asked, with a slight smile, "And what would your Mr. Lincoln think of your interpreters' program?"

The Chief ignored the condescension. "He would be empathic," he said. "I like to think he would be empathic, just as I am empathic. The program is inclusive. I am inclusive and Lincoln was inclusive."

After she'd gone he told me: "Yes, some people think it's eccentric, my interest in Mr. Lincoln. And yes, there's maybe a smirk here or there. Sometimes a joke maybe. But if that's what they're thinking—that it's an oddball thing—they don't have the balls to tell me to my face, usually. I don't rub their noses in it. Even within the Lincoln community it's hard sometimes to get people to understand the relationship. You take a look at Springfield, now."

I said, "I was wondering about Springfield."

He stood up abruptly. "Come on, let's get some lunch. You're hungry, right? Of course you are. We'll eat. Then we'll see more of the collections."

The Chief gets around Rhode Island in an SUV driven by a rotation of sheriff's deputies. An officer named Vito drove us across town to Venda Ravioli, an old-style Italian delicatessen. "The quality here, as the Chief will tell you, is beyond compare," Vito explained to me. "Of course, as you know, here in Providence we're known around the world for having the best dining restaurants in the nation. And you are about to experience one of the finest of these."

And it was fine—everything at Venda's was spectacularly good. A table had been laid out for us in the back. We walked past long glass cases showing hocks of ham and wedges of cheese and grilled peppers and button mushrooms swimming in bowls of olive oil. Cries of *Chief!* rose from behind the counter or from the massed ranks of customers cradling their weekend supply of caprioli and agnolotti. The weather map brightened and he worked the tables like the pol he chose not to be. When there were no hands left to shake he sat down at table. Waiters appeared with plates of food. "Try, try," they said, to the Chief's protests. I asked him about Springfield again, and a dark thunderhead crossed the map.

"You know that Lincoln didn't carry Springfield in 1860?" the Chief said. "Of course you've heard that. He carried the county but not the town—maybe it was the other way around, we can check that. The point is: That tells you something, huh, doesn't it? And it's still the same out there. They're shortsighted, provincial. The parochialism of that city is incredible. Watch out for them, Andy. I didn't watch out. I was unsuspecting and look what happened. Everybody out there's got their own agendas."

"What are their agendas?" I asked, dribbling minestrone.

"Envy," he said. "Envy. Jealousy. And their own self-aggrandizement. That's what they care about down there more than Mr. Lincoln—self-aggrandizement."

Springfield is home to the Abraham Lincoln Association, the country's oldest Lincoln organization. The Chief became president in 1986, landing what is probably the most prestigious position in the Lincoln fraternity; whoever occupies it immediately transcends buff status and becomes a first-rank expert, ex officio. He held on to the job for nearly ten years, serving longer than any other president. When buffs outside Springfield whisper disparagingly about "Springfield," they mean the state bureaucrats and they mean the ALA, which even in Frank's day was deemed sleepy and ineffectual—a social club for Springfield's oldest families. Frank's dynamism evidently roused them from their slumbers, and in 1995, in a series of parliamentary maneuvers and power plays, a rump group of Springfielders seized control of the ALA board, ejected Frank as president, and elevated another Springfielder to the post. It was a signal event in Lincolnworld, opening a fissure between buffs within Springfield and buffs outside it. After more than a decade the wounds are unhealed.

"It was a clash of cultures," he said. "They think he's all theirs. And I disagree. Do you see what I mean? I disagree that he's all theirs. Lincoln is for everybody! What I tried to do was expand the organization. I brought in new people. Outreach. I was inclusive. I was for inclusion. Our membership doubled during my time there. We brought in scholars. I increased the frequency of our meetings. None of this was okay by them. They objected. They don't appreciate him, they don't understand him, but they don't want anybody else to have him either. But he belongs to everybody, not just Springfield!"

He stared into his plate, where the uneaten ravioli was puddling up.

"Yes, it was a shock. But we recovered." The Chief left the ALA and, taking several directors with him, formed a competing national organization. The Lincoln Forum—Hon. Frank J. Williams, chair—

has met annually since 1997 in Gettysburg, Pennsylvania. "In the Forum we do things the Lincoln way. We place a high value on Mr. Lincoln's values—fellowship, civility, friendship. It's more like family."

And indeed, the Forum has been blessedly free of the rivalries and rancor that often characterized the ALA during the Chief's tenure. The relative stability of the Forum, according to the Chief's defenders (including the Chief), refutes the notion that his own dynamism was somehow the cause of the ALA rupture. At the Forum, expanding the membership rolls is a priority; so is "outreach"—advertising and other forms of publicity. Its annual meeting is televised on C-Span, the buffs' favorite cable network. The Forum publishes a biannual journal, sponsors a yearly essay contest for college students, and every year bestows the Richard Nelson Current Award of Achievement. The prize, handed out by the Forum chairman, Frank J. Williams, at a formal banquet, is a statuette by an Illinois sculptor named John McClarey, and its most recent recipients, in 2005, were . . . John McClarey and Frank J. Williams.

Just like a family.

Vito drove us out to the Chief's house, so I could see the rest of the collections. It's a modest split-level affair sided in shingle and set back among a stand of pine trees, outside a rural village thirty miles from Providence—about as far away as you can get from the roiling politics of the capital or the bitter rivalries of Lincolnworld. We entered through the garage and into the tack room, where the "gewgaw and gimcracks" of the Frank J. and Virginia Williams Collection of Lincolniana are kept. Thousands of items were scattered in glass cases and cabinets: the glassware and old syrup bottles, the souvenir plates, thimbles, and spoons sold at tourist traps, coin banks shaped like log cabins or like Lincoln's head, shaving mugs, matchbook covers . . .

"We collect fewer of these gewgaws than we used to," the Chief said. "My wife has a new thing. She collects outhouses now." He saw my surprised look. "I don't know," he said, with uncommon mildness. "She's from Texas."

He seemed to be decompressing as he showed me around. Smooth jazz was piped throughout the house from satellite radio. The bulk of the Chief's collections, I discovered moving from room to room, are books and gewgaws. Still more bronzes stared out from cabinets and shelves. A few Lincoln signatures were mounted on the walls. At last we descended a twisting stairway to another room the Chief described as his private hideaway. He had it specially built as part office, part library. Years ago he hired a bibliographer to work half-time cataloging each item of Lincolniana. The project has taken years and has a Sisyphean hopelessness to it, since the Chief acquires items—newspapers, magazines, books, monographs—faster than a part-timer can log them in. Wheeled library carts loaded with books were lined up awaiting attention.

"It's a mess," the Chief said. He cleared off a stool for me to sit on and parked himself in the room's only easy chair, his legs stretched before him. Here, too, Lincoln statues were everywhere. On one shelf was a limited edition of the statue of Lincoln that Bob Kline had brought to Richmond, the one, as Kline described it, that "simply says, We should love each other." I asked the Chief what he valued most in the collection, of all the 22,000 pieces. His answer was typically idiosyncratic. The autographed copy of the Lincoln Douglas debates? The commission for James Shields?

"The pamphlets from the Civil War," he said. Most of these deal with Lincoln's use of war powers, both pro and con. They're not at all rare—they can be found on eBay routinely, for as little as twenty bucks—but they show Lincoln under fire, the Chief said, undergoing the most withering political and intellectual criticism, and they show him at his best in response—wily in argument, forceful in expression.

"And this is a special piece," he said, pointing to an oil painting that he had set directly across from his easy chair, at eye level.

It was huge, showing Lincoln nearly life-sized. It was painted by the American illustrator James Montgomery Flagg, who's best known for inventing the Uncle Sam "I Want You" poster in World War I. Flagg posed for Uncle Sam himself, and he used himself as a model as well when he rendered Lincoln. But where his Uncle Sam is fierce, his Lincoln is intensely emotional. It shows a Lincoln beyond dejection. His hair is disarranged to look like a bird's nest. He's on his knees in his White House bedroom, his elbows akimbo and his fingers entwined in prayer, his upturned face wet with tears and contorted in agony. It's Lincoln past the point of endurance, wretched in the extreme, turned to the heavens in a final plea that every quivering line of his face says will not be answered. Deliberately or not, it evokes Christ at Gethsemane.

The exaggerated effects are almost grotesque, pathetic and unpleasant to look at—a kind of mawkish, near hysterical Lincoln that few would find appealing. I told the Chief I'd never seen it before.

"No," he said. "It's not well known. That's the original, by the way. But it's very powerful. It shows something, doesn't it, Andy? Doesn't it?"

He leaned back in his easy chair. "Sometimes the frustrations are very intense. You know the time Lincoln was at Fortress Monroe and he became so frustrated with McClellan he threw his hat on the ground and stomped on it. Like that—it's just like that, often. Do the frustrations hurt? Yes. Do they take a toll? Yes. Is it worth it? Ask him." The Chief pointed to the Flagg portrait.

"This is where I escape," he said. "It's my refuge. I come down here, and it's all quiet, and there's no bother, and Lincoln's here, and here, and here," he said pointing to items from the collections piled around the room, next to his chair, on the bookshelf behind him, over by a desk covered in more stacks of books and papers. "And here," pointing to the Flagg portrait. When he sits in the easy chair he's looking directly at it, directly at Lincoln on his knees, at the end of his rope. "He was so human, wasn't he? Heh? Wasn't he? And he knew loneliness. Yet he survived. No matter what they threw at him. The man survived."

*   *   *

Spending time with collectors made me realize why I found it so hard to express what I felt when I stood with Tom Schwartz that evening outside his office in Springfield. "Go ahead," Tom had said. So I did. I lifted up the Gettysburg Address, held it by its cream-colored matting. Lincoln had written out this manuscript as a favor to Edward Everett, who had spoken right before him during the ceremony at Gettysburg. Everett wanted to auction it off to raise money for wounded soldiers. I saw the ink that had turned to sepia, and the lines in the paper that Lincoln used to guide his careful penmanship. It was written with great care. It was Lincoln through and through. And I felt . . . nothing.

Or not nothing—but not very much. Not as much as I expected to feel. Holding the thing, in fact, wasn't for me quite as moving as actually reading the words that make up the address, the greatest public utterance in our history. Lincoln comes to us in different ways. He had come to me as a little boy in my bedroom late at night as I pored over those cheap reproductions, and then later he had appealed to me as someone who loved American history and worried over politics. And he had come into the lives of Louise and the Chief in different ways, too. Lincoln was made real to them by the things they held, and beheld, sometimes as a consolation. Lincoln, I knew, comes to each of us from a different direction. I was beginning to wonder whether it was the same Lincoln.

6

A SEA OF LINCOLNS

From a distance, out on the highway, it was hard to tell which was the statue—Santa or Abe. Santa was tall and roundish, Abe was much shorter but even rounder, with a belly that under the right circumstances would unquestionably shake like a bowl of the sweet stuff. On closer examination, the Santa turned out to be the statue—a painted fiberglass job, set out as a tourist come-on—while the Abe was a regular person, or as regular as a person can be who tries to earn a living by dressing up like Abraham Lincoln even though he's shaped like Santa.

And this person was not alone. In fact, he was just the beginning. I parked my rental car and walked into the lobby of Santa's Lodge, the only motel in the crossroads town of Santa Claus, Indiana. I heard the tinny sound of "Rudolph the Red-Nosed Reindeer," and I saw, on ledges near the ceiling, ranks of pint-sized animatronic elves gaily hammering away at Santa's workbench, and I saw the large Christmas tree and the billows of snowy cotton dotted with little evergreens, and I heard a miniature train whistling by on a tiny track, and I saw more than forty men dressed exactly like Abraham Lincoln staring at me as I walked through the door.

I was prepared for this. In the parking lot I had seen several RVs and cars—older models, American-made—bearing vanity plates: ABE AND ME, ABEFAN1, ITS ABE (twice), ABE L 1, I LIKE ABE, 4 SCORE, ABES R US, HERES ABE, and so forth. Men who dress like Abraham Lincoln, I soon discovered, spend a lot of time in their vehicles, and so it was nothing for them, on this lovely spring weekend, to drive from homes all over the country into deepest Indiana to Santa's Lodge, where, in the lobby, they were registering for the annual national convention of the Association of Lincoln Presenters.

There's not much in Santa Claus aside from a post office, the lodge, a Food Lion, and the Splashin' Safari Water Park, which was closed. But the presenters had come here because Santa Claus is in the heart of Spencer County, where the real Abe lived his formative years, and each year they try to gather near a site with such deep spiritual resonance. This was the organization's ninth convention. It was founded in 1990 by a trio of Abes, including Dr. Dan Bassuk, a retired psychologist from New Jersey who was still serving as the organization's president when they gathered in Indiana. Within its first five years the ALP grew to nearly one hundred members—seventy-six Abes and twenty-two Marys—and they chose to celebrate this landmark with their first convention, in Mary's birthplace of Lexington, Kentucky. By the time they got to Santa Claus, ALP membership stood well over 250, with members from nearly forty states. Roughly 175 of these members work as Abes; another 40 or more are women who impersonate Mary, usually teamed with an Abe; and another 40 are members designated as "patrons"—people who, like me, don't dress up as Abraham Lincoln but like to hang around people who do.

Presenters resist the tag "impersonators" because the word sounds showbizzy—you imagine guys in tuxes saying "You dirty rat" like James Cagney, or, worse, guys twirling a feathered boa like Carol Channing—and they struggle to maintain a dignified, though not solemn, air, which is not always easy. The organization's latest motto, "Would I Might Rouse the Lincoln in You All," is its third. The first was "Now He Belongs to the Stages," which some members thought overly cute, while the second—"Ready, Willing, and Abe L"—proved to be typographically unsettling. All three were conceived by Dr. Bassuk, but everyone seems to agree that the third time was the charm and that the newest one is best. The line about rousing the Lincoln is drawn from the work of the prairie poet and mystic Vachel Lindsay, and it fits the mission the organization has set for itself. The most dedicated presenters hold an expansive idea of Lincoln. For them he's not just a historical personage but also a mystical force, a universal, indwelling presence that's accessible to everyone but is too often obscured by the bustle of the workaday world, and it can be goosed along with the right coaxing—by, say, hiring a man who dresses up like Abraham Lincoln to speak to your organization or appear at your event for a modest fee, usually negotiable.

"If any personal description of me is thought desirable," Lincoln once wrote, "it may be said, I am, in height, six feet, four inches, nearly; lean in flesh, weighing on an average one hundred and eighty pounds; dark complexion, with coarse black hair, and gray eyes—no other marks or brands recollected." This was typical Lincolnian understatement. A good seven inches over average height, always ill-dressed, hair uncombed, loose-jointed and high-waisted, narrow at the upper chest with Gumby arms and enormous hands and feet, Lincoln was by all accounts one of the most extraordinary-looking men any of his contemporaries had ever seen. *Extraordinary* is the least prejudicial term I can think of; others weren't nearly so kind. "I have seen, in Washington and in the West, several public men of rough appearance," wrote his political ally Carl Schurz, "but none whose looks seemed quite so uncouth, not to say grotesque, as Lincoln's." Even as a boy, a childhood friend said, he was "dried up and shriveled." The man who knew him best, Joshua Speed, wrote: "He was a long, gawky, ugly shapeless man." And these were his friends.

Few of the Abes of the ALP take offense, therefore, when you point out that many of the members look even less like Abraham Lincoln than, for example, your grandmother does. Scanning the lobby at Santa's Lodge, I noticed men who were dead ringers for Abe, and many more who weren't. Dr. Bassuk, for example, was short and bald, while Lincoln was neither, and every syllable of his speech betrayed his urban northeastern upbringing, in contrast to what acquaintances recalled as Lincoln's country drawl. But because Dr. Bassuk's understanding of his hero was essentially spiritual—"Lincoln is as close to perfection," he told me, "as any man could be expected to be"—he never considered this lack of height, hair, or drawl to be a deterrent to his vocation.

And vocation is the word; more often than not the call comes unbidden. Dr. Bassuk heard it sometime in the late 1970s. "It began with the beard," he said. He grew the beard—a Lincoln-like affair, trimmed down almost to the jaw line, no mustache—because he liked the austerity of the style, and before too long, he said, people began calling him Abe. Then one thing led to another. Talking to other Abes, I discovered that this is how it almost always happens. A fellow, minding his own business, decides to grow a beard. Soon, multiple people are telling him that he bears a striking resemblance to Abraham Lincoln. It doesn't matter that very often these people are wrong. So strong is the lure of Lincoln that when people tell a man with a beard that he looks like the greatest of all Americans, he believes it. And if he's of a curious cast of mind he begins learning about Lincoln, and pretty soon someone gives him a stovepipe hat as a gag, or asks him to appear at a child's birthday party or a Memorial Day parade. And then he gets it in his head to make a living at it.

By Dr. Bassuk's estimate, more than a third of the Abes in the ALP are full-timers. Others moonlight, snatching a gig here and there to supplement other income, with the hope of becoming full-time eventually. In Santa Claus I met a gardener, two school janitors (though one of them, fudging, called himself a "custodian," and the other, fudging even more, said he was a "maintenance engineer at an elementary educational facility"), two surveyors, a Presbyterian minister, an arborist, a bus driver, several teachers, a man who designs window treatments, and a Pentecostal preacher.

Whatever their station in life, they share an outlook and humor peculiar to themselves. "You don't look like you've been dead for a hundred and forty years!" is a common greeting. In Santa's coffee shop, where the Abes ate their lunches and breakfasts, an Abe might take his seat and say, "Normally I wouldn't sit here. I'm not real fond of Booths."

"I'm so hungry I could split a rail," another would announce, tucking into a plate of flapjacks and bacon. "I'd follow you anywhere," an Abe said to his wife one night in a stage whisper, hoping to be overheard by his fellow Abes, "just don't ask me to go to the theater again!" If you were looking for a particular Abe and asked one of them to point him out for you, he might say: "Just look for the fellow with the beard and top hat." None of these gags, or their many variations, seemed to go over like a lead balloon.

Even to an outsider, the centrifugal pull that draws the Abes together was unmistakable. Working as an Abe is not all glamour, not all parties and parades, pig roasts and ribbon cuttings. It is solitary work, usually, and not lucrative. Abes, I discovered, often spend weeks on the road at a single stretch, away from home and their own beloved Marys and Tads and Willies. They work out of their cars or vans and will sleep in them too, depending on how many expenses the client has agreed to pick up. At night in the parking lot at Santa's Lodge I saw that some Abes who couldn't afford a room were spending the nights in their backseats. They'd emerge with the dawn for a towel bath in the restroom off the lobby, where on Sunday morning I spied a particularly rumpled Abe at the sink, brushing his teeth—followed by a brief comb through the beard, a quick brush over the beaverskin top hat, and a tug on the lapels of the frock coat, a routine executed before the mirror without a wasted movement, like a mime's or a magician's, by way of preparing to face the day.

From this unsettled life the ALP offers a respite—a fraternity, an oasis of fellowship where an Abe can share his life with men who know what it is about. Part of the pleasure is purely superficial, too, of course: just putting on the costume and hanging out with a bunch of other people who like putting on the costume and hanging out. It's the same principle of solidarity that draws nudists together, only with clothes. When I mentioned this to one Abe, he agreed but offered me a friendly corrective. "It's not a costume," he said. "It's a suit. Clowns wear costumes. Any Abe who tells you he wears a costume is not a real Abe." And for those of us in the non-Abe community, the clothes pose a puzzle beyond terminology. When you go to a meeting where every man but you will be wearing a black frock coat, black trousers, black boots, and a top hat, it is impossible, paradoxically enough, to figure out the dress code. When are you overdressed or underdressed? How do you tell? To be safe, all weekend I wore the usual khakis, blue blazer, white shirt, and topsiders—the native dress of my people—and never passed a moment when I didn't feel conspicuous. At such moments, in my experience, a drink is just the ticket. But I quickly found out, at dinner that first evening, that no alcohol is served at ALP functions. Lincoln was a teetotaler, and so are the Abes.

Other than the lack of alcohol, however, and the inescapable Christmas decorations, and the constant echo of the carols from the lobby, and the scores of people impersonating Abraham Lincoln or his wife, the ALP convention was like any other convention. Teamsters, librarians, Abes—the schedule doesn't vary. After registration came the plenary business meeting, followed by the banquet in a large, barnlike hall out behind the lodge, built from corrugated metal and laid with indoor-outdoor carpeting. After dinner we heard a guest lecturer give a talk about one of Abraham Lincoln's brothers-in-law. Then came time to hand out awards. Even Abes, modest as they are, can't resist this customary form of conventioneering self-flattery; indeed, their superabundance of fellow feeling and good cheer would seem to require them to show their appreciation for one another in such a way. When the Glenn Schnizlein Memorial Award for the Best Abraham and Mary Lincoln Team was given to B. F. and Dorothy McClerren, Mr. McClerren rose, much moved, to thank his wife. He noted how long they had been married, and how their bond had only deepened since they had begun performing as Mary and Abe in Civil War reenactments.

"She's seen me get shot over and over again," he said, looking at her with unmistakable pride, "and my Mary goes into hysterics every time."

Abe and Mary duos like the McClerrens have become increasingly common. Bringing along a Mary lessens the loneliness of the road, and wives, naturally enough, are often enlisted for duty, though with Marys, as with Abes, the lack of resemblance between actor and character is a problem not quite successfully overcome with either wardrobe on the part of the actor or lots of imagination on the part of the audience. There were scrawny Marys and there were Marys who could easily smuggle two of the scrawny Marys underneath their hoop skirts, but few that were built according to the original's just-so blend of petiteness and pudge.

Recent years have seen an explosion of reenactors of all kinds, with the result that more and more often these days even an Abe who travels solo might find himself working as a team—if not with a Mary then with a Stephen A. Douglas or Ulysses S. Grant, and occasionally, down South, a Jefferson Davis or a Robert E. Lee, in a kind of equal-time, point-counterpoint arrangement. In an idle moment Friday night, one Michigan Abe showed me an album of pictures of himself with a series of presenters trying hard to look like Mark Twain, both Roosevelts, George Washington, Thomas Jefferson, Patrick Henry, and James Garfield.

"James Garfield?" I said.

"He was a nice man," he said, tapping the photo. "God, he just loved Garfield. And his Garfield was very good—not that I would know, of course." He looked up. "I've wondered sometimes how much business he gets."

*   *   *

Getting business, of course, runs a close second to fellowship as the point of professional associations, so early Saturday morning—will it surprise you to learn that Abes are early risers?—the Abes gathered for a seminar on how to generate publicity, deal with reporters, and other mysteries of public relations. Lincoln himself was cunning with publicity, an early master of the American art of getting noticed. He traveled widely, befriended and flattered reporters and writers, and never passed up a chance to have his likeness made, becoming easily the most photographed and recognizable man of his time. Herndon once found him dropping a ten-dollar bill in a letter to the editor of a country newspaper, as a way of keeping him friendly. In 1859, thinking ahead to his presidential campaign, Lincoln even bought a small German-language newspaper in Illinois, guaranteeing some favorable coverage with an otherwise hard-to-reach constituency.

So it was altogether fitting that his impersonators should be schooled in the same art, a point made by the seminar's host, a former newspaper reporter who had volunteered to speak on the subject. "I know about the difficulties of publicity from both sides," she said. She was both a retired journalist and a wife to an Abe (though she had not yet taken the plunge herself and become a Mary). Her husband, in fact, was the only beardless Abe at the convention, and Americans, perhaps unaware that Lincoln was without a beard for fifty-one of his fifty-six years, will routinely fail to accept any such glabrous fellow as an authentic representation of their greatest president.

"You don't know what frustration is," she said, "till you've tried to convince people that this is Abraham Lincoln, and that they want to hire him, and that he's just as good as any other Abe, even though he doesn't have a beard."

She dispensed advice under the "Ten Bees." Be proactive: don't hesitate to contact reporters. But Be considerate: find out whether reporters like to be contacted by e-mail or fax or phone. Be a record keeper: keep a record of the names of reporters in the towns you visit, also of their husbands or wives or children if you can. Be not a snob: remember that publicity in small papers is helpful too. Be grateful: send a note to reporters who write you up. Above all: Be gracious. "Lincoln was," she said. "He would want you to be too."

After her presentation, which was acknowledged with a generous ovation, the seminar was opened up into a freewheeling discussion on similar themes. Schools, it's generally agreed, present the best profit potential for the entrepreneurial Abe. But how to generate business?

"Get into a car and drive," said a no-nonsense Abe from Georgia. He said he often travels cold to new parts of the country. "There is simply no substitute for it. Sometimes I can hit twenty schools in a day. I might get four or five bookings. That sure pays the grocery bill."

Another Abe from Illinois rose from his chair to disagree with that approach. "Where I come from, you just show up unannounced at a grade school dressed like this"—he flapped his lapels glumly—"and the chances are very high that they will call the police."

"They sure will," said an Abe sitting next to him. His voice seemed weighted down with painful experience.

In that case, the no-nonsense Abe said, when you hit a new town, you should find the superintendent of schools and ask for permission to speak to his district's school principals. "You can try to send a mailing in advance, but that won't work," he said. "Important people get lots of mail. Besides, they want to see you. They want to see Abe! You need to put yourself before the people who sign the checks."

Others suggested attending conferences of educators, event planners, or booking agents, and doing the presentation for them as an advertisement, for free.

"Maybe that works, maybe it don't," said another Abe bitterly, "but oh how they all love that word 'free.'"

This led to the dicey question of money: How much, said one of the younger Abes, should we charge?

There was an awkward silence, followed by some hemming and hawing. Nobody likes to talk about money.

Finally Dr. Bassuk, seated at the front of the room, spoke up.

"Come now," he said. "This is nothing to be ashamed of. As an Abe, you deserve to be paid. This is our livelihood. Of course, we must be reasonable in our fees because, really, this is not about the money. We want to enrich the educational experience of children and adults. That's why they choose us, is it not?" Suddenly Dr. Bassuk seemed gripped by a rhetorical urge. He rose to his feet. "My dear friends, they're tired of the magic shows! They're tired of the dance troupes, the cute animal acts, the disc jockeys! If you've got a good product they will snatch it up!" There were murmurs of assent. "And do we have a good product? Do we? I say we do! This—this—is what they want!" He doffed his hat, and his bald head shone.

There were more murmurs of assent.

"Bottom line," said Dr. Bassuk, returning to his seat, "two hundred dollars an appearance. At a minimum. Please. Let's do try to keep the prices up."

I glanced around the room. Already, in my discussions with other Abes, I had come to know that several of them would have considered "two C-notes" (as one Abe referred to the magic $200) a huge windfall. "Some of us are lucky to get fifty dollars, because we don't talk much or we don't like to give speeches, or because, frankly, some of us don't know enough about Lincoln to impart an educational experience," an Abe told me in confidence. "If you just show up to cut a ribbon or walk in a parade, it's hard to ask for more than fifty dollars. And sometimes, for weeks on end, you feel lucky to get a parade even. Fifty doesn't look too bad then."

Sometimes, not surprisingly, circumstances push an Abe to do something he's not proud of. "I did a wedding once," another Abe told me privately, shaking his head at the memory. "Pronounced them man and wife, just like that. Of course, legally, it didn't mean a damn thing. But

I did it and maybe I'd do it again. But please don't tell the other Abes. They'll think it was undignified."

Just as important as the official seminars were the off-session conversations. Much of the convention was spent comparing notes, telling stories, and passing on tips, whether singly, in casual, Abe-to-Abe interaction, or in larger bull sessions. They traded shtick—bits of business, as they used to say in the borscht belt, that work for one Abe and might work for another. What to do, for example, when a kid asks how you died? Abe can't very well talk about his own death. One Abe from Ohio said he has "Hat's Off Time." He announces "Hat's off!," removes his hat, and goes out of character to talk about Lincoln in the third person; then he becomes Abe again when he puts his hat back on. Dr. Bassuk was happy to talk about his highly successful program "The Man On the Penny Makes Cents"—a lesson in frugality for schoolkids. Others offered ideas for titles of shows. "You've got a title, you sound a little more upscale," an Abe said. "Even Abe needs a catchphrase." They felt free to choose among "Living with Lincoln," "All About Abe," "Getting Honest with Abe," even the discarded "Now He Belongs to the Stages."

Over iced tea or lemonade in the coffee shop Abes would gather to one-up one another with stories from the Abe life. One Abe from Vidalia, Illinois, told of being hired by a ladies' club in a nearby small town to do a team appearance with an untested Stephen A. Douglas.

"It was a big parade," he told us. "Or as big as that town could have. This Steve Douglas they had, well, he was a good man but he was a drunk. He just was. It got real hot and sure enough, before the parade even starts, he drank what must've been eight, ten beers. So we're on our float and he's trying to stay upright, just having a fine old time, waving at everybody, till we turn a corner and head into the very small African-American community they had in this small town.

So Steve Douglas turns back to me and shouts, 'Hey, Abe, here's a bunch you ain't freed yet!'"

The Abes around the table gasped.

"That's right," he said. "I was mortified. Everybody was. When we pulled up to the parade grounds the president of the ladies' club comes up to us and says, 'Well, you two gentlemen can both walk home!' Which I did. And which I did not get paid!"

One Abe warned his colleagues of a new brand of top hat that Wal-Mart had just started stocking. "Buyer beware!" he called out. "Six dollars for a fine-looking hat sounds like a bargain, but it ain't gonna look like a bargain when the brim breaks off and falls around your chin!" Hats were a permanent topic of conversation. How high should the rise of the hat be? Curved brim or straight? A tapered crown, which adds an elegant touch to the line of the hat, or straight-up stovepipe, which can augment the illusion of formidable height, important to the shorter Abe? A good hat can be a source of pride. Dr. Bassuk had a hat with a collapsible crown, impressively high when fully extended, flat as roadkill when pressed down. He liked to push it flat and then pop it up again. "You can crush my hat," he said when he did this, "but you cannot crush my spirit."

Others dismissed the crushable hats as insufficiently tall. "Sure," another Abe from Michigan told me, "everybody would like one you can squash. But right away you run into height problems. We have to live in the real world, and out there in the real world, height is what you need. Say you're out on a battlefield. It's the middle of a reenactment. Soldiers running around, smoke everywhere. You need to be seen. People need to see Abe! You need something with a little lift so you can stand out. I'm sorry, but your squashable hat is not going to do that for you." I noticed his brim was curved, not straight across, Pilgrim-fashion, like some that other Abes were wearing. "Don't get me started on the brim," he said.

The most ingenious tip I learned came from an Abe from Kentucky. I was admiring his extraordinary resemblance to the real Lincoln.

"You're lucky," I said. "You've even got the mole." I pointed to the famous blemish that adorned the crease of Lincoln's right cheek.

"You like it?" he said. "It's yours."

He dug his fingernail into his cheek and tore off the mole and tried to hand it to me.

"Go ahead, take it," he said. "It won't hurt you. All you do, you just clip an eraser from a number-two pencil and stick it on with epoxy. Easy as pie. Don't even need to color it. See? Already flesh-toned."

On the last day, Sunday morning, I went out in the parking lot among the rusted Fairlanes and first-generation RVs to get something from my rental car, and I was headed back to my room when I passed the banquet room and heard singing—vigorous, booming voices. The Abes and their Marys, awake early again, had gathered for a worship service. I came in through the rear door and was pulled up short when I saw that none of the Abes was in his suit. They wore T-shirts and jeans or golf shirts and shorts, sandals and sneakers. Only one of the Abes was suited up, the Pentecostal minister. He rose to the podium to give an impassioned sermon about Barabbas. The narrative was mostly apocryphal, I think. He told how Barabbas, after his release on Good Friday, had himself become a saint by retracing the footsteps of Christ—becoming like Christ by trying to live like him. The minister slipped into first person as the story went on, so that we had the rare pleasure of seeing a professional Lincoln impersonator transforming himself into a Lincoln impersonator impersonating Barabbas as Barabbas gradually began to impersonate Jesus.

The sermon ended in a great expenditure of emotion, with the minister near collapse, but he recovered quickly. Then we sang again. There was no piano in the banquet hall. One of the Abes had a pitch pipe, though, and he stood on tiptoes in front of us—he wasn't more than five foot eight—and he waved his arms as we sang. We sang "The Old Rugged Cross" and "Nearer My God to Thee." We sang "Amazing Grace" and "In the Garden."

They knew all the verses and they sang with passion, these Abes, because they are passionate men. It is the passion that makes the low pay and the constant travel and physical discomfort tolerable for the true Abe. He must agree with Dr. Bassuk when he said, "Lincoln is as close to perfect as a human being could be. That's what gives us a sense of mission. Being Abe is a calling." It would have to be, wouldn't it? Working on his own, freelance, trying to make history pay in a country that is famously indifferent to history, an Abe must be self-sufficient, spiritually. He must carry around within himself his own internal generator of enthusiasm and love, since he is unlikely to draw it from his audience, as other performers say they do.

That afternoon we all piled in our cars and formed a caravan to the Lincoln Boyhood National Memorial, near the site of the Lincoln family farm. When we arrived I could see just a smattering of visitors, three or four families wandering about the enormous limestone frieze that marks the spot. I did a quick calculation. The Abe-to-tourist ratio was easily three to one. It was a funny thing, but at the sight of the tourists—all of them big-butted in the American style, with fanny packs and flushed faces, looking vaguely annoyed that this wasn't a video game—you could see a flicker rise in the eyes of the Abes. *Civilians!* *. . . An audience . . . People who need to know about Abe.*

Soon, a dozen of them had surrounded the families and laid siege.

One was bent over a pair of preteen girls, reciting an autobiographical passage Lincoln once wrote: "My father removed from Kentucky to what is now Spencer County, Indiana, in my eighth year. It was a wild region, with many bears and other wild animals, still in the woods . . ."

"I have often been quoted as saying, 'You can fool some of the people . . .'" said another Abe, having cornered a grandma.

"I am certain," said another, "that you have heard my most famous address, given at the cemetery of Gettysburg . . ."

The parents didn't know how to react. Neither did their children. Some paused politely, others giggled; there were gapes and quick retreats.

"I was raised to farm work, which I continued till I was twenty-two. At twenty-one I came to Illinois."

One mother turned her daughter toward the parking lot.

"Are they crazy men?" I heard the girl ask.

"No, honey, of course not," the mother said. "They just want to be Abraham Lincoln. I don't know why."

7

ABE LINCOLN AND THE
SECRET OF SUCCESS

T he "town square" in Gettysburg, Pennsylvania, is really a
town circle—a roundabout where two major traffic arteries
come together and do a do-si-do for 180 degrees before continuing on their separate ways. We were careening around it in a big
tour bus when the tour guide half-rose from his seat and shot his arm
out the window.

"There it is, folks!" he yelled. "The only known statue of Abraham
Lincoln and Perry Como!"

You can't do justice to *Return Visit,* as the Lincoln-Como statue is
called, from a careening bus. I got a good look at it later on, after the
tour was over. It stands on a sidewalk next to the David Wills House,
once the private home of Gettysburg's most prominent citizen. Wills
was the man who invited Lincoln to help dedicate—to help consecrate—to help hallow—the battlefield cemetery in November 1863. The
night before the ceremony Lincoln touched up his remarks in a second-
story bedroom, and today, below the bedroom window, a bronze tourist
stands frozen in khakis, crew-neck sweater, and sneakers. He really is a

dead ringer for the dead crooner. In his hand he holds a piece of paper—either a copy of the Gettysburg Address or the sheet music to "Hot Diggity (Dog Ziggity Boom)." Lincoln stands next to him, a life-sized six foot four, his lips parted and his hat raised toward the window. They look like a vaudeville team, shuffling off to Buffalo.

Since its installation in 1993, *Return Visit* has proved popular with tourists. As in Richmond, at Tredegar, they gather round for pictures with the A-dude, raise rabbit ears behind his head, duck under his arm, kiss his cheek if they can reach it. Among buffs and art critics, however, the sculpture is taken to be the low point of Lincoln iconography, and the denunciations are ferocious: aside from its technical ineptitude, it's too informal, too cartoonish, too undignified. And *Return Visit* does raise the same knotty, paradoxical question raised by so many contemporary Lincoln sculptures that show Lincoln at ground level, in familiar, everyday poses: If the man is extraordinary enough to honor with a sculpture, why make him look so ordinary? Only greatness, you'd think, could inspire a statue. Yet these statues suggest nothing of greatness.

As depressingly true as this criticism is, it ignores the important, and much less depressing, point of *Return Visit*. Lincoln isn't just standing there, looking unheroically accessible. The focus of the little scene is his engagement with the tourist. Lincoln is pointing something out to the Como person, counseling him in some way. And the tourist, of course, is meant to represent Everyman. (That was Perry Como's appeal, too, when you think of it.) The tourist is a stand-in for *us*—and Lincoln has something he wants to say. Alone among the eye-level Lincolns, *Return Visit* brings Lincoln down to our level for a purpose that doesn't diminish him. It's meant to make him appear—I shudder to write the word, but here it comes—*relevant*. It establishes Lincoln as our contemporary, an approachable fellow who has something to tell us that we need to hear.

Lincoln as a man out of Time, whose practical wisdom is useful for everyone, spanning generations—this is an old, old idea, almost as old as the Land of Lincoln itself, and much older than the recent fad for earthbound statues. It's what brought me to Gettysburg in the first place. For Gettysburg is where Tigrett Corp holds its "Lessons from Lincoln" workshop—a management training seminar for CEOs, vice presidents, and other high-ranking officers from American government and business. Among its clients Tigrett counts big companies like General Mills and Rite-Aid, trade groups like the National Roofing Contractors Association, boutique financial consulting firms, and several agencies fished from the federal government's alphabet soup (DIA, NGA, PTO, FJC, ETC.). They come to Gettysburg for shifts of two or three days. In the meeting room of the Holiday Inn on Cemetery Hill, they turn the story of Lincoln's life into a "learning platform" that "breathes new life into leadership behaviors." They learn, in particular, how to placate clients, massage superiors, and manage the unruly flock of employees that surround them, just as Lincoln did, apparently. And they do this all in hopes of goosing the bottom line—as Lincoln did not do. Against all odds, Lincoln has become a business guru.

Here in the great commercial republic, in this vast dollar-humping, glad-handing USA, such a role for Lincoln was inevitable. The business-guru industry is too large and ravenous not to have swept him up. The industry caters to a peculiarly American type of businessperson, that striving, hope-filled, anxiety-ridden wannabe, the middle-management meatball. Not yet a professional success, but by no means a failure, the meatball leads a difficult life. He suffers in a state of constant competitive pressure. Above him looms the prospect of corporate advancement, below him yawns the abyss of stasis or decline. This drives him to mysticism, the conviction that somewhere out there a trick is waiting to be discovered, a special technique, some bit of knowledge—The Secret!—that will lead to promotion, to riches, to a life of ease and luxury, to the respect of doormen and secretaries, to success. Dale Carnegie, the legendary author of *How to Win Friends and Influence People*, was the first of the gurus, and the first to employ Lincoln in this way, as a kind of Keeper of the Secret, in the 1930s. The Carnegie-Lincoln tradition was given new life by Donald T. Phillips in the 1990s. A mid-level manager for a Texas oil company and a buff who got the Lincoln bug bad, Phillips wrote his *Lincoln on Leadership* in his spare time. After a slow build it became one of the biggest-selling business books of the decade, and perhaps the best-selling Lincoln book ever. Tigrett Corp has taken the tradition into the new century, adding tricks of its own.

Though the name sounds rather grand, Tigrett Corp is really just two people, a married couple named Antigoni and Everett Ladd, the Tig and Rett who combined into a Corp in 1984 and moved the business to Gettysburg in the late 1990s. They live on the edge of the battlefield, in a modest ranch house filled with boxes of books and pamphlets—the tools of their trade—as well as several stray cats they have offered a home. Everett is in his mid-seventies and is the Jack Spratt of the pair, a loose-limbed, exceptionally vertical New Englander with the folksy air of a country banker, which he once was. Antigoni, softer and rounder and a good deal younger, is the charged battery of Tigrett, as well as its academic director. With her degree in philosophy from the University of Chicago, she does the scholarly work of research and lesson planning. Everett mostly handles logistics, accounting, and "client development." It's a big job. The pair does thirty to forty workshops a year, with attendance running up to thirty workshoppers at a time.

We sipped hot tea at their kitchen table on a rainy afternoon, while the cats came and went. Antigoni told me how they got the idea for turning Lincoln into a learning platform, though I never got clear on what a "learning platform" was. The two met in our nation's capital, and their romance followed the typical Washington boy-meets-girl trajectory: lobbyist (Everett) is introduced to trade-association official (Antigoni), they date, they fall in love, they get married, they start a consulting business. Everett had read Carnegie on Lincoln many years ago, but the real inspiration for "Lessons from Lincoln" came from a book, *The Classic Touch*, by an academic named John Clemens.

The Classic Touch was published in the early 1980s. After the unhappy 1970s, capitalism was again in vogue, and publishers were beginning to rediscover the nearly limitless purchasing power, not to mention gullibility, of the management meatballs. A book on any subject— history, science, technology, sports, personal reminiscence—might sell if it were tagged as a business book. (For a publisher, The Secret is per- suading book buyers that its book contains The Secret.) Clemens's specialty was literature, and for *The Classic Touch* he combed through the classics of fiction and mythology and pretended they held lessons for businessmen—not The Secret, necessarily, but lots of little messages that might add up to The Secret eventually. The story of Agamemnon and Achilles became a case study, "Trouble in the Greek Executive Suite," which could serve as a guide to winning power struggles with fellow executives. Plato was described as having written "History's First Consultant Report." The theme of *King Lear*, it turned out, was "Find- ing a Competent Successor." *Macbeth* told the story of a "Promising Career Gone Awry."

"I loved it!" Antigoni said. At the time she was directing her trade association's adult education programs in Washington. "I loved the idea of taking something old and different, yet familiar too, and finding parallels to the people and situations of today," she said. So she asked Clemens if she could build a management training workshop around the book. It was a big success, and she and Everett decided to go off on their own—except they would use history rather than literature as the source of business savvy.

They shopped a few ideas for workshops to potential clients in the corporate world. "We tried Churchill," she said. "We tried the story of the whaling industry as a case study. We tried lots of things. None of them really took off." And then . . . "We hit on Lincoln. Bingo! People loved it. We thought it would be a hobby for our retirement. But it just didn't stop. We could do Lincoln all year round. People just love him.

"But you know that. What are you writing a book about? Lincoln. See? You put Lincoln's name on anything—soap, insurance, whatever—it'll sell."

When I rose to go, Antigoni offered to check with one of her clients to see whether any would let me sit in on one of the workshops. "You really need to see how people respond to this man," she said.

I told her I would love to come. I didn't tell her that the word "workshop" rang in my ears like a fire alarm.

Now and then I have kept myself busy by trying to decide which of the many views of Lincoln is the most far-fetched. Everyone I met wanted him to be one thing or another, a liberal or a conservative, a Christian or a skeptic, a bookish don or a horny-handed son of toil; but whose view was the most wildly implausible? For a long time I thought first place went to those spiritualists who testified to Lincoln's love of séances and his ride atop the grand piano. Then I thought it had to go to the American leftists in the 1930s who celebrated Lincoln-Lenin Day because Lincoln was a proto-Bolshevik. Then I recieved a book in the mail one day, written by a member of the Yogananda Society in California, proving that Lincoln had been reincarnated as Charles Lindbergh.

Lincoln as business guru, though, a management consultant imported from the nineteenth century—this may be the biggest stretch of all. Philosophically and politically, Lincoln was a great champion of capitalism, of course, but whenever he tried his hand at business—and he tried desperately—he failed with soul-flattening finality. Bad luck had something to do with it, but it was mostly a failure of temperament and disposition. Even Herndon, as we've seen, remarked on his lack of "money sense." "He had no head for business," his biographer Benjamin Thomas wrote. Lincoln's first job in New Salem was as a clerk in a general store. The store went broke so spectacularly that its proprietor felt compelled to flee the territory. Some of Herndon's sources recalled young Lincoln trying to start a warehouse business. That didn't work out either.

When he mustered out of the militia after the Black Hawk war, he took his pay and joined with a friend, William Berry, to buy another general store. Competition was stiff, and good money followed bad. He and his partner, Lincoln later wrote, "did nothing but go deeper and deeper into debt." Meanwhile, Berry was dipping liberally into the store's whiskey barrels. In the end he dipped himself to death. After they poured him into his grave, Lincoln found himself owing creditors more than $1,000, at a time when the average yearly wage was about half that amount. He called the burden his "very own national debt." It took him years to pay off. (How many years? Scholars differ.)

But he did pay it off—a testament to his honesty and dutifulness, and also to the lucrative law practice he enjoyed after he'd left New Salem, which generated enough savings to cover the debt. Even then, as a lawyer, he had no patience for figures or ledgers. His law office was a model of inefficiency. He left most administrative details to clerks, aware of his own disorganization and lack of business savvy. In our day, the business guru Stephen Covey has identified exactly Seven Habits of Highly Effective People; they do not include "forget to cash your paychecks" and "keep your most important stuff in your hat." Lincoln's bad habits continued when he became president. As chief executive his handling of subordinates appeared chaotic, an unpredictable oscillation between fussy micromanagement and distracted indifference. His White House office resisted all efforts to impose method and routine, whether from his wife, his cabinet, or his secretaries. "There was little order or system about it," wrote his gifted secretary John Hay. "He was extremely unmethodical; it was a four-year struggle to get him to adopt some systematic rules."

You have to dig through the literature to find them, but there are comments about Lincoln's "management style"—to use a phrase unknown in his day—and none would work as a letter of recommendation to the Wharton School. Michael Burlingame, the Lincoln scholar, pointed me to several hopeless complaints from Lincoln's acquaintances. "Lincoln was without executive ability," wrote the Illinois senator Lyman Trumbull. His attorney general, Edward Bates, wrote in his diary: "It is now evident that the Administration has no system—no unity—no accountability—no subordination. Men are appointed and not trusted—interfered with, and so relieved from all responsibility. Of course, therefore, things run all wrong."

Another cabinet member, Salmon P. Chase, complained of Lincoln's uncommunicative nature, especially as it showed itself in cabinet meetings. "There is, at the present time, no cabinet except in name. The Heads of the Departments come together now and then—nominally twice a week—but no reports are made; no regular discussions held; no ascertained conclusions reached."

Supremely self-confident, Lincoln rarely solicited advice from those around him, as modern managers are always told to do, and even more rarely did he reveal his thoughts until they were fully matured. He evidently had no faith in that essential technique of the modern, nonhierarchical corporation, the brainstorming session, partly because he knew that no one had a brain nearly as big as his. Even his most sensitive decisions were presented to his colleagues as a fait accompli. "As a politician and as president," wrote his Illinois friend Leonard Swett, "he arrived at all his conclusions from his own reflections, and when his opinion was once formed, he never doubted it was right."

None of this, however, worked to deter Dale Carnegie. Somewhere in the unsystematic doings of Lincoln, he thought he'd discovered a way to make people rich.

Carnegie fell for Lincoln relatively late in life. He was in his mid-thirties and living in London at the time. It's strange it took so long. He was born in rural Missouri, not far from Lincoln's home in Central Illinois, in 1888, only twenty-three years after Lincoln's death. Already the country was marinating in Lincoln. For some reason, with Carnegie, it didn't take.

Perhaps it had to do with his upbringing. As a boy Carnegie chafed at the dull rural life to which, he feared, his oafish, ill-educated father had doomed him. He struck off on his own as early as he could—first as a salesman in the Midwest, then as an actor in New York, then as a salesman again, all over the place. He sold Armour bacon, animal feed, shoes, tins of lard. As his own biographers later told the story, the innocent Dale fell into the clutches of a wellborn, cosmopolitan femme fatale—a European countess, no less—who wiled him into marriage and, before too long, revealed herself as a howling shrew. She might have ruined his life. Instead he managed a divorce and escaped to London, where he made a living as a public speaker, giving lectures on "public speaking."

One morning over breakfast, Carnegie came across a newspaper article about Lincoln's life. He was stunned. Lincoln's story, he discovered to his astonishment, was that of a talented, ambitious young lad from the Midwest, stultified by an oafish, ill-educated father, who chafed under the idiocy of rural life and broke free at last, only to be tricked into marriage by a cosmopolitan femme fatale who soon enough revealed herself as a howling shrew. She might have ruined his life. Fortunately, Lincoln transformed the torment she inflicted into the fuel of his own advancement and his eventual greatness.

This, Carnegie realized at once, was "one of the most fascinating tales in all the annals of mankind."

It wasn't just Lincoln's life story (with its eerie echoes) that hooked Carnegie. Within a few decades of his death, Lincoln had gained a reputation not only as a statesman but also as a homespun philosopher. Carnegie himself, like any good traveling salesman of the time, had a ready stock of Honest Abe's cornpone sayings which he would use to jolly up his potential customers. There was no shortage of these in the public record, and some of them are still repeated today: "You can fool some of the people all the time, and all the people some of the time, but you can't fool all the people all of the time." And some of them, though not that one, were actually said by Lincoln.

Lincoln had a Polonius streak. Particularly in his less hectic, prepresidential years, he was always happy to volunteer pithy maxims that might be suitable for any contemporary business book with a title like *Five Steps to Strategizing Time-Management Solutions for Your Organization.* "Leave nothing for tomorrow, which can be done today," he once wrote. "Nothing valuable can be lost by taking time," he also wrote, having forgotten that you shouldn't leave anything for tomorrow. "Always bear in mind that your own resolution to succeed is more important than any other one thing." Not all his aphorisms are as weightless as this, but some of the Lincoln sayings that have been etched in the national canon tend to dissolve into obviousness if you think about them too hard: "If we could first know where we are, and whither we are tending, we could then better judge what to do, and how to do it." Well, yeah.

Bit bad by the Lincoln bug, Carnegie left London and returned to the States, vowing to write Lincoln's biography. There were dozens of Lincoln biographies already in print, of course. Yet none, Carnegie thought, was fitted to the "busy and hurried citizen of today." Understanding the interests and aspirations of this busy citizen, this striving worker bee of the great commercial republic, this prototypical meatball, was Carnegie's genius. As a boy, in bed beneath that wide Missouri sky, he had dreamed of becoming rich and successful, and in time he learned that this ambition of his flowed into an immense continental reservoir where it commingled with the identical dreams of boys just like him, now grown to manhood. The surest way to become rich and successful, he realized at last, was to tap that universal dream of becoming rich and successful by telling people he could teach them how to become rich and successful.

For Carnegie, Lincoln was not only an inspiration but also a teaching aid, an illustration of how a self-made man gets made. His biography, *Lincoln the Unknown,* was Carnegie's first commercially produced book. It was hugely successful and became the best-selling biography of his generation. As a work of history it is almost useless. Aside from its denigration of Tom Lincoln and its exaggeration of Mary Lincoln's howling shrewishness, the book is littered with errors of fact. But there was a method to Carnegie's exaggerations and inaccuracies. Carnegie intensified Lincoln's hardships—instigated by Tom and Mary, mostly—to make the final triumph all the more inspiring. He hoped to capture the great man's spiritual essence, then to distill it to a lesson in "personal relations" that his readers could easily grasp. Lincoln had The Secret.

Carnegie's Lincoln mysticism was thoroughgoing. In his introduction to *Lincoln the Unknown,* he boasted that he wrote up some events of Lincoln's life in the settings where they actually occurred. He wanted to feel for himself Lincoln's domestic torment at the hands of Mary; so he set up his typewriter in the parlor of the Springfield house on Jackson and Eighth, to hear through the wobbling ectoplasm the faint echo of her bitching. Writing of the doomed romance with Ann Rutledge—which Carnegie accepted as the pivotal tragedy of Lincoln's life—the author drove across rutted farm fields to the site of her abandoned, weed-hidden grave, where Lincoln himself had once mourned for long hours. Dale unfolded a card table and little chair and started tapping away, while the ghosts rose like mist around him. "And there," Carnegie wrote, "where Lincoln came to weep, was set down the story of his grief." Stories like these can move units.

The great success of *Lincoln the Unknown* inspired Carnegie's next book, *How to Win Friends and Influence People.* Published in 1936, it has sold more than 15 million copies, making it the biggest-selling book in history that doesn't have God as a main character. It sealed Carnegie's international fame and made his name a byword. Even today, seventy years later, the Dale Carnegie Institute of Effective Speaking and Human Relations maintains branches the world over, instructing eager capitalists in its "rock-solid, time-tested advice up the ladder of success."

In *How to Win Friends* you find the wellspring of two great streams of American popular culture: the self-help movement and the business book. Protestant America had always taken it as axiomatic that good character would be rewarded with worldly success and, on the flipside, that worldly success was reliable evidence of good character. In *How to Win Friends* Carnegie used Lincoln to show how one led to the other. Though never wildly rich himself, Lincoln was "the most perfect ruler of men that the world has ever seen." As president, of course, he didn't have the chance to exploit this talent commercially, being preoccupied with Union-saving and slave-freeing. But you, too, Carnegie promised the reader, can be a ruler of men. You, too, can be like Abe—minus the war and the wife.

Lincoln looms large from the opening pages. He illustrates the first of "Three Fundamental Techniques in Handling People": *Don't condemn, criticize, or complain.* Carnegie begins with a negative example, the tale of "Two Gun" Crowley, who one night was enjoying a "necking party" with his best girl out on Lover's Lane. Surprised by a patrol officer on his nightly rounds, Two Gun "cut the policeman down with a shower of lead." He was arrested, convicted, and sentenced to death.

And what were the gunman's final words in the electric chair at Sing Sing? "This is what I get for defending myself," Two Gun said.

"There you are," Carnegie wrote in disgust. "Human nature in action. Wrongdoers, blaming everybody but themselves."

Carnegie's point wasn't just that a shower of lead is totally inappropriate as a Fundamental Technique in Handling People. He wanted to encourage self-criticism, while also discouraging the much more common habit of blaming others for one's own mistakes. "Criticisms of others are like homing pigeons," he wrote. "They always return home."

Then Carnegie—a master of the stark contrast—jumped from Two Gun grousing in Sing Sing to Lincoln lying mute on his deathbed, surrounded by admirers overwhelmed with grief.

How, Carnegie asked, had so many come to love this man so much?

It's true, he said, that early in life Lincoln had indulged in blame-shifting and buck-passing. Often he criticized others instead of him-

LAND OF LINCOLN   179

self. But Lincoln learned from experience, and by the time he was president he had developed the maturity to set aside the habit of faulting subordinates and criticizing coworkers. Even provoked to the uttermost by incompetent generals and lazy underlings, "he almost never criticized anybody for anything," Carnegie wrote. "He had learned by bitter experience that sharp criticisms and rebukes almost invariably end in futility."

So Lincoln moved on from his hard feelings, never letting them rankle or disturb his relations with others. Lincoln not only knew the Three Fundamental Techniques in Handling People, he illustrated the Six Ways to Make People Like You, the Twelve Ways to Win People to Your Way of Thinking, and the Nine Ways to Change People Without Arousing Resentment. That makes for Thirty Techniques / Ways in all. Yet Carnegie insisted he wasn't "advocating a bag of tricks. I am talking about a new way of life"—Lincoln's way, and properly managed, it would lead to success and happiness. It was Lincoln's kindness, his generous spirit, and his self-control, Carnegie said, that led Teddy Roosevelt, whenever vexed with a problem, to ask himself, "What would Lincoln do if he were in my shoes? How would he solve this problem?" WWLD?

This question, Carnegie said, should never be far from the mind of a man pursuing worldly success. When we meet a moment of perplexity, he wrote, "Let's pull a five-dollar bill out of our pocket, look at Lincoln's picture on the bill, and ask, 'How would Lincoln handle this problem if he had it?'" WW$5D?

A couple months after our interview I got an e-mail from Antigoni. A client had agreed to let me attend one of the Lincoln workshops, asking only that I not identify the client company or the employees who would be attending. I was happy to agree. I was less happy about the prospect of spending two and a half days in a workshop. I don't like workshops.

I don't even like the word. In *Jake's Thing*, a novel by the great, grumpy British writer Kingsley Amis, an even grumpier character says, "If there's one word that sums up everything that's gone wrong since the war, it's 'workshop.'" Whether in diversity training, team building, time management, or skills development, the workshop has become an unavoidable ritual of American business. On a horrifying handful of occasions, an employer has enrolled me and colleagues in "routine" workshop training. Each time I approached the date with clammy palms and sandpapery tongue; I expect the worst and I have never been disappointed. I dislike being thrown together with strangers in close quarters under the watchful eye of a facilitator. I dislike being told to "leverage the brand." I dislike the forced chumminess, the coerced informality, the deceptively gentle, vaguely totalitarian expectation that any natural reticence or hesitation "to share" one's feelings is somehow suspect. I dislike facilitators.

Workshops have always been a lowest-common-denominator enterprise, intellectually, but the past decade has seen the introduction of a software program that makes them even dumber. As workshoppers know, PowerPoint distills all information and concepts into a bulleted list of easily digestible phrases of no more than three or four words each. Supposedly PowerPoint aids memorization and note taking; I take it as a professional threat. If you're someone who tries to make a living by writing sentences and stringing them into paragraphs, and then attaching one paragraph to another to fill up a page, PowerPoint will make you feel the way a blacksmith must have felt watching the first horseless carriage pass beneath the shade of his overspreading chestnut tree. It's a dagger thrust at the vitals, a pitiless sign of inevitable obsolescence.

And it seems absurdly ill suited to Lincoln, one of the greatest American prose writers, who is already revered for his gift of compression. The Gettysburg Address manages to distill the meaning of war, sacrifice, the United States, and representative government into

272 words. This is about as much distillation as a writer should be asked to do. Any more distillation and *pfffffffft*.

VISION: BIG PICTURE
- 4 x 20 + 7 = 87 years ago
- Forefathers ⇒ continent ⇒ new nation
- Key Proposition: *Everybody* Equal
- Civil war ⇒ long endurance test
- Battlefield = cemetery (final resting place) = hallowed ground
- Caveats: cannot dedicate
  cannot consecrate
  cannot hallow
- Action step: new birth of freedom

And sure enough, when I got to the ballroom at the Gettysburg Battlefield Holiday Inn the screen was already up and aglow with PowerPoint phrases. "Ballroom" is overstating it, by the way. It was a long space segmented by movable dividers, under a low ceiling. The walls were covered in mirrors and the mirrors were crisscrossed in lattices unwisely painted in a pukey peach. And the Holiday Inn is probably the nicest hotel in town.

Gettysburg, to which every buff makes a pilgrimage sooner or later, is inexplicably short on visitor amenities. The tourist trade is a potential gold mine—two million people a year—but there are no grand hotels or good restaurants, no upscale shops for the carriage trade. One hundred and seventy thousand men once converged here over a three-day span in hopes of killing one another, and eleven thousand died in the attempt, and even now, 143 years later, the town still doesn't know what hit it. It has a dazed, dull feel to it—the consequence, I suppose, of taking a scene of blood-drenched horror and unspeakable heartbreak and trying to make it a pleasant vacation spot. Many of the town's schemes for capitalizing on its fame strike an off-key note. One morning I found a flyer tucked under my windshield.

Come on the "Orphan Tour"!

A Walking Tour Taking You Down in the Cellar of a Haunted
Orphanage, Where Children Were Abused and Chained to the Walls

Adults $7.00 Child (6–8) $5.00
Buy Tickets Early
Don't Be Caught on the Outside Wishing to Get in!

Antigoni and Everett had spaced six round tables around the meeting room and covered them in white linen. In the middle of each table was a tray of hard candy and a little American flag. Each workshopper was assigned a team, and each team a table. My teammates had come to the workshop from various parts of the country, but they all worked for TekaDyne, as I'll call it, a nationwide "information processing" concern whose business was as mysterious to me the day I left Gettysburg as it was when I arrived. Unless you're the one doing it, office work is incomprehensible.

"They updated the 10-20KR?" one of my teammates was saying when I sat down. "When was that?"

"Dude—like, last quarter. *Hello?* If you thought the 260 was bad, just wait. The decrypt function on the new system totally destroyed my FYs. Every freakin' one of them. I had to obso all my 11-50s and re-up a whole new ECI. Nightmare. Total nightmare." Incomprehensible and unbelievably boring.

Antigoni began the workshop as workshops always begin, with personal introductions—another reason to dislike workshops. Everyone was asked what they hoped to learn over the next two and a half days.

"I want to learn as much from Mr. Lincoln as I can," said a prim, thin-lipped woman next to me. She kept her purse in her lap. Her sucking up to Antigoni was so relentless I came to think of her as the Apple Polisher. "Everyone at TekaDyne who's been to your workshop," said Apple, "has just come back so enthusiastic and full of praise for your work."

Next to her was a middle-aged man in a short-sleeved shirt. When he introduced himself you could see his scalp flush through the bristles of his flattop haircut. "Just here to listen—to learn if I can maybe . . ." he said, shrugging. "My division v.p. thought I might get something out of it . . . so here I am." He looked as though he was deeply committed to proving his boss wrong.

"We've got a lot of issues, and I think it's time that we at TekaDyne just came out and admitted it," volunteered another of my teammates. She talked very fast—a real Motormouth. "There's a lot of competitive issues, ever since the re-org. There's an issue with clash of cultures. There's communications issues. There's service issues. We have issues with new hires . . ."

"We'll get to all those issues, trust me," Antigoni said, interrupting, but Motormouth was telling us that an entire new acquisitions team had been transferred to her division with inadequate training, and when they tried to do the sycrons before backing up the 10-50s, the system crashed and . . .

Antigoni sat back in her chair, listening intently. She has the dedicated air of someone who never stops caring, even though she has heard it all before; the best therapists have this air, priests also. The workshoppers didn't know it at the time, but many of the "issues" they described—the difficulty of reorganizations, trouble with new technology, uncooperative coworkers, ill-prepared subordinates, bullies from other departments—played right into the hands of Antigoni and Everett Ladd, their Lincoln facilitators.

If you want to make Lincoln *relevant* to a contemporary business audience, you've obviously got to find parallels between the situation a commander in chief of a nineteenth-century war-torn republic found himself in and the situation a middle manager in a twenty-first-century corporation finds himself in. This requires a lot of ingenuity. Antigoni, in her role as chief facilitator and Tigrett Corp's academic director, had found a parallel so comprehensive it served as the theme of our entire workshop. It's her theory that the first eighty years of the USA's existence, the decades leading up to the Civil War, were just like the life of a small business that has really taken off. The PowerPoint that glowed from the screen at the front of the room made this explicit:

> ➤ USA as a fast-growth company

"Think about it," Antigoni says. "It's 1860. Lincoln's about to take office. There's been a revolution in this company, the United States. In 1776, we were a Mom and Pop company. Small potatoes. Eighty percent of our population worked in agriculture. By 1860 our output in manufacturing is equal to our agricultural output. In 1776 we had two million employees. By 1860 we're talking 31.1 million. This is incredible growth. And the company is feeling the strain."

The company—I mean the country—has been creating new operating units, Antigoni says; historians call them "states." It's acquired other companies, what historians call "territories." The workforce is diversifying—four million new hires ("immigrants"), without any diversity training workshops. The company is coping with new technologies: railroads, oil refineries, sewing machines, Bessemer converters —even elevators! The country's got elevators!

Antigoni's enthusiasm filled the room. The PowerPoints zipped by. Her talk was so lucid, and the slides so simple, that no one stopped to ask what a real historian might think of trying to cram the organic growth of a nineteenth-century nation-state into the categories of Stephen "Seven Secrets" Covey and Tom "In Search of Excellence" Peters. No one even stopped to ask what a Bessemer converter was. At the same time, though, by painlessly talking business, Antigoni was trying to implant real historical knowledge. Quickly and crisply she explained the Gadsden Purchase, the Missouri Compromise, the *Dred Scott* decision, and the Kansas-Nebraska Act, all of which, she said, transformed the company's organizational structure as it struggled to cope with rapid change.

"This is TekaDyne," said Motormouth suddenly. "This is TekaDyne to a 't'!"

Antigoni leaned back on her stool again and let my teammate talk. ("You get somebody who's dying to say something, let them say it," she had told me. "It's much easier than trying to shut them up.") Besides, Motormouth was doing Antigoni's work for her—establishing that the United States in 1860 was a lot like TekaDyne in the twenty-first century. "I've got to tell you," Motormouth said, looking around at her colleagues. "I'm pretty blown away by all this." She seemed stunned to discover that in all of American history there had been a situation almost as difficult, as stressful, as dealing with the new acquisitions team at her office.

"Now let's step back for a moment," Antigoni said. She switched off the PowerPoint. From a bag she took colored felt pens and turned to an easel supporting a huge pad of white paper—low-tech tools that are as indispensable to the facilitator as PowerPoint. "Let's think about this. Change is forcing our company to come apart at the seams. What kind of leader do we need for this situation?"

"We need a leader who has very strong leadership qualities," Apple Polisher volunteered.

"Absolutely," said Antigoni.

"He or she absolutely has to have the ability to lead people and make people believe in his or her leadership skills," said Apple.

Flattop crossed his arms again and squinted at her.

"Yes," Antigoni said. "Excellent. Now let's get down to specific qualities."

In a looping hand she filled several of the vast sheets on her easel with suggestions called out from the workshoppers. A leader should be "compassionate," she wrote. A good listener, someone suggested. Patient. A big-picture guy, said someone else. Visionary. Knows where he wants to lead the organization. Good communication skills. "Excellent," said Antigoni. She capped her pen. "Keep these in mind for later."

For our last module of the day we broke up into our teams for discussion. The room erupted in cross talk. Sometimes I think that workshops have proved popular because people get to talk a lot, much more than they get to talk at the office. Other times I'm not so sure. No workplace that included Motormouth could enforce a gag rule, for example. And there was the opposite example of the table next to ours. That team was cursed: it was all male. Evidently none of them had met before the workshop, and each man looked equally uneasy. They were silent.

My heart went out to them. I'd seen this before. Workshops are built on what even female sociologists agree are feminine styles of communication. Arguing and contention are frowned upon, and there's lots of sharing and unburdening and sympathetic give and take. For this and other reasons, men find workshops less congenial, as a rule. Lincoln himself, as one of his friends said, was the "most shutmouthed man I ever met." For a time the guys pretended to read several sheets of statistics that Everett had handed out. Then one reached into his satchel and brought out the sports section of *USA Today*. After five minutes or so, while the other teams bubbled with chatter, the guys had all stopped pretending to read their sheets and were staring into the middle distance, managing to avoid eye contact. They tried not to slump. Their legs jiggled up and down. They had that unquestionably male look of polite impatience, fists cocked at belt level, next to their hip phones, wondering how long it was till they could go get a beer.

At our table, discussion proceeded at Motormouth's direction. Antigoni had asked us to identify Lincoln's Vision, Mission, Action Plan, and Goals and Objectives. These terms are familiar to every workshopper; they pop unbidden out of the PowerPoint template.

"Vision?" said Motor, pen poised over paper. She had appointed herself team secretary. "That's easy. This is a man who wanted his company to succeed."

"His vision was to make this the very best country it could be," said Apple.

Flattop ran his hand over his biceps. "I don't really think so," he said. "If that's his vision, then why's he forcing half his company to stay when they don't want to?"

"He's not forcing anybody to do anything!" Apple said. She gripped her purse.

"He's waging the bloodiest, most savage conflict in the history of the world up to that time," said Flattop. "That sounds like force to me."

Flattop wasn't a buff. Motor tried to turn the conversation back to the acquisitions team at TekaDyne, and how their bullheadedness reminded her a lot of some of those Confederates, while Apple stoutly defended Lincoln, about whom, she added, her daughter had just written a report in history class. But Apple was outgunned. Flattop released a flurry of economic statistics that sounded vaguely familiar to me. Later, he told me I had to buy myself a copy of *The Real Lincoln*, by Thomas DiLorenzo. "That's a book that can question a lot of your assumptions," he said.

"Maybe you can explain it to my son," Flattop said to Apple. "This boy is ten years old. My son says to me, 'Dad, there's one thing I don't get. If it was okay for us to split away from England, then wasn't it okay for the South to split away from the North?' I'll tell you, a ten-year-old boy stumped me with that one."

"Antigoni?" Apple said, her voice rising. Our facilitator came over to our table. "I think we have a misunderstanding here," said Apple, apologetically. "There's a . . . a *disagreement.*"

Flattop repeated his question—or "his son's" question.

"Sounds like you're having quite a discussion here!" Antigoni said. "I love it! But, look, we're not here to refight the Civil War. Okay? This is not a workshop about Abraham Lincoln. This is a workshop about how to lead within an organization, using Abraham Lincoln as a case study. What's his Vision? What's his Mission? His Goals, his

Objectives? How does he Implement and Interact? I'm not asking you to agree with everything he did."

Flattop took a Jolly Rancher from the candy tray and popped it in his mouth. He looked unappeased. Apple Polisher appeared shook up. Lucky for us, it was soon time for our bus tour of Gettysburg.

Dale Carnegie died in 1955. As *How to Win Friends* was revised for newer audiences, who were presumably less interested in history, Lincoln's presence faded from the text; stories of his patience and self-command were pushed out by fresher accounts of strivers like "Karen Kirsch, a TWA flight attendant from Rancho Palos Verdes," who memorized the names of all the passengers on all her flights—and became incredibly popular as a result! Meanwhile, among businessmen, Carnegie's folksy, friendly approach to success was being eclipsed by "scientific management," an approach to discovering The Secret that was, at first glance, more reputable intellectually, more rigorously objective. It was also much less friendly and folksy.

Scientific management theory was the perfect companion to the age of automation and assembly-line mass production. It advised breaking production down into its most elemental tasks, and workers, each trained to a particular job, could then be handled like interchangeable units. A good manager, for his part, was trained to manipulate the units and calculate the inputs and outputs necessary to success. The outputs and inputs could be tested, quantified, and easily replicated from workplace to workplace—and, just as important, taught in business schools, to which America's meatballs had begun to turn, seeking shortcuts and academic credentials. Intuition, sympathy, individual judgment, and other such unpredictable elements were smoothed away beneath the steamroller of quantifiable efficiency. The Secret was still out there, of course, and the meatballs were still intent on figuring it out. But now it was a logarithm.

The Carnegie-Lincoln tradition never disappeared altogether. Scientific management was too bloodless and unsatisfying to dominate forever. Also, it didn't work. As the decades wore on, American corpo-rations felt competitive pressures from Germany and then Japan, and the scientific method of business management proved itself too rigid in a globalized turboeconomy. Meatballs, even those in the business schools, hungered for homegrown wisdom, something more all-American, a business technique that could allow full play to a manager's creativ-ity. By the 1980s, Carnegie's method—stripped of its corny and senti-mental particulars—was easily revived. The key was the word "leadership." Suddenly the pursuit of leadership, or "leadership skills," was all-consuming, pointing the way to The Secret. And once again the example of Lincoln proved indispensable.

"Management is doing things right," Everett Ladd said to me one day. "Leadership is doing the right thing." Whether consciously or not, in this singsongy formulation Everett was echoing Donald T. Phillips, the man who single-handedly returned Lincoln to the search for The Secret and made him a hero for the modern meatball.

Phillips was trained as an engineer, which might have made him a per-fect apostle for the scientific rigor of management theory. But his mother was a Lincoln buff, and she raised him to be a Lincoln buff too. He grew up in Arlington, Virginia, across the Potomac River from Washington, where the Lincoln Memorial glowed on summer evenings. "Studying Lincoln appealed to my creative side," he said. With his engineering degree he found work at an oil company in Texas, in the exploration division. "I was good at finding oil and gas, and because I was good at that they put me on a management track."

But the Peter Principle was at work: he wasn't a particularly good manager, he said—at least not at first. "I wanted to get better at it. So I started reading the books that were available, all the management theory. I didn't much like the attitude in those books—it was all 'my way or the highway.' And very technical. This business-school man-agement type approach didn't apply to what I wanted to do."

Meanwhile, he continued reading about Lincoln for pleasure. "I saw, well, here's a guy who knows how to manage people, but he's doing it in a totally different way from what I'm reading about." He first noticed it when he studied Lincoln's presidency. "I found I had a hard time placing him—I mean placing him physically. Day to day, I didn't know where he was, and the books didn't say."

Like a good engineer, Phillips plotted a big graph on a conference table in his basement, tracking Lincoln's whereabouts during his presidency. On another time line he plotted the major events of the war. "Suddenly it became very apparent what he was doing," he said. "He was moving constantly—going where the action was. I thought he'd just been sitting in his White House office. But he wasn't. He was off visiting the battlefields, seeing his generals, meeting the troops, checking the telegraph office for news, getting to know his people." The graph was eventually reproduced in *Lincoln on Leadership,* under the title MBWA—"managing by walking around," a formulation from Tom Peters that became a buzz phrase of the 1990s.

"I thought, Lincoln managed by walking around, I'll do what Lincoln did. I'll get out of the office more, get to know the people who were working for me. Other managers weren't doing that. But it worked." Phillips dug deeper into the Lincoln literature, reading through the eight volumes of the *Collected Works of Abraham Lincoln* and acquiring books filled with secondhand anecdotes, like *Abe Lincoln's Yarns and Stories* and *Life on the Circuit with Lincoln.* "I read about all these stories he would tell. That's how he influenced people—by telling stories. He'd use a story to clinch an argument or persuade somebody or to maneuver one way or another."

So he began keeping a card catalog of Lincoln's stories, several hundred of them, filed under the categories Patience, Consistency, Decisiveness, Honesty, and many other leaderly attributes. "I started trying them on the job, and I found I could build friendships and relationships. So both of these things—telling stories and getting out in the field more—they were quite successful." Seeing Lincoln as a better guide to good business than the management books stacked up in the bookstores and libraries, Phillips decided to write a book of his own.

"The book needed to be written," he said. Too many businessmen were still in thrall to scientific management, and he looked on his own book as a kind of reclamation project—not of Carnegie necessarily, but certainly of Lincoln, and of an earlier, preindustrial, pre-management-theory way of dealing with people. "Scientific management was just a phase of the industrial revolution," Phillips said. "Lincoln was the last preindustrial leader, before that period of industrial change. When Henry Ford came along with the assembly line and workers had to be dealt with in large numbers, that's when the management theory began and people were thought of as objects. That pervaded business for years. But people aren't objects. They aren't units. And Lincoln showed a way around that."

In the dining room of his house in suburban Texas he assembled his graphs, his time lines, his card files with Lincoln stories. Writing the book took nine years of weekends and evenings, vacations, and occasional time off. He started it as a bachelor; when he finished he was a married father with two kids. Warner Books released the book in 1992 and it remains one of Warner's perennial big sellers, having become a staple of business-school reading lists and military officer training schools. Early sales were given a boost by Bill Clinton, another man with buff tendencies, when *Time* magazine identified the book as "his private bible of how to govern."

The success of *Lincoln on Leadership* could have made Phillips a star. He quit his job with the oil company, and he might easily have ended up squeezed between Suze Orman and Dr. Wayne Dyer during PBS pledge week, or strutting the stage on one of the road shows put together by the quasi-Christian motivational speaker Zig Ziglar, stopping only to bag the cash as it rolled in. But Phillips is an oddly mild-mannered man, gentle and soft-spoken. He lacks guile, the essential quality for megasuccess in the guru business.

"I started getting a lot of requests for public speaking," he said. "I did that for a while. There are people out there who will pay you a gazillion dollars just for a speech about Lincoln and leadership. But after a while I just had to say no, no, I'm not doing this anymore."

I asked him how he could turn down such easy money.

"Those are golden handcuffs," he said. "I could have made a lot of money in the oil business, too, but money's never been the driving force for me. Not for Lincoln either. I wrote the book because I wanted to change things. But these businesspeople would hire me to come and talk, and they'd say they wanted to change, but they didn't want to, not really. You could talk and talk and nothing would change."

He's a writer full-time now, having worked on books with Mike Krzyzewski, the Duke University basketball coach, and Greg Norman, the golf pro. He even spent two terms as mayor of his small town in Texas. He makes a nice living, he told me, but he's not in Dr. Wayne Dyer's league.

If Phillips makes for an unconventional business guru, his book is odder still. A few weeks before I was to go up to Gettysburg and get workshopped by the Ladds, I picked up a copy of *Lincoln on Leadership* and read through it. Most business books are like self-help books: PowerPoint presentations that the author has inflated into a staggering length of two hundred pages. *Lincoln on Leadership*, by contrast, is a real book, written in recognizable, though sometimes misty, English prose. The cover carries all the come-ons of the business book—promising "how Lincoln can help you to run your organization." But there are no pie charts, no schematics, few graphics of any kind. The unavoidable bullet points are mostly free of jargon or cute turns of phrase—nothing about "unleashing the Abe Within" or "emancipating Your Inner Slave."

Instead, the substance of the book is all Lincoln. The chapter headings are in the imperative mode, and illustrated with events from Lincoln's presidency. Under "Exercise a Strong Hand—Be Decisive," Phillips explained Lincoln's insistence on provisioning Fort Sumter in

1861 over the objections of his cabinet and even at the risk of provok-
ing the South to war. In "Never Act Out of Vengeance or Spite,"
Phillips cited Lincoln's lengthy record of commuting prison terms and
issuing pardons during the war. In fact, the book is so loaded with Lincoln that it seems much more a work of popular history than a book
about managing a business.

   As I read it, a stray thought occurred to me: Phillips is teaching history by subterfuge. Just as God had to invent professional sports so men
would have something to talk about other than sex, in the same way
He may have had to invent an author like Phillips, and a book like *Lincoln on Leadership*, so business-obsessed Americans would sit still long
enough to learn their history, in the guise of learning The Secret to
success.

   That was my thought, anyway, till I went to Gettysburg. There I
finally realized what it was that the Ladds—and Phillips, and Carnegie,
too, for that matter—were really doing, whether they knew it or not.
They weren't just teaching history, and they weren't really teaching
business techniques either. They were teaching something else that,
nowadays, is harder to come by, and harder to make stick.

The Ladds had given every workshopper a slender briefing book, and
after a day of workshopping and bus-touring and a leisurely commu-
nal dinner we were supposed to retire to our rooms and read assigned
chapters. I was expecting Ziglar-like expositions on "Six Foundations
to Building a Better Team" and charts spouting arrows and tangents.
Instead, the text was drawn almost entirely from Lincoln's own writings, and the excerpts that weren't from Lincoln's hand came from biographies of the first rank. The booklet made for a quick but
comprehensive primer on Lincoln's presidency and the Civil War. And
it had the welcome effect of elevating the subject matter. If you wanted
to know how to "Clarify Goals for a Splintered Organization," for
example, the booklet let you watch how Lincoln himself clarified his

view of slavery and states' rights for his splintering country, by offering chunks of his famous Cooper Union address and the Lincoln-Douglas debates.

The reading material was just one of the pleasant surprises of the Ladds' workshop. The pleasantest surprise of all was what we weren't asked to do. We didn't have to do role-playing or team-building exercises, and no one was pressured to "share" his feelings. No one said "leverage the brand." Instead we were treated to stories about Lincoln's own difficulties, particularly in personnel matters. The generals, cabinet officers, and politicians with whom Lincoln dealt were variously brilliant, corrupt, incompetent, imaginative, petty, and condescending toward him, and his dealings with them, as explained by Antigoni, were wise, comprehensive, sympathetic, and often kind. To illustrate the point we watched scenes from the movies *Gettysburg* and *Gore Vidal's Lincoln*. Could there be a less painful workshop? Even Amis might be delighted with the Ladds' handiwork, if he weren't dead.

On our last morning Antigoni asked us to break up into our teams for a discussion of how to deal with difficult coworkers. Motormouth was in full acceleration when a door swung open and a Lincoln presenter, fully suited up, ambled through.

"Mr. President!" cried Antigoni. Apple gasped and stood at attention, placing her hand over her heart. Her purse tumbled to the floor.

This was a man named James Getty, a legend in the field of Lincoln presenters for his gentle air and his dead-on likeness, from the dangling lobes of his significant ears to the peak of his eyebrows. Getty has realized the presenter's dream: he has a steady paying gig close to home, a regular and exclusive engagement at a theater reserved just for him in Gettysburg—much as, in Branson, Missouri, Tony Orlando and Yakov Smirnoff have had dinner theaters dedicated to them, as certifications of general excellence. I had seen Getty perform at the Battle Theater, which sits a few hundred yards from where General Pickett launched the insanely suicidal charge that bears his name. Just downstairs a restaurant bears the general's name too—a further honor—

and up those stairs and into the theater, from morning to night, float the scents from the grease trays and the steam tables of General Pickett's Buffet, as well as the last surviving nutrients from the string beans, carrots, and broccoli florets that are being boiled unto death in the kitchen below. Getty's performance conquers all such distractions.

It was a few moments before Apple regained her composure. "He looks so, so alive!" she said, taking her seat. Antigoni told us we were privileged to be at a presidential press conference and should feel free to pop questions. She went first, asking how to "establish avenues of communication" with truculent employees. Not surprisingly Lincoln-Getty responded with answers that closely followed the lessons Antigoni had been teaching us.

"You have to value people for what they can offer, for their peculiar talents, and forget the rest," Abe said. "You're not in the business of changing personalities. Some things are beyond your control, and that's one of them."

Flattop asked a pointed question about Sherman's "rape of the South" on his March to the Sea—"Oh, there were abuses, no doubt about it," conceded Abe—but otherwise the questions were friendly. "Mr. President, I've always loved your work," Apple said, once again rising to her feet. "Particularly your Gettysburg Address. Can you tell us, my gosh, what on earth inspires you to write with such eloquence?"

Whatever the question, Getty never broke character. "I wanted my people to challenge me," he said. "I wanted lots of new ideas, and when they worked out I didn't hog credit, either. I was never jealous—or at least not so it showed—and I was never vindictive. You can't manage people that way, now can you? I once said, 'I shall do nothing in malice. What I deal with is too vast for malicious dealing.' A good lesson."

By the time he left, the fix was in. We broke back up into our groups for a final session. Antigoni asked each group to list the qualities that Lincoln had exhibited as a leader.

"Let's forget Lincoln the president, the great man, the icon," she said. "Let's see him as a CEO. He's new to the company. He's just stepping into the job. Half his employees have walked out on him. He's never had a job like this before. No experience. Terrible resume. What resources can he call upon to help him deal here? What's he got? It's got to be something inside. Something inside himself. Some values or beliefs that carry him through this fragmented culture he's stepped into."

"I will grant you that the man was a leader within his particular organization," said Flattop. "He was cognizant of human nature. His communication skills were just excellent. He didn't let the little things get to him." It seemed like an astonishing confession, and Apple looked pleased. "But," he added quickly, "I'm still not convinced about all his rationales for not letting the South do what the South had every right to do under the Constitution."

Motor explained that Lincoln seemed like a patient man. "And believe me, this is something I need to work on," she said. "He kept his eye on the vision of what he wanted to accomplish. He ignored the personal aspects, and he tried to be understanding. He looked at what's good for the organization as a whole."

Antigoni had her easel ready and her marker in hand when we came back into general session. Of course the characteristics we had discovered in two and a half days of learning about Lincoln turned out to be the same ideal characteristics we'd listed on the first day. All the workshoppers seemed to have something to say, and as before there was plenty of complaining, only now the workshoppers included themselves among the objects of complaint.

"You read Lincoln," someone said, "and you see he spoke to, not at, other people—I need to learn to do this in my own situations sometimes."

"Just because someone questions what you're doing, that doesn't mean they're attacking you personally," another workshopper said. "If Lincoln took everything so personal, nothing would have gotten done."

"He didn't dwell on what people said about him," said still another. "He just got back to business."

"You can't change other people," said Motor. "You *can* change how you react to them. You have to let other people be different." She said that was going to be her vow with her new team. "I'm trying it—I'm trying it."

After a final, hurried lunch, the workshop was over. People gathered their booklets and papers and headed to their rental cars for the ride to the airport—though not before Apple had gotten everyone's address and phone number, in hopes of having a reunion some day. I hung around the quiet ballroom while Antigoni and Everett packed up. I told them about Motor's vow, and I wondered how her acquisitions team— young, inexperienced, annoying—were going to react to the new Motor; I wondered whether there really would be a new Motor.

"Who knows?" said Antigoni. "She may forget it the minute she gets back. That's why we go at them from so many different directions— the movies, the bus tours, the readings, the Lincoln presenter. In my experience what happens is this: sooner or later they'll be having a rough time with some coworker or an employee. Something will re- mind them of a scene from one of the movies. Or a light will go off and they'll remember something Jim Getty said, or something I said, or something from one of Lincoln's letters. 'Oh, yeah! Lincoln used to handle these people this way! I should just learn to appreciate that per- son for the gifts they can offer and stop with the criticism.'" Antigoni shrugged and smiled. "That's the hope, anyway."

"We just want them to stop and think about it," Everett said. "Lincoln's qualities of leadership are the very things we should do but we find very hard to do. You have to stop and think instead of just reacting knee-jerk to people. You need patience. You need to listen. You need to consider you might be wrong sometimes. These aren't easy things to do. Some- times we have to force ourselves to do them. But if you want to be a suc- cessful leader, that's what you've got to do. That's what Lincoln did."

Once I asked Don Phillips what he really hoped his readers would take away from *Lincoln on Leadership*. Without hesitation he said: "I want them to know they can become better people."

It took a while for this to sink in, but it did, finally. Business wasn't really the point at all. Dale Carnegie, Phillips, the Ladds—they had something else in mind. They've taken the most American of pursuits, and potentially the most crassifying—getting ahead, making lots of money, climbing the greasy pole of success—and turned it into an occasion for painless, gentle moral instruction. Lincoln lets them do it. It turns out that in capitalism's sea of uncertainty and flux, in this churning, buck-hustling country, there really is The Secret, or, in any case, this secret: *You can always try to become a better person.* Maybe that's what Lincoln is whispering to Perry Como on the Gettysburg town square.

Antigoni had said: "Put Lincoln's name on it, and you can sell anything." Even kindness and sympathy! Even courtesy and patience!

And best of all, this being America, there's always a meatball willing to buy.

8

HOT ON THE TRAIL

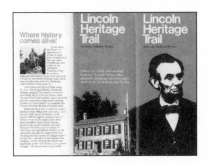

L incoln buffs often speak of their obsession as a kind of benign
contagion that spreads from one like-minded person to another.
I was wondering whether it was a heritable trait, passed from
generation to generation, so that my children might grow up to share
in the pleasures and exhilaration of a life touched by Lincoln, as I had.
Failing that, I was wondering whether I could ram it down their throats.

My instrument would be the Lincoln Heritage Trail. After my father
had taken us on the Trail forty years ago, the trip stood alone among
the limp, defeated ranks of car-trip memories. Other trips I recalled only
for the heat or the boredom, the wisecracks and backseat torts committed willfully against my person by my older brothers, the badly timed
bathroom breaks, and the roadside baloney sandwiches and warm waxy
boxes of milk. But thinking of that Lincoln trip I recall no unpleasant-
ness at all, not a single moment. I remember the sun pouring down on
our convertible as it glided on roads laid like ribbons through fields bil-
lowing with Burpee Silver Queen, and I remember the growing pile of
souvenirs I kept in a small duffel in the back: miniature log cabins, mus-
ket balls, parchment paper, cap pistols, quill pens, a coonskin cap, and
several shot glasses imprinted with the profile of the Great Teetotaler.

The Trail was an artifact of the era. You used to see signs marking it all over the three states where Lincoln spent his life before Washington and war. The markers were austere in design: handsome white squares, two feet by two feet, laminated in reflector paint, raised up on metal poles by the side of county roads, with Lincoln's profile etched in a bronze circle. The profile was pre-beard, and it was touched up to make him a bit handsomer than he really was. An inscription read, "Lincoln Heritage Trail." There was no other explanatory text—but when you saw it you knew you were in a place that Lincoln had known, or so went the implication.

Forty years on, the markers are scarce. I found one on the outskirts of Pontiac, Illinois, one day a few years ago, with the paint chipped where the rust hadn't eaten through. I saw another one flattened in the weeds of a railroad crossing south of Springfield. Seeing such dereliction filled me with nostalgia and regret that the Trail had been lost, and I hatched the idea of reviving it, at least for my own purposes, and dragging my family along as my father had dragged us—with, I hoped, the same happy results: a freshly kindled interest in Lincoln to enrich our family life. It seemed like a nice summer vacation trip. Doing my research on Lincoln over the next few months, I asked around about the Trail, but no one seemed to know how it had started or why it had fallen into disuse, or how a person could go about piecing it back together.

I had almost given up and resigned myself to improvising when I got a call from Nicky Stratton, the director of the Springfield Visitors Bureau. "I've got your guy," she said. "He knows everything you want to know." The man who'd put the Trail together back in the sixties was still alive, living up in Champaign in eastern Illinois. She gave me his number.

Robert Newman is in his early eighties, more or less retired after a life in and out of state government. When I called him up he said he was delighted to talk about the old days—or anything else. His voice crackled with energy. "Ask me what time it is, and I'll tell you how to build a watch—that's what people say about me," he said. I told him about my interest in the Lincoln Heritage Trail. I said I thought it was a shame people had let it go to seed, because it betokened a time when Americans really cared enough about Lincoln to mark his memory by retracing his steps, by touching the important places of his life; there was a seriousness about the past back then that's lacking today, I said, and I told him I was proud to be talking to the man who had invented the Trail.

"Why, thank you," Mr. Newman said after a slight pause. "You know, don't you, the whole thing was cooked up by the marketing guys at the American Petroleum Institute."

"It was?" I said.

"They wanted to get people traveling," he said. "Get 'em into their cars, get 'em buying gasoline. So in the early sixties they came up with the idea for these heritage trails around the country. Back east there was a Washington Heritage Trail, for George Washington, and a Hiawatha Pioneer Trail in the upper Midwest, around Minnesota, northern Iowa. They had a hard time with that one because, you know, let's face it, Hiawatha didn't exist. He's just in a poem. They had to make it up, the whole thing. There was an Old West Trail—that was a long one!— and this Lincoln Heritage Trail. The petroleum people went to the governors of the states—Illinois, Indiana, Kentucky—and said, you come up with some money to finance it, and we'll match the money, help you get up the brochures and whatnot, and we'll promote tour- ism and get people coming to your state. In their cars! Buying gaso- line! I was about to become director of tourism—the first one in the history of the state of Illinois—so it fell into my lap."

The governors of the three Lincoln states were alert to the main chance, as governors always are. The celebrations to mark the Civil War centennial were in full swing by 1961, and the Lincoln connection of- fered the three states a ripe opportunity to exploit what Mr. Newman called the "dollar potential" of historical tourism. Attended by their respective bureaucrats, the governors held a summit meeting one summer weekend at the resort of Kentucky Lake. Like Woodrow Wilson at Versailles after World War I, they pored over maps and divided the Trail evenly, along with its spoils. Each governor was allowed to appoint ten members to the Lincoln Heritage Trail Foundation board. "They liked that," Mr. Newman said. "Another committee they could appoint their friends to."

The main Heritage Trail was mapped out at 960 miles—a number chosen in part because it was divisible by three. Each state got 320 miles worth of Lincoln's life. The problem was that Lincoln had not distributed his life around the three states with the same meticulous evenhandedness. He spent seven sedentary years in Kentucky before his family moved to Indiana, where he spent another thirteen years, seldom wandering more than twenty miles from home. He lived the balance of his prepresidential life, nearly thirty years, in Illinois, traveling the state almost constantly, spending the night in this hotel or arguing a case in that courthouse, scattering the countryside with more future Lincoln sites than even the most Abe-crazed tourist could hope to absorb.

Kentucky and Indiana ran out of their Lincoln heritage long before their 320 miles were used up. So they improvised.

"Some of these places didn't have anything to do with Lincoln," Mr. Newman said. "Well, a lot them, actually. Maybe most. Santa Claus, Indiana, was a stop on the Trail. Have you been to Santa Claus?"

I said I had.

"There was a theme park there—Santa's Village, or something. Kentucky wanted Churchill Downs on the Trail. That's not exactly a Lincoln site. But I guess I could see the point. Why go to Kentucky if you're not going to see Churchill Downs?"

Nicky Stratton had sent me an old Heritage Trail brochure she'd found in her files. As it happened, Mr. Newman had written it, decades ago. I looked at the map on the back. He was right. A lot of the stops didn't seem to have much to do with Lincoln: the Indianapolis 500 Speedway, Waveland ("the restored estate of Daniel Boone's great-nephew"), the golf course at Lake Cumberland State Resort. In fact, there were lots of golf courses. Lincoln didn't play golf. The Trail looped across the three states, describing lazy switchbacks and zigzags that a family could burn a lot of gasoline trying to trace. There were plenty of campgrounds along the Trail, making for an inexpensive vacation. Gas was cheap in 1964.

The Trail was a hit. Mr. Newman, who spent much of his career as a press agent, hatched promotional schemes to keep it in the public eye. The foundation commissioned a solid silver Lincoln Heritage Trail Memorial Coin, which was sold at banks across the three states. He produced a travelogue for local television stations, narrated by the actor Ralph Bellamy. He hired a film crew to follow the governors as they biked the Trail and taxied junkets-full of reporters from Springfield to Lexington, Kentucky, and back again, wining and dining them as best he could. (Neither wining nor dining, as opposed to drinking and eating, were easy to do in the rural Midwest.) "We made the front page of the *Chicago Tribune* three separate Sundays in 1964," he said—accounting, I suppose, for how my parents got the idea for our trip. "We tried to measure the economic impact, and let me tell you: it was significant," he said, in the emphatically hopeful words of tourism officials the world over.

Then came the 1970s. Interest in Lincoln waned. "People had other things to worry about," Mr. Newman said. The petroleum institute stopped promoting tourism when the oil embargo hit. In time the original governors left office, retiring or failing reelection or getting indicted. State bureaucrats turned their attention elsewhere. Eventually the foundation died away, and one by one the markers came down.

"Nowadays people don't care too much about that kind of thing," he said. "The family car trips aren't such a big option as they used to be. Now it's all computers and Game Boys—things you do inside, without leaving home.

"But I'm glad we did it. I got imbued with Lincoln lore. One Lincoln buff told me that somewhere in the world another Lincoln book is published every day. Every day! I don't know if that's still true, but it tells you something, doesn't it? This Lincoln legend, it waxes and wanes but it never goes out. But you've got to market it carefully."

In the summer of 2005, gasoline became more expensive than it had ever been in the history of the United States. A low-pressure front, or maybe it was a high-pressure front—I'm never sure which is which—stalled indefinitely over the Midwest. Heat and humidity climbed to record levels.

"Kids," I announced, "we're going on a car trip to the Midwest."

I carefully unfolded the aging Lincoln Heritage Trail brochure on the dining room table. I offered a reading of Mr. Newman's prose. His style relied heavily on ellipses. "You'll come to know Mr. Lincoln a little better . . . ," I read, "dot dot dot . . . not only the Lincoln recorded in the pages of history books, but the raw-boned lad and the lonely man . . . Do the things he did . . . walk the rooms of the only home he ever owned . . . follow the path he took to visit his mother's simple grave . . . cool yourself in the shade of the mighty Boundary Oak near the cabin of his birth . . . share the everyday experiences of the man whose compassion, wisdom and courage were reflected in his greatest triumph . . . the preservation of this nation."

My son, then thirteen, and my daughter, then eleven, had so far indulged my Lincoln interest as a harmless eccentricity (I have others). Suddenly, with the prospect of two weeks in a rented van parting thickets of heat through the deepest Midwest, my eccentricity seemed not so harmless. It seemed actively insane. For them it raised the possibility—to use a phrase my daughter had recently picked up from a cop show on TV—of child endangerment. At this point early in the summer they were watching friends go off to Disneyland, to mountain sojourns and adventure camps, to beach cottages and dude ranches. The alternative I proposed was unthinkable. They reacted with the latest and most effective weapons in their arsenal: irony and sarcasm. All children today are experts in irony and sarcasm, from long hours of *SpongeBob SquarePants* to *South Park* and . . . worse.

"What are we doing for our summer vacation?" my son asked a colleague of mine who had come to dinner one evening. The boy was being rhetorical as well as ironic. "We're going to drive around the Midwest. We're going to see Lincoln sites. We're going to see a mighty Boundary Oak! And lots and lots of farmland." He tapped an imaginary windshield. "Oh, look: a cornfield. And over there: another cornfield. Hey, what's that? Oh my God, a cornfield."

My colleague thought it was funny and so did my wife, but I was uneasy. If I had got this idea a few years earlier, when my children were far more pliable and much, much cuter, the prospect would have seemed unobjectionable. In those days they were always happy to tag along, cheerfully unaware that they had no choice. Now I could see days of bitter contention and knotted difficulty—motel room squabbles, backseat sulks, the hairy-eyeball gaze boring through the back of my skull as the kids slumped along the Trail behind me.

I developed two schemes. The first, designed to inject some dramatic pacing and purpose into our itinerary, was to move backward through Lincoln's midwestern life: beginning our trip at Springfield, where he lived for twenty-five years before moving to Washington, we would follow the Trail leisurely to such earlier Illinois haunts as New Salem, then cross the Wabash River into Indiana, where Lincoln had spent his formative teenage years, and at last reach the man's essence, and the trip's climax, at the place of his birth, the famous rough-hewn log cabin that sits encased in a magnificent marble temple on a wooded knoll outside Hodgenville, Kentucky.

They gazed at me dully.

"All right," I said. "How about this."

My second scheme was a barter system. Whine-free days visiting Lincoln sites could be purchased with promises of more conventional vacation-like pleasure. "Give me a morning in Hodgenville," I told my daughter, "and I'll make sure you get a day at Kentucky Horse Park, in

Lexington, Kentucky, all expenses paid." The old Santa's Village that Mr. Newman had told me about, in Indiana, had changed its name to Holiday World and Splashin' Safari Water Park, as I'd seen during my weekend with the presenters. "Follow me around the Lincoln Boyhood Home National Memorial in Lincoln City, Indiana," I told my son. "Join me as we pay respects at the graves of Nancy Hanks and Lincoln's sister Sarah. In return, I can guarantee you an uninterrupted afternoon riding the Raven, voted America's third-best all-wooden roller coaster, not to mention many thrill-packed hours on Zoombabwe, the world's tallest enclosed water slide." The ratio of Lincoln to Fun was never perfectly one to one. They got the better of the deal. But before long they seemed pacified; an entente was reached; the bitter pill was sufficiently coated in Aspartame for the kids to choke it down. Whether our entente was temporary, I didn't know or want to know.

Packing for the trip I realized that the little brochure of Mr. Newman's, with its schematic map and elliptical descriptions, would be an inadequate guide to the Trail. As a supplement I grabbed from my shelf a travel book I had only paged through, *In the Footsteps of the Lincolns*, written by one of my heroes, Ida Tarbell, and published in 1923. Those who remember Tarbell nowadays know her as the great muckraking journalist, whose exposé, *The History of the Standard Oil Company*, finished off the Gilded Age of unbridled capitalism and inspired the trust busting of the Progressive Era. But Tarbell saw further and deeper than muckrakers do. She'd been classically educated in France, which helped; but more important she was too sympathetic, too largehearted to be a crusader. She never settled for sensationalism or mere scandalmongering; even her book about Standard Oil betrayed a tenderness that made John D. Rockefeller seem nearly human.

She fell in love with Lincoln early in her life and never quite let him go. In 1893 she published, in two volumes, what became for thirty years thereafter the standard Lincoln biography. She used Herndon's methods but revised his conclusions. She took a brighter view of Lincoln's early life and the role of the frontier in shaping his character. She revered Lincoln's father Tom, whom Herndon had dismissed as little better than a shiftless vagrant, oafish and cruel. She had the idea that to belittle Lincoln's rural beginnings, as others had done, was to belittle something elemental in the nation itself.

In writing about Lincoln, she said, she meant to refute "the tradition that his childhood and youth were passed in hopeless and sordid poverty and hardship. There were poverty and hardship, but they were never hopeless, therefore never sordid. They were regarded as a necessary stage in the great undertaking of opening, taming, and developing a new land. These men knew what they sought. To treat them as vagrants is to fail to understand the spirit of the pioneer. Abraham Lincoln's youth was passed in one of the most daring and promising struggles to which American men ever have put their hands." For her, the character of Lincoln was all mixed up with the character of the United States, making it hard to tell where one left off and the other began. She wasn't the first to feel this way nor the last.

As a biographer she refused to stay home. She was tireless in her travels, running down documents and pestering sources; it was she, for example, who finally fished out Tom and Nancy Lincoln's wedding license from a dusty cubby in a tumbledown courthouse, dispelling once and for all the whispers of Abraham's illegitimacy. Nearly thirty years after her Lincoln biography was published, she retraced her research trips and wrote a first-person account in *Footsteps*. She was an old woman by then, but she was still tireless, still expansive in spirit, and this made her a boon companion for me on the Trail. In our motel rooms at night, with my wife dozing and my son and daughter frozen in the glow of the in-room video, I would settle under one of the dim little lamps and pass time with Ida, following her as she retraced her earlier efforts to trace Lincoln's life. The next morning, I'd be made more aware than usual of the way history deposits itself in sedimentary layers, like a coastal shelf. At the bottom, of course, was Lincoln's life, but then just above it were the tracks of another hero, Ida Tarbell; and forty years after her my father and his family, my mother and my brothers and me, rolling over the same terrain, and now my own family, with me in my father's place . . . a resonance that deepened until the last morning, when we pulled through the entrance at the Lincoln birthplace, in Hodgenville.

This backwards itinerary that I had concocted had an additional benefit. It offered a unique perspective on the patterns of early frontier settlement—and another hint of the heroism that Ida Tarbell found in Tom Lincoln's generation. The migration of the Lincoln family from Kentucky defies all contemporary expectation, not to say common sense. Whether you approach it from Chicago, to the northeast, or from St. Louis, to the southwest, Central Illinois is almost unimaginably flat, as though the whole country had been smoothed out by a rolling pin. Along this meridian the deciduous forests of the eastern United States thin out and the grasslands of the west begin. Now tamed into fields of corn and soy and alfalfa, the land in Lincoln's time sprouted a sea of prairie grass, each shaft of which was stiff as cardboard and sharp as a handsaw. It rose chest high or higher, retained the damp heat of summer, and spawned colonies of locusts, crickets, and leaping bugs of all kinds—until the prairie farmers managed to conquer it with their scythes and plows. Back then, in other words, the prairie was even less attractive and more forbidding than it is now. If a man could tolerate life here, he could tolerate anything.

Yet old Tom Lincoln not only tolerated it, he sought it out. So did the numberless families who migrated in the same direction. As my family and I retraced the Lincolns' steps in reverse, from Illinois prairie to the river valley of Indiana to the hummocks and dells of Kentucky, the land grew lovelier. Tom hauled his family the other way, with the landscape getting more and more unsightly, calculating that the less inviting the land was, aesthetically, the more potential it held, financially. He must have scanned each new neighborhood and thought: verdant bluffs, meandering creeks dancing with sunlight, hidden hollows and twisting pathways swept by cool breezes—too pretty! We'll never make a buck here! Pack it up! And so on, till he finally found a place ugly enough to earn a living.

A century and a half later, the descendants of these Illinois prairie farmers have taken upon themselves a difficult task of their own. They have tried to make the prairie appealing to tourists. The simplest way to do that is to make it an object of nostalgia. The interstates running through Central Illinois are lined with "Prairie Grass Preservation Areas," patches of ground designated and protected by state bureaucrats as a way of nurturing the weed that their great-grandparents almost killed themselves trying to obliterate. The forerunner of those Interstates, the famous Route 66, was decommissioned and left to crumble in the 1960s, but the remaining stretches of it, buckled and cracked and sprouting knots of crabgrass, are now an object of international veneration. Route 66, what's left of it, draws thousands of tourists a year to Central Illinois. They come from all over the world to see the pavement. Most of the foreigners are Germans, who thereby relinquish the right to make fun of the French for their love of Jerry Lewis movies. "We're very lucky in Illinois," Nicky Stratton, the tourism lady, told me. "We have more surviving contiguous mileage of Route 66 than any other state in the country." So they have made it pay. The Route 66 obsession has spawned Springfield's Gas Station Museum, which is a museum dedicated to the American gas station and which, unbelievably, is not the prairie's strangest museum. Any German who gets tired of Route 66 can make a run up to Atlanta, Illinois, where the Grain Elevator Museum is open for tours on Sundays from one to three p.m.

This urge to commemoration, this desperate attempt to conjure something interesting from the prairie, settles most naturally on Springfield's Lincoln sites. There are half a dozen of these, including major sites like the tomb and the home, and lesser ones like the Benjamin Edwards house, which contains the horsehair davenport that tradition identifies as the courting couch of Abe and Mary. We chose to begin at the new Lincoln library and museum. It had been several months since the grand opening, and attendance numbers already were wildly exceeding expectations. We ran into the director, Richard Norton Smith, in the lobby. "Sixty thousand and counting!" he said, gesturing to the lines snaking toward the theater showing *Lincoln's Eyes,* the multimedia extravaganza that introduces visitors to Lincoln's life. And indeed the lines were impressive.

Even my kids almost thought the wait was worth it. After *Lincoln's Eyes,* they rendered their verdicts of the quaking seats and smoking cannon barrels. "Cool," said my son. "Good," said my daughter. But my wife's critique drew me up short.

"Did you notice there weren't any facts in there?"

"What do you mean?" I asked.

She said, "I mean that aside from the information that he had four kids and was born in Kentucky and moved to Indiana and then Illinois and presided over the Civil War and got shot by a racist nutjob, there are no facts in there. No dates, no time line, no names of important people or other politicians or places or battles."

"They can only do so much in fifteen minutes," I said, a little defensively.

"No," she said. "They're scared to death of making it seem like school. I think they think real information will scare people off. It's all about feelings—how he felt, how people felt about him. Nothing concrete. Nothing that might make a kid think, 'Oh, no! Is there going to be a test later?'"

And so began my campaign of parental pedantry. Along the Trail I took every opportunity to give my kids dates and names and facts, and to show them the places that might make the facts more memorable. This is harder to do on the Trail today than I would have supposed. Over the next day and a half in Springfield I walked the town without pity, the family dragging behind. We went to the restored law office of Lincoln & Herndon and to the old state Capitol, where Lincoln delivered his "House Divided" speech ("on June 16, 1858," I said). At twilight we stood on the tracks alongside the old train station where he had given his beautiful farewell address on his way to Washington ("having won only 39 percent of the popular vote but winning the electoral college handily, with his running mate Hannibal Hamlin").

Each place was given respectful attention. But I began pressing my luck. Lincoln's Springfield exists on many different levels of historical interest, with the surface made up of the sites that have been rebuilt or preserved, and below them, the places where maybe one interesting but less than seminal event happened, and below that level the places where even more obscure, pretty much completely nonseminal events took place. Having drunk deep from Ida's *Footsteps,* supplemented by tourist brochures and guidebooks, this is the level at which I tended to see Springfield, and I took to pointing out sites that weren't, technically, sites, at least by any normal definition of tourism. One warm morning I brought them to a half-empty parking lot downtown.

"Right here is where the Globe Tavern stood," I said, "just about here in the middle of the block."

There were several seconds of conspicuous silence. "What's the Globe Tavern?" the boy asked at last, with an icy dread in his voice. From the corner of my eye I saw him wince against the torrent of information he knew would follow.

"It's where the Lincolns moved right after they got married!" I said. "They spent their wedding night here. They got married on November 4, 1842. Abe was thirty-three. Mary Todd was twenty-four—considered old for those days. Robert Todd Lincoln was born here, on August 1, 1843, exactly nine months after they got married. And right here is where it all happened—right here!"

I made a grand gesture of the kind that I had never before made toward a parking lot. Then I had them walk another couple blocks to where Lincoln's first law office had stood, which, I pointed out as we moved along, was near the building that housed the Joshua Speed store where Lincoln first lived when he came to Springfield, on April 15, 1837. Both buildings were torn down a century ago. I next took them down to the grounds of the new state Capitol, where Lincoln's brother-in-law Ninian Edwards had lived, in a house that was torn down in 1917. By the time we broke for lunch I realized with a start that, though we'd been sightseeing most of the morning, we had yet to see a site that was still standing.

"Now, if I may have your attention," my daughter said, stopping suddenly. She patted the brick wall next to her. She had had enough.

"You'll notice this fire escape here," she said. "Mr. Lincoln taught Springfield all about fire escapes. He rescued hundreds of orphans, many of them disabled, from terrible fires. To your right, you will see a mail box." She made a grand gesture. "On many occasions, Mr. Lincoln leaned against this mail box, usually only when he had a tummy ache. The jokes he could tell about that! And across the street here—a window! Mr. Lincoln loved windows! Unfortunately, many of his windows were torn down hundreds of years ago."

The wisecracks were slightly sharper than ones tossed around forty years ago by my brothers, who hadn't the benefit of soaking themselves in today's irony marinade, but the general tone was the same and, like so much else, served as a reminder of that earlier trip along the Trail. Walking through Springfield I wasn't just looking at Lincoln sites, essential to the history of the country, I was revisiting sites that made up a cherished bit of my own history. Leading my kids down the street toward the Lincoln home, I was spooked by the image of my father doing the same with his kids, with my brothers and me, under the same trees, down the same street, to the same destination. It was a powerful feeling, and it stayed with me no matter how much the Trail had changed.

When we visited the Lincoln house in the 1960s it had yet to fall into the hands of the National Park Service. Later I learned, from an informative monograph by Timothy Townsend called *The Site Adrift in the City*, how it evolved from locally run tourist attraction to a federally maintained National Historic Site. When the Lincolns moved to Washington, in 1861, the place quickly became a curiosity. During the war, soldiers stationed nearby sought it out as a window into the domestic life of their commander in chief and the nation's most famous family. After Lincoln's martyrdom it became a place of pilgrimage—and a source of income. Robert Todd Lincoln, who inherited title to the house, left it in the hands of a caretaker, Osborn Oldroyd, who slept upstairs and filled the first floor with relics of Lincoln and the war. The admission fee he charged for his trouble, and kept for himself, was gladly paid by sightseers eager to worship at the shrine.

The profiteering infuriated Robert. He fired Oldroyd and offered the house to the state, on the condition that it be opened without charge to all who cared to visit. The state accepted the offer, and to manage the property the governor promptly rehired the crafty Oldroyd. Unlucky for him, the caretaker's job was considered patronage. When the state government, and hence the Lincoln home, fell into the hands of Democrats, a decade later, Oldroyd was replaced by a timeserver with more sympathetic politics. Oldroyd packed up as many of his artifacts as he could and moved to Washington. There he rented the Petersen house, the three-story town house across from Ford's Theatre where Lincoln had been brought to die. Before long Oldroyd had filled the parlor with his stuff and was welcoming sightseers into the sacred back bedroom—for a fee.

Back in Springfield, the state took care to preserve a respectful environment around the home. In 1908 the city passed a zoning ordinance prohibiting any "bone factory, soap factory, brewery, distillery, lumber yard, bowling alley, shooting gallery, skating rink or dance hall" from being built near the house. Even so, when my father brought us to the Lincoln house, in the sixties, it was still in a living neighborhood, still knitted into the city's warp and woof. People came and went, moved in and out, raised their children and opened shops, tore down a house here and put up a new one there. Most of the buildings dated to Lincoln's day, however, and organically this was still the neighborhood Lincoln had known—connected by an unbroken flow of life from his day to ours. Newer neighbors recalled older neighbors who had known families whose parents had known Lincoln. On hot afternoons they would cool themselves on their front stoop, languidly watching the tourists line up at the famous house on the corner.

The neighborhood had grown shabby by the 1960s; even I, Lincoln-sozzled and young though I was, could see that. The city built a cul-de-sac at the foot of one of the cross streets, to discourage traffic. A for-profit museum across the street featured dioramas of scenes from Lincoln's life—much less skillful than the ones in Chicago, at the historical society, and carelessly maintained: the figurines were lumpy and clumsy under a film of dust, and dead flies lay belly up along the tiny streetscapes, totally out-of-scale, like winged raptors in a Japanese monster movie. Next door to the Lincoln home was a bookshop whose disarranged shelves held every Lincoln title imaginable, and a glorious souvenir store in which my brothers and I dawdled for what seemed like hours but, given my parents' impatience, couldn't have been. On the gift shop's porch a spectacular row of battle flags flew—including Old Glory and the Stars and Bars, welcoming tourists of every inclination.

Now all the funkiness is gone. Lincoln's home has been sealed in a pretty, parklike setting. The streets are all closed off to traffic now, their surfaces swept clean and coated in a rubberized material made to look like 1850s dirt. "Noncontemporaneous buildings"—meaning houses built after Lincoln left—have been torn down, leaving vacant lots, covered in grass, in their place. Picket fences enclose the mowed lawns. The houses that remain are either empty shells or government offices. The shabby museum and the gift shops are gone. All private enterprise has been squeezed out, and so have the old families, along with every sign of unauthorized activity. It's as tidy as if Martha Stewart herself had worked the place over with a toothbrush. There is no chipped paint, no blade of grass out of place, no rust, no hint of the ramshackle or the human; nothing seems lived in. The old charm is gone, and the scene looks frozen and drained of life—a butterfly under glass.

What happened? Reading Townsend's excellent monograph, and wanting to blame someone for this duded-up look, I settled on Richard Nixon. (When in doubt, blame Nixon.) In 1969, in an elaborate ceremony at the old state Capitol, Nixon signed a bill deeding the Lincoln home to the National Park Service. The state was happy to offload the property, and the Park Service, flush with the new science of historic preservation, was happy to go to work. Preservation professionals seem to think that the easiest way to reconstruct a historical period is to eliminate anything that links that earlier moment to our own. The rangers immediately set about subduing the human ecology of the place. Eminent domain was declared, the four surrounding blocks were seized, and the families were sent elsewhere. The cobwebs were broomed away, along with all signs of the accumulated past.

Anyone who wanted to see the Lincoln home used to walk up and stand in line, and before too long the line would snake through the front door into the parlor and around the back through the dining room and then up the main stairs to the bedrooms and then down the back stairs through the kitchen and out the back door. Docents in each room would answer questions as you shuffled past. Nowadays visitors are funneled first through a visitors' center, where they're placed in groups and issued timed tickets. The visitors' center is one of those one-story brick-and-glass creations of 1970s architecture; it could pass for a library, a jail, or a parking garage for municipal vehicles. Inside, a small theater shows an orientation movie, in keeping with the assumption that no historical sight can be enjoyed by people who haven't seen a video of

what they are about to enjoy. Just enjoying it, without precondition-
ing, is very pre–Nixon administration.

The reigning ideology of the Park Service is party poopery—a
constant vigil against anyone taking unauthorized pleasure in a Park
Service property. The authority of the men and women who enforce
this ideology is only slightly diminished by forcing them to dress like
Smoky the Bear. Their job is not so much to introduce the public to
historical properties as to protect the properties from an unpredictable public. The rangers don't let on that that's what they're about,
though. The lights go down in the little theater and a warm voice says:
"During your visit, your safety is our primary concern. The area you
are about to enter reproduces a nineteenth-century environment and
you will encounter surfaces that may seem unusual: brick sidewalks,
uneven stone paving, and boardwalks. Remember: Walk, don't run.
To reduce risks of heat exhaustion, sit in shady areas and drink plenty
of water. A heart defibrillator is located in the visitors' center.

"Trash receptacles," the voice goes on, "present a special hazard,
drawing bees and other insects during the summer months. Please
keep clear of trash receptacles. [Here there was a menacing shot of a
trash can.] If you are stung by a bee, be sure to notify a park ranger.
If you've parked in our parking lot, please take elementary precau-
tions. Lock your vehicle. Be aware of your surroundings. And when
leaving the parking area, remember to fasten your safety belt and drive
safely." And then in a valedictory cadence: "Remember safety when
you experience . . . your America."

From the visitors' center our group was ushered outside to a seat-
ing area and holding pen. Trash receptacles were everywhere. Before
too long our ranger showed up. She told us that we were to be careful
inside the house. A rubber mat was laid to guide our passage from room
to room. Any movement beyond the mat, she said, would set off alarms.
"I hope I don't have to scold anyone," she said. "And now welcome to
Mr. Lincoln's home!"

She was young and chatty, with that overrehearsed quality that tour guides acquire in a final, desperate attempt to hide the bone-crushing boredom of their jobs. She might have memorized her script in French and then translated it back to English, because all the inflections were misplaced. "We *are* now in the parlor," she said, once she had herded us inside. "This *is* the room where Mr. Lincoln did receive word *of* his nomination *to* the presidency."

In the late 1980s the house was covered in scaffolding and tarp, taken apart and reinforced with steel beams and cooled with air-conditioning, then put back together using as much of the original material as possible. The house is neat as a pin. You can hear the hum of the a.c. As you enter the front door you see a famous and haunting image in the hallway: a stovepipe hat and Lincoln's shawl, hung carelessly on a wall hook. And for a moment in this wired and air-conditioned and refurbished house you can almost sense an old human presence, as though he had just come home and slipped back to the kitchen to see what was for dinner.

But the impression doesn't last and we were soon hustled onward. What I would have given for a rotted floorboard, a creaking stair, some whiff of age or sign of use! "Folks, let me point out as you approach the stairway here, the railing *is* original to the structure, so you *will* get to touch something that Mr. Lincoln did touch." ("This is ecstasy for you, isn't it, Dad," said my son, as I placed my hand gently on the railing.) Mary and Abe had separate bedrooms, his and hers. "It *was* a sign of real high social standing in those days for the guy and the girl to sleep in separate beds," the ranger said, "although"—she gave us a naughty look—"remember the Lincolns did have four children." She winked and then motioned to the corner, to the impossibly small desk Lincoln used. "Mr. Lincoln worked long hours at this desk, and in fact the Dividing of the House speech *was* written here." Down the hall were the kids' rooms: "Mr. Lincoln did spend his whole life doing away *with* slavery, so that is one of the lessons he would have been teaching his children as he played with them in this room." Every now and then a piercing beep would go off, signaling that one of the tourists had passed an unapproved foot or hand through the vast no-fly zone. The look that our guide gave one old couple who had briefly doddered off the mat was enough to give you, or them, a coronary. That's why there was a defibrillator back at the visitors' center.

"There used to be a really cool museum over there," I told the kids when we were back in the open air. "And there were houses in these empty lots, real houses where people had lived for a hundred years. And in front of the gift shop there was an amazing row of flags . . ." But then I gave up. I was showing them sites from my own history rather than Lincoln's. And I was still showing them things that weren't there.

Before we left Springfield I drove the kids out to Oak Ridge cemetery to see Lincoln's tomb. For generations a trip to the tomb has been obligatory for Illinois schoolchildren, and remains so even now. There's a lot for a kid to like. The base is adorned with sanguinary statues of Civil War violence, and the obelisk rises beyond the highest trees. To reach the sarcophagus you enter a hallway of gleaming pink granite and are greeted at intervals by small reproductions of the finest Lincoln statues—Saint-Gaudens from Lincoln Park, Daniel Chester French from the Lincoln Memorial, Anna Hyatt Huntington from the gate at New Salem. The walls are so thick you can't hear the kids pretending to slaughter one another outside.

A giant bronze bust of Lincoln stands watch at the entrance. It was sculpted by Gutzon Borglum, the lunatic who got the idea of rappelling across the face of a limestone bluff in South Dakota, dynamiting as he went, until it looked like four presidents—George, Thomas, Theodore, and Abraham, snuggling cheek to cheek like a group of high schoolers in a photo booth. The bust at the tomb is a knockoff of the one on Mount Rushmore, and tradition requires that kids rub the tip of the nose. Exposure to the elements has turned the massive head to brown; but the tip of the nose, polished by millions of hands, gleams like gold. It looks like a bad case of ski burn.

I held my daughter up and she palmed it vigorously, as my father, years before, had held me up—and as his father, I remembered with a jolt, had uplifted him, when they visited the tomb in the 1930s. There was a snapshot of it in a cardboard box in an attic somewhere, the two of them paying homage to history and to Lincoln, my father somber in short pants and bangs and his father in a tie and fedora, and I tried to recollect the details of the photo and reproduce it, with my wife taking a picture of my daughter and me, paying the same tribute in the same place to the same man, seventy years on.

Just beyond the entrance to the cemetery we found another landmark of the Trail, a barnlike building done up in round logs, stuck with a sign reading, simply, "Lincoln Souvenirs." At this late date my interest in souvenirs was purely clinical, but it remained keen. Had standards of tastelessness been maintained over forty years? I quickly found a coin bank shaped like a toilet bowl, with the words "Greetings from Springfield" stripped across the tank. (Yes!) The children's enthusiasm was less focused but just as intense. I was watching them gorge on rubber chickens stamped with Lincoln's profile, commemorative plungers saying "Come Again!," and plastic paperweights you could shake to unloose a mighty blizzard over a tiny plastic Lincoln's tomb, when I glanced out the doorway and saw, across the road, a small one-story building set back among a stand of cedar. A long drive led up to it from the road. The sign in front read: MUSEUM OF FUNERAL CUSTOMS.

"I thought we were going to New Salem," my daughter said as I led the family across the street.

"We are," I said, "but we have to see this first."

"It's a funeral museum," my wife said. "We're not going to pass up a funeral museum."

The building is in a neoclassical style, modestly proportioned and quietly attractive. Inside, the air-conditioning was turned up very high—cold as a meat locker. A display case in the anteroom held relics distantly tied to Lincoln. The centerpiece was a swatch of cloth identified as a "fragment of a flag hung in one of the cars of the Lincoln funeral train for the duration of its stop at Indianapolis 4.30.65."

In the small lobby, I paid for our tickets while the kids and my wife moved ahead, around a corner into the exhibit room.

As I collected my change I heard my daughter's voice, a little too loud, edged with alarm. "Mom," she said, "what's embalming?"

The ticket taker smiled warmly.

"That's where you'll want to start," he said. "Our first exhibit: 'Embalming—the Art and Science of.'"

I rounded the corner and found myself in an embalming room, circa 1928. It had been extracted whole from a mortuary in Monmouth, Illinois. I'm fairly sure that's what the sign said; I didn't read it closely. I had never seen an embalming room before. This one looked perfectly preserved; you could almost smell the formaldehyde. Everything was lit a little too brightly, like an operating theater or the set of a porn movie. A metal rack rested on a grooved ceramic table, and both rack and table were slanted toward a drainage sink that sat on the tile floor. A white smock hung from a hook on the wall. Rubber tubes sprouted from a pump near the table. A diagram showed how the body would rest on the rack, the fluids would cascade through the slats of the rack and flow down the drain. . . .

My wife was coming toward me. She had hurried through the embalming room to the other exhibits and now was rushing back, toward the door. "If I stay here any longer I'm going to pass out," she said.

"Wait," I said.

"There's lots of Lincoln stuff back there," she added over her shoulder.

"Thanks," I said.

The kids brushed by, trailing her.

"See ya, Dad."

"See ya, Dad."

I turned back to the "Pioneers of Embalming" display. There was a selection of old embalming fluids, from the 1920s and even earlier, cloudy in their original vials. I walked on to the "Prosthesis and Cosmetology" exhibit, which showcased the fake hair, false eyelashes, and "restorative noses" that were often necessary to restore a comely appearance in the aftermath of a good, thorough facial draining. Old newspaper ads for rubber embalming cloaks were pinned to a display board. The grainy photos showed the cloaks modeled by a stout, impassive embalmer, his shoulders thrown back as though he were on a parade ground, a rictus of grim satisfaction set in his face.

The museum took pains to honor "diversity and difference," as all museums do in our multicultural age. There was an exhibit on "Women Pioneer Embalmers," another on "The Black Funeral Home," and a brief nod to Indian burial rites. I moved on to the back of the hall, where I found the Lincoln corner. A life-size (if that's the word) reproduction of his casket rested on a bier draped in black ruffles. The casket was studded in silver, and a plastic pink rose lay wrapped in a lace doily on top. From hidden speakers a tinny wind ensemble played the funeral march commissioned for Lincoln's burial.

I picked up a brochure entitled "The Embalming of President Lincoln: April 15, 1865."

"Embalming immediately followed the autopsy," I read.

Henry P. Cattell first positioned the body, closed the eyes, arched the eyebrows, and set the mouth in a slight smile. He also shaved the face except for a short tuft at the chin. After closing the cranial incision, he began the arterial embalming. Cattell drained the blood through the jugular vein and then used the femoral artery (in the thigh) to inject the embalming fluid. [I skipped shakily down the page.] *Lincoln did not receive any cavity treatment, as it was not a common practice at the time. Soon, Lincoln's body hardened to a marble-like state, ready for the amazing journey in store for it. Persistent problems with skin discoloration around the eyes resulted from the grim nature of the murder. Due to a phenomena called*

*transmitted force, the bullet's impact as it entered the back of the head
cracked both of the skull's orbital plates, bruising the . . .*

"Boo!"

My daughter had come back.

"Can I have one of these?" she said. She held up a small coffin made
of chocolate and wrapped in cellophane. "It's a dollar fifty."

I dropped the brochure and turned and made for the door. The ticket
taker emerged from an office and cut me off. "Have you visited our gift
shop?" he asked.

He was very pale, but also so polite and eager that I didn't dare be
rude. The chocolates were in a box on a shelf by the door, next to a
stack of books and videos ("Cryptic Clues") for sale. There were souvenir pencils inscribed with the museum's name, casket key rings, and
a refrigerator magnet that said: "Each departed friend is a magnet that
attracts us to the next world."

I bought four chocolate coffins. The coffins had a chocolate mummy
inside, arms folded, at peace. My daughter bared her teeth and took a
big bite.

"This is your first visit?" the ticket taker asked.

Like you've ever had a return customer . . .

"This chocolate is yummy," my daughter said.

"They're made exclusively for us," he said. "One lady bought several boxes for her wedding."

He was not only the museum's ticket taker but also its director. He
told me the museum had opened fairly recently, and he had come aboard
only a few months before. For years the collection—bottles, tubes,
racks, fake hair, restorative noses—had been languishing in a warehouse, seeing the light of day only rarely when sections of it would be
hauled around the state in a traveling exhibit. At last the Illinois Funeral Directors Association had raised enough money to build a permanent home, and now they had set about the business of bringing in
paying customers from among the thousands visiting the Lincoln sites.

"The location," he said, pointing toward Lincoln's tomb outside, "simply could not be better." He was in a talkative mood. "And we're making progress with the museum. Some serious errors were made before I got here. There's not enough storage. There's not nearly enough exhibition space. We have serious problems with the lack of amenities for guests. The restrooms are too small. This gift shop is hopeless. There's no room for a snack bar or restaurant."

A restaurant?

"In case people get hungry," he said.

I thanked him and steered my daughter to the door.

"You're interested in Lincoln?" he said. "Because if you are, we've got lots . . ."

"No," I said, "not terribly."

I felt a little guilty at my lie, but I saw through the door that my wife was at the wheel with the motor running.

Lincoln lived in New Salem for six years. The village sprung up a few years before he arrived and was abandoned only a year or two after he moved on—as though it had emerged from the mist, Brigadoon-like, to help him along, then faded away once it had fulfilled its purpose.

That fleeting quality, the evanescence of the village, gives it an almost mystical significance in Lincoln lore. Shortly after World War I, a group of local boosters formed the Lincoln League in hopes of rebuilding the little town on its original site, on a bluff overlooking a milldam on the Sangamon River. Writing in 1920, Ida Tarbell noted these plans with pleasure, though she passed through here before they could be realized. "The most unique, and I am inclined to believe the most popular monument that ever will be erected to Abraham Lincoln, is the restoration of the town of New Salem," she wrote. The rebuilt cabins are set along either side of an old sunken road, and the old road runs through a forest, and the forest leads down to the lazy stream. To most buffs, leafy New Salem rivals the birthplace in Hodgenville for its ability to conjure up the essence of the man. Yet even here in this re-created space, cut off from the sites and sounds of the present, that sense of Lincoln's elusiveness—that will-o'-the-wisp feeling I briefly got in his Springfield home, as though you've just entered a room that he's left only a moment before—is impossible to shake.

In fact, it's consciously reinforced. The essential unknowability of Abraham Lincoln the man has become a theme of the New Salem state park.

Early on, the park's Lincoln relics—dazzling stuff like his old surveyor equipment, the dinnerware from the Rutledge tavern where Abe met Ann—were laid out in heavy wooden display cases in an old stone house near the center of the reconstructed village. Now a new museum stands at the entrance to the park, and the stuff, following trends in curatorial science, is more complicatedly displayed. The old museum was built around a straightforward narrative of Lincoln's time at New Salem, lifted whole, pretty much, from the Mark Twain–like account in Herndon's original book: footloose, the awkward but ambitious young man arrives by flatboat, and then endears himself to his new neighbors by winning a wrestling match with a local tough named Jack Armstrong; he falls in love with Ann, works variously as a store owner, surveyor, and town postmaster, and tries his hand at politics before leaving, six years older and much wiser, for Springfield and a career in law.

The new museum offers nothing so comfortable as a straightforward narrative. It instead applies the Rashomon effect to Lincoln's New Salem years. There's lots of text in the museum, on story boards here and there, quoting friends and neighbors from Herndon's archives and elsewhere. The displays recount the most famous incidents of Lincoln's time in New Salem—yet more often than not, as we've seen, the testimony conflicts. There are two versions of how Lincoln happened to come to New Salem, for example; both are offered up to the visitor without prejudice as to which might be true. No fewer than six accounts, from six different witnesses, are offered of the wrestling match with Armstrong; some say he won, some say he lost, some call it a draw.

Another display gives the contradictory testimony from Herndon's records about Abe's relationship with Ann. Two views are given of Lincoln's early business partner, an itinerant named Denton Offutt, who might have been a rascal or a hardworking entrepreneur—take your pick. The visitor who bothers to read all this scrupulous scholarship will be extremely well-informed but ultimately out of luck. Any hope he had of nailing down the story of Abe in New Salem has been dashed. The effect is vertiginous, in the postmodern manner.

Reconstructed New Salem was forty years old when my parents first brought me here, and already showing its age. The logs in the cabins were splintered and weathered to gray. Now it looks newer than ever. One day a few years ago, a docent told me, the federal government served notice that the dirt pathways, which were susceptible to potholes and raised clouds of dust in summer, had to be paved over to comply with the Americans with Disabilities Act. Wheelchair access ramps were built to the cabins. By now, in its eighth decade, the place is more than the reconstruction of a historical artifact; it is itself a historical artifact. It has become a great favorite of historiographers, the historians who study the study of history.

And for anyone who clings to romantic notions of New Salem, who believes in its power to summon the spirit of Lincoln, these historiographers can be brutal. New Salem was once considered a fine example of historical reconstruction. Back in the 1920s, the Lincoln League worked from a map drawn by a man who had lived in the village as a child. Along with the state government, the League hired archaeologists to find the foundations of as many old cabins as they could, and the work of raising up the old village proceeded with care and even reverence. More recently, however, two historiographers who work at the park, Richard S. Taylor and Mark L. Johnson, have been undercutting the authority of those efforts with what looked to me like an unseemly relish. Their history of the reconstruction, published in the *Journal of Illinois History*, was called "A Fragile Illusion." The title gives the game away.

New Salem, the park, isn't what it claims to be at all, the historiographers have discovered. Promoted as a historical project, it was in truth an exercise in early-twentieth-century bourgeois propaganda. Johnson and Taylor quote one of the project's early champions: "The purpose of the restoration is not only to honor Lincoln, but to instill civic virtue, honesty, hope and perseverance into the heart and minds of our people." This is not good, apparently. "By reconstructing New Salem," the historians write, "the Lincoln League was responding to a debunking, skeptical, and relativistic age by creating a three-dimensional icon that promised direct or experiential access to an objectified past."

Surely, though, when it comes to skepticism and relativism, the 1920s had nothing on our own era, overrun as it is by academic historians using words like "objectified" and "experiential access." Not much that gives pleasure in New Salem survives the meat grinder of Johnson and Taylor's debunking. The Lincoln League's pretensions to historical accuracy were a sham; the old man's map was a con; many of the houses were inaccurately sited, and an entire section of the village was most likely misplaced. No one really knows who lived where. The hewn-log construction of the cabins is all wrong—most of the buildings were made from round logs. The funding of the project was tainted with political opportunism. The design of the rebuilt village is littered with "nationalist meanings." And where'd all these pretty trees come from? "The New Salem that Lincoln knew," they write, "was most likely perched atop a hill made barren by its builders, not a village nestled amidst a picturesque forest rendered visitor-friendly by hiking trails, trailside shelters and comfort stations." They didn't have restrooms for tourists in the 1830s? Who knew?

And so modern historiography renders a final verdict on the old-time buffs who built the new New Salem in the 1920s. Their "definition of authenticity as visual verisimilitude was, in fact, itself a historically contingent construct produced and sustained by a technologically driven visual culture." It was, in the end, "a fragile illusion ever subject to disclosure and subversion."

This is party poopery of a different sort from the Park Service's, but no less dispiriting. And it stands on one side of an unbridgeable divide, historiographically speaking. The people who rebuilt New Salem eighty years ago wanted their history to inspire and uplift a visitor, to illustrate moral truths about courage and enterprise, and if it didn't do that they worried that the history they were telling was somehow illegitimate, or a failure. That was their working premise, anyway. The people who have inherited New Salem today work from an opposite premise: history that uplifts or gives comfort or inspires is suspicious on its face, and the job of an academic historian is to take it apart, piece by piece.

I'm not sure the new way spells progress, but of course I didn't be-labor it with the kids. Running through the forest, darting from cabin to cabin, loitering in the shade of an old oak outside the inn where Abe courted Ann—if Abe courted Ann, and if the original inn was really on this spot and not somewhere hundreds of yards away—both son and daughter seemed genuinely delighted, full of questions. They didn't know they were imbibing historical contingencies. But I did. Lincoln seemed harder to get hold of than ever.

Here and there along the Trail I felt the vibrations of a great slumber-ing creature rousing itself—some long dormant beast beginning to stretch and yawn and lift a drowsy eyelid to peek around. There are hints of a new era of Lincoln commemoration. The first signs suggest it would be much different from the earlier one. Old New Salem was a good example of the earlier era and the earlier attitude. Like the Lin-coln Memorial in Washington, D.C., or the first Lincoln exhibits at the Chicago Historical Society, it was a place conceived in Lincoln wor-ship and an urge to evangelize—to offer moral instruction through the story of his life. Back then commemorations of such ambition and expense could have been inspired only by an irresistible awe and rev-erence. The new Lincoln museum in Springfield was an example of the newer era. Nowadays commemorations of such ambition and expense could be inspired only by economics.

The apparent success of the new museum has induced other communities along the Trail to begin to exploit their own Lincoln associations—though on a smaller scale, of course, with expectation of a smaller return. The renewed enthusiasm comes after many years of letting Lincoln lapse. On our way to Indiana from Central Illinois we stopped in Decatur, twenty miles to the east of Springfield. Few towns in Lincoln's life were so important for so long. This is where Tom Lincoln and his family, newly arrived from Indiana, first settled in Illinois, when the town was just a cluster of shacks and tents and guttering campfires, and here, according to legend, Abraham climbed a stump and gave his first political speech, rebutting some gasbag who had dared to slander his great hero Henry Clay.

The farm that Lincoln helped his father lay out was a few miles from town. "Here they built a log cabin," Lincoln wrote later, in a third-person biographical sketch, "and made sufficient rails to fence ten acres of ground." Thirty years later, in 1860, those same rail fences were found, dismantled, and liberated by enthusiastic political supporters, who carried them triumphantly into the Decatur convention hall, where the state Republican party nominated Lincoln as its candidate for president. The rough-hewn logs became a symbol of his commoner background. Decatur is the place where he got tagged as "the Railsplitter."

"When one is on a Lincoln pilgrimage," Ida Tarbell wrote in *Footsteps*, "he has the first sense of being in a living Lincoln country when he reaches Decatur. It is the first place where there are still people who really knew him, and is one of the four or five Illinois towns which treasure most sympathetically and intelligently its Lincoln contacts, which seem not only to revere but love the man." In 1918, Tarbell attended an Old Settlers reunion in Decatur where no fewer than 150 old-timers claimed to have known Lincoln or at least seen him in the flesh. They're all gone now, of course, and gone too—in recent decades at least—was the love and reverence.

The spot where the Lincolns first pitched camp, and where Abe gave his first speech, is marked downtown by a statue in Lincoln Square. Lincoln Square is more a traffic island than a square. The streets have been widened and widened until they've pretty much consumed the patch of land they originally surrounded, like a piece of cake being eaten from all four sides. The statue and a bench sit lonely in the swirl of traffic. The statue is called *Lincoln's First Speech*. Looking young but intrepid, Abe crouches by a stump gazing off into the middle distance. The sculptor probably wanted to suggest a young man peering into the limitless future, spying a dawn of unimaginable promise, but now that the future is here the young man is actually peering across two lanes of traffic into the window of Nancy's Lingerie and Intimate Apparel Shoppe.

There's not much here for buffs. A reconstructed cabin once marked the spot outside of town where the Lincoln farm was located, but it burned down twenty years ago and has yet to be replaced. Downtown is a honeycomb of empty storefronts and cul-de-sacs and closed-off streets—the remains of the pedestrian malls that seemed, to the desperate urban planners who reached the end of their rope sometime in the 1970s, like a good idea at the time. The intimate apparel shoppe stands at the end of a block-long revitalization effort, with benches set out in front of a candy store and a card shop, under the sketchy shade of linden trees struggling to stay upright and leafy. But the city fathers hope that Abe can do what half-assed attempts at urban renewal won't. The local papers were full of ideas about expanding and reconfiguring Lincoln Square as a "premier" Lincoln attraction.

"The initiative is about positioning our historic assets to help redevelop and reenergize the downtown area and tap into the enormous tourism industry," wrote Paul Osborne in an editorial in the *Decatur Tribune*. Osborne's editorials are highly influential with city government, since he is both the paper's editor and the town's mayor. "How we market our links to Abraham Lincoln will determine whether downtown will be a 'destination' or a 'drive-through' for decades to come."

"It's not about nostalgia," he concluded, with admirable candor. "It's about marketing nostalgia."

Yet history has taught that Lincoln doesn't always pay, as we were soon to discover. If Mayor Osborne wanted to know about that, he could simply cross the border one day and visit the state next door. He could ask the Hoosiers.

9

A WHOLE LOTTA LINCOLN

The Lincolns crossed from Indiana to Illinois at the Wabash River, near the old Hoosier capital of Vincennes. And so did we, except in reverse, of course, in keeping with my backwards scheme. "As we move back in time, it's like we're peeling back the layers of Lincoln," I instructed the kids, glancing at their blank faces in the rearview mirror. "From the successful Springfield lawyer to the New Salem frontiersman to the young Hoosier, all the way to the toddler in Kentucky, see—we're digging down to his roots, stripping him down to his essence."

There was a silence.

"What?" said my son, at last.

"Did you say 'stripping'?" my daughter said, momentarily disengaging from her iPod. "I don't think so!"

A graceful stone bridge arches over the river and links the two states. I am not a Hoosier but my wife is, having been born and raised in Fort Wayne. Thus under the Indiana Law of Return, our children are technically Hoosiers too. They have cemented their status with frequent trips to see their grandparents. But what we saw down here in the southwestern toe of the state was an Indiana unknown to them. Fort

Wayne lies in Indiana's northeast quadrant, smoothed out by ancient glaciers and still caked in ice for much of the year. Southwestern Indiana, though, rises and dips its way through a broad valley between the Wabash and the Ohio rivers, and my son and daughter were astonished at the rolling hills and lush meadows. Here Indiana is so beautiful it's a wonder the Lincolns stayed as long as they did.

Indiana is the forgotten stepchild of the Trail—though of course it has its full, 320-mile share of the Trail's 960 miles. Illinois gets most of the Lincoln attention, as it should, and Kentucky, site of his birth, comes in a distant second. Indiana scarcely rates mention in some of the guides. This is deeply unfair, but it is partly Indiana's fault. The Trail here, as Mr. Newman had warned me, splays through the state to take in every tourist site it can, Lincoln connection or no Lincoln connection—from the home of Booth Tarkington, author of *Penrod,* to the 500 Speedway in Indianapolis, to the memorial to Virgil I. Grissom, the second American astronaut in space, down in Mitchell. Another tangent spikes up to the headquarters of the Lincoln Life Insurance Company in Fort Wayne, where there's still a Lincoln museum the company built fifty years ago. Lincoln never set foot in Fort Wayne, however. The best the city fathers have been able to do, according to a sheepish placard in the museum, is raise the possibility that he just might have perhaps "switched trains" there once, maybe, in 1861.

Ida Tarbell sensed Indiana's status as an also-ran and, characteristically, responded by becoming a great booster of the state—almost an honorary Hoosier, which is another reason she made such a pleasant companion each night when I settled down with *Footsteps.* She was shown around the Indiana trail by a grandson of the Crawfords, who were the Lincoln family's closest friends during their time here. In 2005 we followed her as she had followed him, along the river where young Lincoln worked for a while as a ferryman and then back into the woods to Pigeon Creek, where Tom and his family staked their claim and built their farm.

*   *   *

Abe was seven when the Lincolns arrived from Kentucky, and he was twenty-one when they left for Illinois. A lot happened in those fourteen years. Ida was adamant in her belief that Indiana formed a kind of hinge point in Lincoln's life. She surmised the state must have been a jolt to Abe's imagination: "How it must have pulled at his head and heart and at all the young passions in him!" Arousing passion, historically, has not been a specialty of the Hoosier state, and even Ida conceded that Indiana's greatest importance for Lincoln lies in what didn't happen here—in the opportunities he avoided and the paths he refused to take as adulthood opened up in front of him.

"If he had been 'born' to farm, here was his chance," Ida wrote; likewise, "if he had had any strong craft sense," he would have come to it here, in Indiana. Instead Lincoln decided he wanted nothing to do with farmwork or with a life in carpentry. The work he enjoyed was the kind that kept his mind in motion. As a seventeen-year-old ferryman bringing travelers across the Ohio, he was exposed to a range of human life rare in the experience of a frontier boy; the same happened to him as a flatboatman, when he carried a load of grain down the Ohio and then the Mississippi to New Orleans and glimpsed for the first time the possibilities of cosmopolitan life (if not the horrors of a slave auction). An Indiana neighbor offered the fateful loan of a law book. By the time the Lincolns left Indiana for Illinois, he was well on his way to becoming a worldly man—well on his way to becoming Lincoln.

Hoosiers have never been quite sure how to handle this legacy, which is, after all, mostly negative. It's hard to take pride in your state because it's the place that one of the greatest Americans who ever lived couldn't wait to leave. The hub of Lincoln in Indiana is Lincoln Boyhood National Memorial, where I'd watched the presenters corner the hapless tourists one afternoon. It's deep in the sedimentary layers, too, for this is the only Lincoln boyhood site that Lincoln himself ever bothered to revisit. In 1844, by now thirty-five and a prosperous lawyer and politician, he came to southwestern Indiana to campaign for his hero Clay, then the Whig presidential candidate, and he spent a day wandering the old homestead, just as visitors do now, hoping to catch a shadow of his life as a young man. Lincoln was the first Lincoln tourist.

Today a bronze casting of the cabin's foundation logs and stone chimney sits where the Lincolns lived. It encompasses an amazingly small space—small but standard for the time: eighteen feet by sixteen feet. When Lincoln returned in 1844 to sightsee, the old cabin must have still been there, though apparently abandoned. We know this because Lincoln himself memorialized it in a poem.

"My childhood's home I see again, and sadden with the view," the poem begins. Then it gets even more depressing:

> Nearly twenty years have passed away
> Since here I bid farewell
> To woods and fields, and scenes of play
> And playmates loved so well.
>
> The friends I left that parting day,
> How changed, as time has sped!
> Young childhood grown, strong manhood gray,
> And half of all are dead.
>
> I hear the loved survivors tell
> How naught from death could save
> Till every sound appears a knell
> And every spot a grave.
>
> I range the field with pensive tread
> And pace the hollow rooms;
> And feel (companion of the dead)
> I'm living in the tombs.

Not a lot of fun on a car trip, that Abe.

Those fields that felt Abe's pensive tread in 1844 have mostly reverted to woods now, and back among them, a few hundred yards across a two-lane state road from where the old cabin stood, sits the most ambitious of all of Indiana's Lincoln landmarks. The Lincoln Amphitheater was built in 1987, and every year since it has staged an original open-air musical called *Young Abe Lincoln,* put on by students from Indiana State University (with the occasional help of a few professional ringers imported from Broadway). The show runs from early June through early August.

On the Internet before we'd left home, I'd gotten tickets for the last show of the season. Quite a surprise for the kids! I sprung it on them in our motel room, as we unwound after the day's drive from Vincennes.

"A musical about Abraham Lincoln?" my daughter asked. "Abe is going to sing? He's going to *dance?*"

I said I wasn't sure, but we would soon find out. My wife, mom-like, remarked how fun it would be. My son was quiet for a long time. Finally, as we left for an early dinner on our way to the amphitheater, he spoke up.

"How long will this Lincoln musical be?"

I said probably two hours, maybe two and a half.

"Two and a half hours," he said, with a barely perceptible shudder. "That's a whole lotta Lincoln."

Yes, it was! Lincoln's life has been pressed through the filter of every imaginable narrative form: children's books, morality tales, religious parables, Hollywood melodramas, journalistic debunkings, paperback romances, epic poetry, even TV sitcoms. *Young Abe Lincoln* proved it could survive a Broadway musical too. The state commissioned the show from a man named Billy Edd Wheeler. As his name implies, Billy Edd Wheeler writes country songs for a living. On the side he writes summertime outdoor extravaganzas based on American folklore—Johnny Appleseed, the Hatfields and McCoys, and Lincoln. His tunes rely heavily on the guitar-centered conventions of country music, but the exuberant theatricality of the show,

the grab-the-folks-by-the-lapels-and-hold-on-till-they-go-limp enthusiasm, is pure Kander and Ebb.

The basic problem with musicals is well known. With intimidating
regularity, the characters suddenly start singing and dancing just at
those points when normal people would be talking and sitting, or keeping quiet altogether and lying down. Billy Edd and the kids from Indiana State couldn't quite get around these difficulties of believability and
verisimilitude, but not for lack of effort. They were a high-spirited
bunch. They showed the same upbeat, fresh-faced wholesomeness that
used to send people screaming from their living rooms when the
Osmonds or Up with People would appear on the *Ed Sullivan Show*.
In lumberjack shirts and gingham dresses, carefully color coordinated,
the pioneers danced and danced—they danced when the Lincoln family arrived from Kentucky and they danced when they left, they danced
when someone got married or died, went a-huntin' or a-courtin', and
even, in a particularly confusing dream sequence, when someone fell
asleep. Happy Feet replaced Milk Sick as the greatest threat to public
health.

The larger problem, though, involved Indiana's ambivalent place in
Lincoln's life. The plot ran through all the changes as Herndon recorded
them for us: from the death of Nancy Hanks and the arrival of Sarah
Bush Johnston to the death of sister Sarah and the departure for better
land in Illinois, including all of Abe's childhood hijinks and his day-
dreams of something beyond the hardscrabble life. To provide moral
heft and dramatic tension, a slave couple wandered in and out of the
story. They were on the lam from their brutal owners across the river
in Kentucky. This gave the Hoosier audience several opportunities
to note, with deeply satisfying revulsion, the barbarity and vicious-
ness of Kentuckians.

The crowd loved every high kick and unlikely chorus. So did my
kids, from what I could tell. I was most struck by the setting itself, this
glorious amphitheater in the twilight. The proscenium opened out into
the woods, so with showtime approaching you could see the trees

darken as the sun set. Then the lights came up and the story unwound to a nighttime chorus of cicadas and crickets, coming in wave upon whispering wave from the dark forest beyond. And watching Abe's youth pass by, you'd suddenly realize: This is where it all happened, the pranks and the funerals and the celebrations and the yearning too, in real life, on this very ground! Early in the second act Tom Lincoln, recalling the death of Nancy Hanks, gestures stage left and looks out over the footlights and says: "We buried her up on that knoll over yonder," and there was a special tremor; for on that knoll over yonder, just past the parking lot and across the state road, Nancy Hanks really does lie buried, in the plot the real Tom chose, in the grave that he and his little boy dug for her.

Of course, as I was discovering with clocklike regularity, no Lincoln commemoration is just about Lincoln. As Mayor Osborne of Decatur put it, it's not about nostalgia, it's about marketing nostalgia. But for the Hoosiers it was about something even more. *Young Abe Lincoln* was less a tribute to Abe than a means of restoring civic pride. More than any state I know of, Indiana suffers from a crippling inferiority complex—more than North Dakota, more even than West Virginia. Ida had sensed this, too, eighty years ago. Hoosiers struggle desperately to prove to themselves and the world that they have a higher function than simply filling up the space between Cincinnati and Chicago. The insecurity shows itself in a dozen poignant ways. Hoosiers compulsively compile lists of Famous Hoosiers, for example. You can find them in guidebooks, on postcards, and all over the Internet. Glance through any of them and you'll be struck by their comprehensiveness: no one within even shouting distance of fame has been left out. There are many Hoosiers that any non-Hoosier will concede are pretty impressive (Cole Porter, Theodore Dreiser, Hoagy Carmichael, Eugene V. Debs), but included also are Hoosiers that no self-respecting state would want to claim (Michael Jackson, Jimmy Hoffa) and Hoosiers that no one but another Hoosier could bother about (Jermaine Jackson, Florence Henderson).

And aside from growing up in Indiana, all these famous Hoosiers have one thing in common: they left. The great Hoosier Diaspora is at once a point of pride and an unending ache for those who've stayed behind.

Lincoln represents them all—a synecdoche for every Hoosier who went elsewhere. Here at the amphitheater they were using him to reconcile the contradictions in Indiana's view of itself: the pride it takes in being a cradle for the great, and the vague uneasiness it feels in being the place that the great can't wait to get away from. The show began with a voice rising plaintively from offstage to claim Lincoln as ur-Hoosier.

"Has anybody here," the voice sang out in the silence and the dark, "seen a long-legged boy named Abraham? / Kind of a lanky lad, he just might be / he just might be the best we ever had."

Better than Jermaine, you bet. Two hours later, the refrain reappears in the show's grand finale, with all hands on stage—except that now Abe and his folks aren't coming but going, eager to cross the Wabash into Illinois and what can only be a better life (in Decatur!). Suddenly a bearded, older Lincoln appears from the woods backstage. The dancers part to make way.

"Here I grew up," old Abe says, as the cellos weep behind him. "Not much to look at, is it? Kind of an unpoetical place. But it inspired me to write poetry—so I guess part of my heart is here, and always will be here, in Indiana."

The chorus swells: "My heart will be in Indiana . . . forever . . . and that's a long, long time."

The show got the standing ovation it deserved. After the lights went up, the crowd spilled down the aisles to the stage to greet the cast, but it was stopped short when the actor playing the bearded Abe took a microphone. He looked to be on the edge of tears. The crowd fell back and went quiet.

This would be the last performance of *Young Abe Lincoln,* old Abe said—not just for the season, but forever. The state legislature had cut its annual subsidy for the show and the theater. The administration at Indiana State took that as an opportunity to slip out from under its financial obligation, too. The actor made some halfhearted attempts at rallying the audience—we could write the governor, he said, and our state senators, and of course the president of Indiana State University, to let them know how important the show, and Lincoln, had been to us all, and to all Hoosiers—but it didn't look like even he, even Abe, thought it would do much good. "We cannot escape history," Lincoln had once said.

Even for those of us who had never seen the show before, and who couldn't imagine when we would have had the chance to see it again, this was sad news, and my heart filled watching the young cast members wander the stage with an aimless air, coming together to hug one another good-bye and then parting and wandering till they found someone else to hug. In his lifetime Lincoln met every demand his country and history had made on him. He saved the Union. He freed the slaves. And now for seventeen years, in this quiet woods so dear to him, "these fields and scenes of play," he had been asked to repair the self-esteem of the Hoosier state. Some jobs are simply too big for one man.

In Kentucky we stopped first in Lexington, where Mary Todd was born and raised and where, on the edge of downtown, her girlhood home still stands, handsomely restored and open for business. I once heard a story about James G. Randall, a respected Lincoln biographer from the University of Illinois, and Randall's wife. In the late 1940s Mrs. Randall was writing a biography too—of Mary Todd, just coincidentally the wife of the man her husband was writing a biography of. A Southern woman herself, a proper and well-bred lady married to a famous, self-absorbed, and hardworking man, Mrs. Randall identified with Mary and held a correspondingly high opinion of her—so high indeed that

Lincoln scholars dismiss Mrs. Randall's book as too gauzy and romantic to be much use to anyone in search of the real Mary.

Mrs. Randall was big on atmosphere. She wanted to see the house where Mary had lived as a young woman, to walk the floorboards she had walked and gaze out the windows of her childhood bedroom. Neither of the Randalls could drive a car, so they enlisted a young student to drive them down to Lexington from their home near the University of Illinois in Champaign. They arrived after a long journey over the state roads. The historic preservation movement had not yet moved south of the Mason-Dixon line, and it had not yet occurred to Lexingtonians to make a tourist destination out of the home of the wife of the man who, by their reckoning, had destroyed nearly everything they treasured. The young student saw when he pulled the car up to the curb that the house was in bad repair. But he sensed something odder than dilapidation. He advised the Randalls to stay in the car while he went to ring the bell.

An older woman in heavy makeup answered the door. Behind her, shadowy figures moved languidly through darkened rooms. The young man pressed ahead. He gestured to the old couple in the back of his car. "They would very much like to come in," he said.

The woman at the door considered for a moment. "Well," she said, nodding toward James G. Randall, author of *Constitutional Problems Under Lincoln* and the magisterial, four-volume *Lincoln the President*, "tell the old feller he's welcome if he's got the money, but the gal best wait outside."

The house still rests at the edge of the curb, hard up against the main road into town, but it's much changed from when the Randalls made their visit, as is the town around it. Downtown Lexington, which begins just south of Mary's old doorstep, is an unsettled place, a victim of the whipsaw life cycle of America's uncertain attempts to revitalize its cities. Forty years ago, blocks of what were once attractive storefronts were slowly abandoned and then leveled by urban planners plotting urban renewal. They were replaced—temporarily, it was thought—by parking lots, acres and acres of parking lots. The parking lots were separated here and there by squat, angular office buildings tacked together from glass and poured concrete, on the theory, I suppose, that all those people who parked their cars downtown would need somewhere to work when they were done parking. Then the urban planners realized, too late, that the parking lots and angular monstrosities were bad for business—even more demoralizing and depressing than the abandoned storefronts—and the last remaining older buildings were bought up and hollowed out and used as a backdrop for the pedestrian malls that would (the planners now hoped) bring people back downtown.

But the pedestrian malls turned as gloomy and windblown as the parking lots that replaced the gloomy and windblown storefronts. So they have fallen from favor, too. Most recently the urban planners have reopened the streets to the old mix of foot, car, and bus traffic, in hopes of saving the downtown by re-creating what the earlier generation of urban planners destroyed while trying to save the downtown. The cruelest of the many ironies is that on block after block the freshest thing, the most welcoming thing, is likely to be the oldest thing: a brick clock tower or Georgian town house, an old bank of rusticated limestone or an apartment house with a cast-iron facade, warming the chilly present with a breath from the past—from an age long before anyone got the idea of urban renewal.

The tardy, frantic effort to retrofit what was left of Lexington's past is what saved Mary Todd Lincoln's girlhood home. After the brothel closed it became a grocery and then a warehouse. It was several times set for demolition till the third phase of urban renewal, the gentrifying phase that hungered for any building made of old brick, reached the edge of the urban core. A foundation bought the old house in the 1970s and restored it—too late to have been included on the original Lincoln Heritage Trail. Too bad, because the results are lovely. Though fronting the road, Mary's house backed into fields and orchards and flower gardens. Those fields are now taken up by a grocery store, a garage, and, of course, parking lots. But inside the genteel flow of antebellum life is carefully simulated. The caretakers, all ladies, have filled the sunlit rooms with lace and bone china. Much of the interior's original fabric of plaster and wood trim survives, including, our docent stressed, the banister leading to the second floor. This was the very same banister that Mr. Lincoln gripped on climbing the stairs during his frequent visits.

She glided a plump hand along the polished wood. "You're free to touch, and don't be surprised if you feel a chill," she said. "You're shaking hands with Mr. Lincoln."

"More banisters," my son said behind me, as we climbed the stairs. "What is it with Lincoln people and banisters?"

Actually, I don't think the docent was really a Lincoln person—or, rather, she was clearly more a Mary person than an Abe person. Sometimes the great divide that Mary cleaves in the land of Lincoln forces you to choose: people who love Mary extravagantly feel it necessary to slight Abe, the way friends will take sides in a divorce. It's much easier to feel sympathy for Mary if you view her as a woman wronged, who had married beneath her, and such were the apparent feelings of our docent. She was a large woman with apple cheeks and wire-rim glasses. She made sure to tell us that Mr. Lincoln, as father and husband, spent many months away from his Springfield home, year after year, leaving the family to fend for itself. Mary's response was often to pack up the kids and come home to Lexington for company, she said. And indeed Mary might have enjoyed the use of the Todd house forever, into the dark years of her dotage. Unfortunately, after the untimely death of Robert Todd, her father and the family patriarch, one of Mary's brothers filed a vindictive lawsuit that forced the sale of the family home.

"The suit tore the house out of the family's hands, with much bitterness," she said. "It destroyed the family, really." A slight arch of the eyebrow and purse of the lips. "The suit was filed on behalf of Mary's brother, incidentally, by Mr. Lincoln."

Now, as I later learned, Mary acquiesced in the lawsuit as well—it was an ugly dispute among members of an extended family, common then as now when pots of money are at stake—but the docent preferred to stress Mr. Lincoln's role in the dismemberment of the family fortune. She mentioned Mary's excellent education, her love of art and music, and her fluency in French, so different from Mr. Lincoln's untutored background, uncomplicated tastes, and backwoods manner. She also mentioned that the house was serviced by slaves in Mary's time. Mr. L., whatever his later reputation as an emancipator, had shown no uneasiness about the arrangement. "He was a tolerant and open-minded man, I guess," she said—another arch of an eyebrow.

She led us into the gift shop at the back of the house, where the air of femininity grew even more fragrant among the jars of potpourri, the handmade soap wrapped in tissue paper, the cross-stitch kits, and the cloth dolls in gingham dresses. Books were displayed for sale in a hutch. I couldn't find the one I was looking for: *The Emancipator's Wife: A Novel of Mary Todd Lincoln.* It had just been published and I thought it might kindle my daughter's interest. I asked the docent, who had taken a seat behind the cash box and was smoothing her hoop skirt.

"That's not the kind of book we would stock in this house," she said.

"It's not?"

"They sent us a copy from up in New York, the publisher did," she said. "They said, 'Won't you please sell this in your gift shop?' We took one look at it and we said, 'No, we will not, thank you very much.'"

I guess I still looked surprised.

"Have you read it?" she asked.

I said I hadn't.

"On one of the very first pages the author says Mary Todd married Mr. Lincoln because she was pregnant! Now, I ask you!" She looked around at us with a look of mock amazement, as though it were an eternal puzzle how such idiocy could survive in a rationally constructed universe. "You just wonder about people!" she exclaimed. What about natural selection! Shouldn't evolution have bumped these people off?

"That page was all we had to read, I can tell you that. One page and it was, 'No, thank you very much, we will not sell your book.' I'm sorry but that's not something we can have here."

In the car, my wife said, "No sir. We won't sell *that* kind of book in an old whorehouse!"

The Mary Todd house was a detour from the main Trail, and predictably enough, with all the lace doilies and brocaded cushions, it didn't carry much Abe-like resonance, the banister notwithstanding. But when you move down into Kentucky, you are entering into the loam from which Lincoln rose, the elements he was made of. From Lexington we headed south, into the magically beautiful hill country of central Kentucky—magically beautiful and scarily remote. Even by the standards of the nineteenth century, Abraham Lincoln was born in the middle of nowhere. Nowadays nowhere is more like somewhere than it was then, thanks to those mighty Interstates, which can take you right up to the edge of nowhere if no farther, and thanks also to the arrival of Costco and Wal-Mart, which ensure that people who live in the middle of nowhere don't have to go all the way to somewhere to buy a curling iron or a George Foreman Grill.

In the nineteenth century, though, nowhere really was nowhere. Thinking of Lincoln as the first modern president, a great figure of literature, the unequaled prose stylist steeped in Shakespeare and Byron, the corporate lawyer and professional politician, commanding armies from the White House, it's hard to recall that his life was rooted not only in the primitive prairie of New Salem but even deeper, in the savage, untamed frontier that preceded it. On the civilizational ladder, this was life just a few rungs up from the bronze age. Abe's grandfather, also called Abraham Lincoln, moved to Kentucky from Virginia and tried to stake a claim not far from present-day Louisville, in the state's northern hump. He was clearing a field one day with his five-year-old son Tom, later to become Abe's father, when a band of Indians emerged

from a nearby woods, took aim, and shot him dead. Lincoln's grandfather was killed by wild Indians! And they would have done the same
to Tom, too, but the eldest of old Abraham's sons, Mordecai, made it
to the edge of the clearing with a long gun of his own. He dropped one
of them, and the rest scattered.

Mordecai gathered up Tom and his other brothers and brought them
and their widowed mother, a woman with the fearsome name of
Beersheba, seventy miles south, to central Kentucky. He built a house
for Beersheba on a hillside sloping down to Beech Fork creek, on a site
now christened the Lincoln State Homestead Park. When Ida Tarbell
first came through this country she could knock on doors and find
people whose grandparents had known Beersheba and her sons. The
region in Ida's time was already thick with Lincoln lore, and a number
of communities competed to be declared the birthplace of President
Lincoln. "Like Homer in Greece," Ida wrote, "Lincoln in Kentucky is
claimed by, if not seven, at least several different places." This was
especially true of the Beech Fork neighborhood. She told of stopping
for directions at a cabin and finding a woman still abed with her new-
born baby. "Prove Lincoln was born here!" the woman pleaded. "I want
my son to have been born near him. Maybe then he could grow to be
like him."

That hope is not just a glimmer from a hundred years ago; it's still
there. We reached the Homestead Park after we'd turned off the Inter-
state and been driving for more than a half hour, having seen nothing
but woods and cut fields scattered with hay bales. The historical part
of the park consists of cabins spaced along the hillside and a little
gatehouse near the road. In the gatehouse two elderly ladies manned
the cash box. They were cheerful and dressed in gingham skirts and
frilly bonnets, eager to be of help and utterly helpless when it came to
explaining what the park had to show. One of the women pointed out
Beersheba's house, just down the hill from the gate, and beyond it was
the "Berry Cabin," which had been moved there half a century ago from
its original location a mile or so away, and which was of particular

interest to me. Neither of the ladies could tell me how much of either building was original, and I felt churlish and pedantic for asking.

"And there's one other thing we cannot tell you for absolute sure," one of the ladies said. "Was Abe Lincoln born here, on this spot?" She had a conspiratorial twinkle in her eye. The answer, I knew, was no; we were twenty miles from the birthplace at Hodgenville. But she didn't seem to be convinced that this was the right answer. "Yes, people have said that Mr. Lincoln was born right here. And yes, some people in a position to know do still say that. There are others who favor Hodgenville"—yes, including every reputable historian, I might have added, if I were a bigger jerk than I am. "But I will not hazard a guess," she continued. "Maybe you can inform an opinion for yourself as you enjoy your visit."

We were definitely beyond the influence of the National Park Service here. There were no orientation videos, no rope lines or motion detectors, no posted warnings about treacherous trash cans and killer bees; just friendly docents who were happy to confuse the customers with wild speculation. The park was deserted. We were free to wander in and out of the cabins unmolested. I was eager to see the Berry house because it was here that Richard Berry and his family had taken in the young orphan girl Nancy Hanks, later to be Abraham's mother. This is where she was raised and where, years later, Tom Lincoln wooed her and finally proposed to her, in the front room before the open hearth.

The two cabins, Beersheba's and the Berrys', are filled with treasures—a corner hutch made by Tom (his initials are carved in it), rough-hewn wooden bowls also from the Berry and Lincoln families, and a broadax that Tom used to clear the fields. My daughter and I climbed the loft in the Berrys' house. But for the yellow safety tape at the edge of the stair treads, the place seemed untouched by the world outside. The room had the musty smell of the old lumber it was made of. In the middle, eighteen inches off the floor, was a rope bed, no more than five feet long. Its wood slats were smoothed by age to a lacquer-like finish. "The Bed Made for Nancy Hanks by Richard Berry" read a sign framed on the wall above it. In the frame was a certificate of provenance, detailing the ownership and whereabouts of the bed from the Berrys' day to the present. The certificate explained that the bed was Nancy's in her childhood, and up here in the loft she lay awake at night, thinking whatever thoughts of the future an orphaned pioneer girl permitted herself to think.

I was impressed—though maybe aghast is the better word. This precious item sits in the loft untended. Gingerly I sat on the edge of the bed, then got up quickly. After some coaxing my daughter agreed to stretch out on the straw mattress so I could take a picture. She clowned at first, but in a moment the jokiness left her and she became still. The air up here was rich with the scent of wood smoke rising from the hearth downstairs. Cobwebs filled the spaces among the rafters. This moment might have been the first one in all our trip when the weight of the past pressed in on her.

"Abe's mom slept in this bed?" she said.

"Two hundred years ago," I said. "Right in this room."

"For real?"

I told her Nancy was an orphan girl who had come to live with the Berrys, and Mr. Berry had built the bed for her, and she'd lie up here each night and go to sleep with the moonlight coming through that window.

My daughter was quiet again for several moments. Then she sat bolt upright and swung her feet to the floor.

"Too creepy," she said. "Let's go."

"Did you see the bed?" one of the ladies asked when we got back to the gift shop. I told her we had. "Quite a thrill," I said.

"People do get a kick out of that," she said. I was dying to ask her how it came about that the bed, and Tom's hutch cabinet, and the bowls that Tom had made, and the house itself were left out here more or less unsupervised, free and open for people to enjoy and wander and commune with—all of which made it so different from so many other Lincoln sites. A ranger from the National Park Service would have an aneurysm.

Then I realized that the alternative—to fence the place in, stock it with watchful docents, possibly wire it with closed-circuit cameras—may not have occurred to the authorities of the Commonwealth of Kentucky. Or maybe, owing to a tight budget, they couldn't afford it and were willing to take their chances. Either way, I didn't want to press the point.

We had one more stop before we got to the birthplace in Hodgenville. Abraham spent most of his Kentucky years, from the age of two to six, on a farm next to Knob Creek, on what was then the heavily traveled turnpike from Louisville to Nashville. It was the first home he had memories of. The field the Lincolns tilled can still be seen on a shelf of land set between a creek bed and high wooded hills. Ida Tarbell was first led here, on foot, by the editor of the local paper. She wanted to re-create as closely as possible the experience of the peripatetic Lincolns, so she had the editor lead her through those hills "on a long and dangerous winding descent" into the Knob Creek valley. Ida was sixty-six years old when she did this, considerably older than I, but I didn't even try to force our family to follow her route. We were close to the end of our journey, and a kind of stupefied quiet had descended over the backseat of the van, broken only by occasional halfhearted grunts of protest whenever we pulled over to read another historical marker. A long and dangerous winding descent by foot was out of the question, even assuming I could get the kids out of the car.

Ida did remark on how lovely the place was in 1922, and "how close to the tide of Lincoln's day" it remained. Nor had the neighborhood changed much by the mid-1960s when my parents brought us here on the way to the birthplace at Hodgenville. I told the kids that I still had the most vivid memories of the Knob Creek property. A year or so after

Ida passed through, a local family called the Howards bought the farm, and they owned it still when I first got there, though by that time the family's interest had taken a commercial turn. In the sixties the farm was hung with all the trappings of a tourist spot, and its impression on me was indelible; in my memory it evokes a fragrant tastelessness that I can savor even now, like a Proustian MoonPie.

A log cabin, meant to resemble the Lincolns', had been reconstructed between the road and the creek. The farmland drifted away behind it, spreading between the bluff and the riverbed, then tapering as it disappeared around a bend. Next to the little cabin, I remembered, was a much bigger cabin, the size of a dance hall, sided in fake round logs, and inside were a lunch counter selling burgers and hot dogs and, just as memorably, one of the most sumptuous gift shops I'd ever seen. The junk was astounding. It hung from the rafters—kites and blankets and banners—and overflowed deliriously from wooden bins: tomahawks and trolls in buckskin, miniature liberty bells and cherrywood paddles inscribed with grimacing faces and legends like "Shut Uppa You Face!" The cheeseburgers were mashed by expert hands on a crusted griddle, flipped and mashed again, then wedged into steamed buns and wrapped in wax paper. My parents and brothers and I ate them at picnic tables indoors.

I was describing those burgers to the kids, enticing them with descriptions of how the grease and melted cheese clotted in chewy little lumps that stuck to the wax paper; I was inspiriting them with word pictures of this gift shop and its bounty, when we swung round a curve and the Knob Creek farm suddenly appeared, up against the road as it had always been, with a flagpole and an iron marker defining the spot. The parking lot was empty.

A few years ago the Howard family, having tried for half a century to make a buck off of Knob Creek, at last gave up. The only taker for the property was the National Park Service, which evidently doesn't know what to do with it. The barnlike hall that housed the gift shop and lunch counter was shuttered, and the log cabin, closer to the creek, had been fenced off so no one could get near. The wire fence was papered with warnings about safety and the dangers that enveloped us: wasps, poison ivy, creek banks so slippery and treacherous that a careless visitor risked plummeting into the three-foot abyss below. Notices tacked to a bulletin board told us where we shouldn't go and listed the penalties that awaited us if we tried. I got close enough to the big old building to look in the windows. Upended tables were scattered about the dusty floor, an old refrigerator stood open in a corner, and a stack of bins of the kind that had once held the tomahawks and bronze log cabins had tipped over empty near the door.

Another notice announced that appropriations were pending to restore the property. I headed back to the van. Once funding comes through the Park Service will arrive to sweep the last traces of the magic away, and the place will be improved beyond all recognition, not only as a landmark from Lincoln's childhood—this is what I was thinking, selfishly and a bit narcissistically—but as one from my own.

It put me in a sour mood, seeing this place I'd recollected for so many years fallen to disrepair and, worse, doomed to progress. The pall carried over from Knob Creek and probably darkened how I felt about what happened next, at Hodgenville. Nostalgia was pressing in on me. In the motel room the night before I'd read Ida's moving account of coming to the birthplace, but as we drove over the hills I was thinking less of her than of the convertible my father drove in the 1960s, and the scarf my mother wore in the front seat to preserve her hairdo from the wind, and the leap my strange young Lincoln-besotted heart took as we turned off the state road by the flagpole and the split rail fence and into the national birthplace park.

And here I was doing it again, forty years later, past the same split rail fence, the same flagpole. "This is it, guys," I said into the rearview mirror. "The real thing. Where it all began."

"There are few more precious birthplaces on this earth than this, where Abraham Lincoln first saw light," Ida Tarbell wrote. Coming to

Hodgenville in the 1920s, she thought she'd arrived at the wellspring of Lincoln's greatness. "It is a deep satisfaction," she went on, "to know that at last the spot is honored as it should be." Tarbell herself had a hand in making sure that honor was shown to the birthplace. She had been one of several public figures—along with Mark Twain and Teddy Roosevelt—who had helped found the Lincoln Farm Association in 1905. At the time, the farm was in bad shape, and the little cabin, the actual birthplace, appeared almost beyond repair.

"For many years men talked of its sacredness," Ida wrote, with unaccustomed heat, "but they were less energetic than men who realized that the cabin might be made a money-maker. It was the money-makers who first laid hands on the Lincoln cabin." Actually, Ida didn't know the worst of it. The story of the farm, in its earliest chapters, is a landmark episode in American commercialism.

Kentucky stayed in the Union throughout the Civil War, of course, thanks largely to Lincoln's sharp maneuvering. But still it was a slave state, a cauldron of Southern sympathies. After the war Kentuckians in rural Hodgenville had no more desire to preserve their Lincoln associations than did their counterparts in cosmopolitan Lexington. Locals knew the location of the farm the Lincolns had owned in 1809, and for a fee they would lead an occasional party of pilgrims to the Sinking Spring woods outside of town where the nation's savior had been born. To a good capitalist of the Gilded Age the thing must have looked a terrible waste, a blown opportunity. And sure enough, in 1894, a restaurant owner from New York, Alfred Dennett, got the bright idea of turning the farm into a resort, complete with spa and hunting lodge. He bought the property through a local agent, a Methodist preacher named James Bigham, who discovered that in the 1850s Lincoln's birth cabin had been moved to a neighboring farm a mile away. On Dennett's orders, Bigham dismantled the cabin and carried it by wagon to Sinking Spring, where he rebuilt it on the little knoll that old folks fingered as its original site.

And there it sat. Both Dennett, working from long distance, and his man Bigham, working close in, had trouble rousing the tourist trade.

Indeed, it seemed that the only people who were eager to make the long trek from civilization to Sinking Spring were vandals seeking a chip or a splinter from the sacred structure and who, being vandals, were unwilling to pay for the privilege. Dennett grew desperate to make good on his investment. These were the days when the nation's leaders were working to lay to rest the last lingering feuds of the war. The two entrepreneurs conceived their own grand gesture of reconciliation. Fewer than a hundred miles from Sinking Spring they found a cabin said to be the birthplace of Jefferson Davis. They bought the precious shack and immediately tore it apart.

The possibilities, they saw, were explosive: reconstructing, side by side, the humble beginnings of the two leaders of the late conflagration! And so both cabins were moved to Nashville and reassembled on the midway of the Tennessee Centennial Exposition of 1897. Yet again box office was disappointing. Discouraged, Dennett had both cabins dismantled and brought back to Manhattan, where the logs were stacked together in a rented warehouse on the Lower East Side. They were brought out occasionally, appearing at the Pan American Exposition in Buffalo, New York, in 1901, and later on at the amusement park in Coney Island. By then ownership of the cabins had changed hands, falling eventually to a pair of promoters who, after a year or two, realized they hadn't a clue what to do with them. Their eagerness to sell inspired Ida and her fellow celebrities to found the Lincoln Farm Association, in hopes of saving the cabin and the farm and removing them once and for all time from the greasy paws of commerce.

The LFA launched a nationwide drive to raise funds. Subscriptions went for a quarter apiece. One thousand dollars was all it took, and in 1905 the Lincoln logs were disentangled from the Davis logs and loaded on a train that took them on a long, winding trip back to Hodgenville. Advance men blanketed the route in publicity. At each town the train would pull to a siding where reverent crowds had gathered. In solemn ceremonies a few logs would be unveiled. Men would doff their hats and hoist their children to touch the splintered wood. When the train arrived in Hodgenville, a brass band serenaded the logs and a crowd of thousands swarmed to get close. A caravan snaked its way to the knoll above the Sinking Spring. What happened to the Davis logs, nobody seems to know, or care; his team lost.

The humble cabin was hammered and grouted back together again. Soon it was smothered in experts hired by the LFA and employing the most advanced scientific methods to prove or disprove its authenticity. The verdict was conclusive: this was it, the cabin that Tom had made and in which Abe had been born. The LFA next commissioned a grand memorial from John Russell Pope, a young architect trained at the École des Beaux-Arts, who would go on to design such majestic piles as the National Archives and the National Gallery of Art. Classicism was in the air, and Pope was a neoclassical man from the strap of his gaiters to the tip of his top hat. The memorial was to sit on the knoll where the birthplace stood. Pope conceived a Greek temple—it's not clear whether John Russell Pope could conceive of anything else—resting at the summit of a grand stairway of fifty-six steps, one for each year of the martyr's life. And inside it, in a sanctum sanctorum, the log cabin would be reassembled, sealed off from wind and weather, preserved for all time.

If there was an incongruity between the rustic origins of the frontiersman they were celebrating and this stout, Zeus-like box of gleaming marble set in the middle of a second-growth forest peopled with extras from the cast of *Deliverance,* no one dared mention it.

Well, not no one: Ida thought it was odd and said so. Though she'd been educated in France, her long contemplation of Abraham Lincoln had dissolved the unwholesome affectations of her schooling, and her tastes had grown toward the simple and unadorned. She declined to attend the dedication of the temple in 1911, and when she finally decided to visit, ten years later, she approached the place with great uneasiness.

"I dreaded to see it," she wrote in *Footsteps,* "for when I learned that it had been decided to build upon the farm a Greek temple, I shrank from the idea of the connection. I did not know what should be done, but in my ignorance it seemed to me that they were doing what should not be done."

The thing was even odder than she knew. When the temple was finished and it came time to reassemble the cabin within its central hall, Pope decided that the cabin was too big for the sanctuary (please note: he didn't decide his sanctuary was too small for the cabin). The old structure's rustic dimensions were eighteen feet by sixteen feet, standard for nineteenth-century frontier cabins. Yet they unbalanced the Pythagorean perfection of the temple, Pope said. Of course the logs were sacred; so sacred that thousands had escorted them on their return to this place of honor; so sacred indeed that Pope himself had been commissioned at great expense to design a classical temple to house, protect, and preserve them. But not so sacred they couldn't be cut to fit. So a couple of feet were lopped off each log. The cabin was reassembled in the temple, sixteen by fourteen feet, a more diminutive and neoclassically apposite size.

Ida describes stopping before the marble temple, at the bottom of the fifty-six steps. I stopped with my kids at the same spot, thinking of Ida's dread and excitement as she made her way up. Viewed one way, the entire scheme, the broad staircase and the thudding marble and the stacked columns, seems wildly grandiose; viewed another way it seems restrained, even austere. The most obvious thing for the designers to have done—that is, erect a massively heroic statue of the man himself at the entrance of the building to overawe the visitor—is something they consciously declined to do. There's nothing representational at all, no friezes or mosaics, just the stairs and the temple and the hushed green countryside all around. It's magnificent and simple, all at once— exactly what the men who built this thing thought Lincoln was.

Ida was delighted to discover that, from the outside, the temple was beautiful; she didn't think it was overblown at all. "It is a triumph of perfection. Its proportions are right, its size is right. But in the exultation of finding it so beautiful, I dreaded an entrance. Would not the little cabin seem mean? Would not placing it inside this perfect thing make it ridiculous by contrast?"

Everyone will have his own answer to Ida's question. We lumbered up the steps. My daughter counted each one—"just to make sure," she said, hoping to catch the architect and builders in a colossal and unforgivable error. At the top of the stairs the heavy bronze doors are inset with mirrored glass. The glass reflects the sky and the flags flying on high poles directly behind you. The last thing you see before you step into the temple, therefore, is a reflection of Old Glory over your shoulder, either at rest or unfurled in the breeze. The effect is almost overwhelmingly patriotic. And then you're through the door and facing the cabin.

"It's so small," my son said. It rests on a stone base, roped off by iron stanchions and a looping black chain. The logs are cracked with age and the chinking of red clay shows through. It has a single door, maybe five and a half feet high, and a single window in one wall. It's impossible to imagine anyone living in it, through winter and summer, but you're forced to imagine it. Under an alabaster skylight, and a coffered ceiling studded with rosettes, and surrounded by polished marble walls inlaid with brass fixtures, the little house should look absurd, a chip of gravel set in a jeweled diadem.

"Would not placing the cabin inside this perfect thing make it ridiculous by contrast?" Ida had wondered, and she answered herself straightaway: "The beauty and wonder of it is that it is not so. It somehow belongs. Why, I do not know; but it stands there so simply what it is, a thing without pretension but of an extraordinary dignity in its simplicity. You have only the native log structure, the clay chimney; but every stone of the chimney, every timber of the cabin is there because it was needed. Never have I been so impressed with the dignity of the thing which fits the need."

I sat there for a long time, as Ida had. The kids went out the rear door to run on the grass behind the temple. When Ida came here at last she thought she had Lincoln pegged—she had written a beautiful two-volume book about him, after all, and in her own time she had met every surviving friend who knew him intimately, she had held his intimate artifacts and his greatest writings in her hand—but she thought this cabin where he was born summed him up in the profoundest way.

The Park Service ranger on duty noticed me jotting in my notebook. "You understand, this is the symbolic cabin," he said.

"I'm sorry?" I said.

"That's what we call it now. A long time ago you would've come here and we would have said it was the real thing. Then we used to say, well, it might be the real thing, it might not be." He turned his hand palm up and then palm down. "Now we say it's symbolic."

"Why is that?"

He told me about the story of Dennett and Bigham and Coney Island and the rest. I told him I'd heard all that—and also about the forensic scientists hired by the Lincoln Farm Association, who'd issued an unequivocal verdict of the cabin's authenticity.

"Yes sir, that's why we would say, 'Yes, this is the cabin,'" he said. "Then we got a call from the History Channel."

It was a show called *History's Mysteries*. For the first time in seventy-five years, the Park Service agreed to let scientists remove core samples from the cabin's logs. It didn't take more than a week to prove that the cabin dated from the 1850s, more than forty years after Lincoln was born.

"So the thing is . . . a fake?"

"Not a fake," the ranger said. He looked offended. "Symbolic."

I went back outside. As my sour mood got sourer I wondered whether there wasn't something summary about this, traveling to the temple, ascending the steps, entering the Holy of Holies, and finding within the marble walls a well-meaning . . . mistake. Put there from the best of motives, of course, but nevertheless a thing that wasn't what it was supposed to be. If it's a symbol, I thought, it's a symbol of the fate of any search for Lincoln. Even when you thought you had him nailed, even when you'd chased the story back to its source, traced him from tomb to birthplace, he slipped away like quicksilver. Lincoln the man never seemed to be where, or what, you thought he was.

The kids were back in the parking lot, waiting for me to unlock the car. My daughter gestured grandly toward a trash can.

"Young Abe Lincoln once carried this garbage for fourteen miles in the snow," she was saying. "He did it to repay a farmer who had lent him a stack of phone books that he would read by the fireside. Suddenly, he was attacked by bees . . ."

I never did mention to my kids that the cabin wasn't the real thing. We made our way home, and swamped by the onset of a new school year and the return of friends from Disneyworld and lake cottages, the Lincoln Trail receded in memory. I couldn't be sure whether the trip qualified as a success or not, but I knew my hopes of re-creating my earlier family trip had been silly. You can't go home again, said the novelist, but he might have mentioned that you can't go on vacation again, either—at least not the same vacation, as of course I should have known.

Over the months that followed I discovered the kids doing unexpected things. I saw the boy on the couch one afternoon with an old paperback I'd left lying around, *Citizen of New Salem*. Half an hour later he was still there, still reading. Passing the closed door of my daughter's bedroom one evening I heard show tunes I couldn't quite place. I knocked and entered to find her huddled over her CD player, studying the sleeve to the sound track of *Young Abe Lincoln* and humming along with the Hoosiers.

They were trying to pin down the elusive Lincoln for themselves.

Over dinner one night that fall I mentioned I might go back to Springfield as part of my book research, and maybe even to the funeral museum to learn more about Lincoln's funeral.

My daughter spoke up.

"Lincoln was shot on April 14, 1865," she said, "and he died at seven-twenty-two the next morning, April 15, 1865."

I told her how pleased I was she knew that.

"Well, what do you expect?" she said. "I can't help it. It's like old Abe has taken up a whole segment of my brain."

"It's worse than that," said the boy. "It's like there's a whole history museum inside." He shuddered so hard I could feel it in my bones. "And an entire wing is devoted to Abraham Lincoln."

They were complaining. I was delighted.

10

IN DEFENSE OF THE ICON

There was one last statue to see. Even buffs are slightly embarrassed by it sometimes, for it can strike the contemporary viewer as overripe, too grandiose, a bit pompous, aggressive in its unapologetic hero worship. Yet the huge Lincoln that sits in his memorial at the foot of the National Mall in Washington, D.C., is the most famous depiction of Lincoln there is. It's the unavoidable Lincoln. Anyone who wants to understand the Land of Lincoln has to account for it.

It's nineteen feet high and carved from glowing Georgia marble. It weighs 340,000 pounds, and if the seated figure rose, as he seems poised to do, he would stand at twenty eight feet. The chamber in which the statue sits is sixty feet wide by seventy-four feet deep, and, through its front entryway, it remains open to the wind and the weather no matter the season.

This is a place that was made for the camera, it begs to be photographed, and visitors come seeking the ideal picture. They don't clown around in here, at least not much. Here Lincoln is too big to throw your arm around; only a mountain climber could try to put the rabbit ears behind his head, and any pinkie finger would be lost in his footlong nostril. Instead the visitors walk in and look up and stop. Traffic congestion—foot traffic—is a problem, day or night, so when it comes time to snap the picture, the challenge is to arrange a tourist-less space in front of the statue, and then another clear space between the person taking the picture and people having their picture taken—one long, open line from photographer to visitor to Lincoln—and this is always too much to ask. Some clueless stranger will wander through the frame, or a clutch of rival tourists crowds in, or a Park Service ranger mills about, or the photographer gets bumped by another photographer hoping to get a clear shot of his own. It never works out. The ideal picture is always elusive. They keep coming here anyway, the tourists do, getting the picture that they'll take back home, where it will end up in one place or another, moving across a computer desktop or pinned to a kitchen bulletin board, and Lincoln will be there, a mute presence at home or at work, glimpsed now and then from the corner of the eye.

What they'll glimpse is Lincoln the icon—and the icon, I've discovered, is no longer considered the optimal Lincoln. Though the term is used to the point of cliché—we have pop icons like Shakira, sports icons like Derek Jeter, racing icons like Richard Petty—icons are usually viewed skeptically when they arise from our past. We're too wised-up to fall for historical or national icons. Regarding Lincoln I heard the word used only as a term of disparagement. "You go to the Lincoln Memorial, you get an icon," the director of the new Springfield museum liked to say, "but here [in the museum] you get the man." (And he's made of rubber.) "I'm not in the icon business," Bob Rogers had said with disdain. "Sure, we could have had some kind of icon," I was told when the little statue was unveiled in Richmond. One scholar had favorably compared the life-sized Lincoln at Tredegar to the "triumphalist icon" in Washington. Even the Ladds, at the seminar in Gettysburg, said they weren't interested in "Lincoln the icon." At the Chicago Historical Society, Russell Lewis had said, "We've been less interested in the icon, more interested in a Lincoln that's much more human . . . That, to us, is much more interesting."

Interesting maybe; but not as valuable, and—consider the possibility—not as true. What if Lincoln the man was, as I'd come to suspect, unknowable, as most men are 140 years after their death? And what if the icon—big, grand, unmistakable—is more real than the much smaller, custom-fit Lincolns that each of us creates for ourselves? Whenever I returned to Washington after a trip exploring Lincoln and saw the memorial sitting solid and immovable by the gliding Potomac, I was grateful for the icon. I was happy to find a Lincoln that was simpler and more plausible than the ones I'd gotten from scholars, haters, publicists, and buffs. I'd look up at him and think: this big fellow certainly doesn't look bipolar. There are no hints here of psychological vulnerability or marriage problems, no suggestions, whatever those might be, of gayness; not much of humor or dark rumination or business savvy, no sign of racism or dictatorial tendencies, no personal disorders of any kind. You can't tell whether, by today's standards, he'd be a conservative or a liberal. Gone, when you get down to it, is all nuance, all shadings and fine distinctions that might distract us from what the memorial says is the essence of Abraham Lincoln.

Maybe that's why icons are dismissed as unreal these days, why so many historians and buffs brag that they're going beyond the icon, peeling back the myth, to find the living, breathing, three-dimensional person beneath. Icons aren't complicated enough for the wised-up world. Nuance fits the times. We can be consumed by nuance, argue about it on TV, blog about it, fill our scholarly monographs with its infinite refractions—even when, like the forest and the trees, our obsession with it obscures the bigger, unarguable facts that are plain in front of us. And that's what the Lincoln Memorial is for: the brute, uncomplicated facts of Lincoln's public life. On the paneled wall of the south chamber are etched all 272 words of the Gettysburg Address, in which Lincoln declared that the Union would be preserved by renewing its allegiance to its founding proposition, that all men are created equal. Opposite to it, in the north chamber, are all 702 words of the

Second Inaugural, in which he claimed that the renewal had behind it a mysterious and providential power.

The designers of the memorial chose these two inscriptions with great care. They were unveiled to the public officially on a bright and breezy morning in May 1922. More than thirty-five thousand people showed up for the dedication ceremony. The guest of honor was Robert Todd Lincoln, Abraham's only surviving son, frail and nearly deaf at the age of eighty. It was a rare public appearance for him; always aloof, he had declined, for example, to come to the dedication of the Pope temple in Hodgenville ten years earlier. And when asked beforehand to make brief remarks to dedicate the memorial in Washington he refused. It was enough for the large crowd merely to see him there, sitting between the Corinthian columns in a straight-backed chair, looking out over the mall and the modern city: it was wired with electric lights now and bustling with automobiles, unrecognizable as the lamplit town of mud streets and carriages where, twenty blocks away and fifty-seven years earlier, his father had said good-bye to him on his way to the theater.

Washington in 1922 was being transformed into a capital worthy of a wealthy and newly imperial republic. A panel of engineers and aesthetes called the McMillan commission, which had drawn up plans for rebuilding the city in 1901, chose a monument to Lincoln as its crowning feature: "erected to the memory of that one man in our history as a nation who is worthy to be named with George Washington—Abraham Lincoln." It took ten years to arrive at a design, and another ten to build it. The site was unpromising, at the edge of a landfill dredged up from the muck of the river flats. But as good fortune or providence would have it, both the architect, a North Carolinian named Henry Bacon, and the sculptor he chose, a New England Brahmin named Daniel Chester French, were geniuses uniquely suited to the task.

Bacon was a creature that's not supposed to exist in nature—a modest architect—but he had the brass to resist the first plans that other designers had concocted for his grand chamber. They suggested placing a giant reproduction of the standing Saint-Gaudens Lincoln, from Chicago, in the center of it. Bacon wanted an original statue, something that no one had ever seen before, and he wanted French to sculpt it. He got his way by arguing that the proportions of Saint-Gaudens's statue would be destroyed if they were expanded to fill the temple chamber. More important, he said, the conventions of classical art required that only warriors be memorialized by standing figures, and Lincoln should not be remembered as a warrior, at least not here. Statesmen, philosophers, and poets, on the other hand, were always shown seated, in repose, an attitude better suited to their contemplative calling, and to the contemplation the statue was meant to inspire in others.

So this is what he got. This is not, however, what sophisticated critics have seen. They were able to decode the real meaning of the big marble pile from the start. The temple had been open only two years when the architecture critic Lewis Mumford gazed down upon it from Olympian heights and pronounced himself appalled. Far from being a tribute to Lincoln, he said, it was instead a strained act of vanity on the part of self-justifying politicians. "One feels not the living beauty of our American past, but the mortuary air of archaeology. The America that Lincoln was bred in, the homespun and humane and humorous America that he wished to preserve, has nothing in common with the sedulously classic monument that was erected to his memory. Who lives in that shrine, I wonder—Lincoln, or the men who conceived it; the leader who beheld the mournful victory of the Civil War, or the generation that took pleasure in the mean triumph of the Spanish-American [War], and placed the imperial standard in the Philippines and the Caribbean?" Like a lot of us, Mumford had his own preferred Lincoln—folksy, humorous, homespun—and he was offended to find him missing.

More recently, a specialist in semiotics has gathered his graduate degrees about him and managed to glimpse many of the same encrypted meanings. The figure in the temple, he wrote, is "a confection of a cultural and political elite bent on stripping Lincoln of his earthly imperfection and his war of its bloodiness, to make it and him into prototypes of the progressive and (for some) imperial nation that Republicans of 1901–1912 hoped to shape." Just so, another of these wake-up-and-smell-the-coffee demystifiers said that Bacon and French were "seamless political reactionaries who sought to bend the chance to build a national memorial to the iconic Lincoln to their politico-cultural program of controlling the populace by sedative, pacifying mythology."

What's most impressive about these appraisals (there have been lots of them) is their condescension; you can't help but envy the ease with which the critic convinces himself that he understands what our predecessors were doing better than they understood it themselves. As it happens, though, they were quite self-aware, these starchy old fellows, and in raising up the icon they actually knew what they were doing. Three men made speeches at the dedication in 1922. The remarks by former president William Howard Taft were gaseous and forgettable—as overblown as former president William Howard Taft. The remarks by then-president Warren G. Harding were much better—and not merely because of the pleasing irony that comes from hearing our greatest president praised by our worst.

Harding's theme was that there was no real opposition between the human being and the icon—and not because the human being was flawless. Indeed, Harding even made admissions that might delight Brag Bowling, Tom DiLorenzo, and the other Lincoln haters, who have convinced themselves that the "Lincoln cultists" admitted no human imperfections in their hero. To the contrary: Harding acknowledged, for example, the vastness of Lincoln's personal ambition, and he pointed out that Lincoln's popularity, while he was alive, was a fifty-fifty thing.

"No leader was ever more unsparingly criticized or more bitterly assailed, lashed by angry tongues and ridiculed in press and speech." Yet none of this should be surprising, according to Harding's account. "Lincoln was a very natural human being," Harding said, "with the frailties mixed with the virtues of humanity. There are neither supermen nor demigods in the government of kingdoms, empires, or republics. It will be better for our conception of government and its institutions if we will understand this fact."

Behind Harding as he spoke loomed Daniel Chester French's statue, which, if you looked closely, underscored the point. French worked hard to make this huge Lincoln look like a man instead of a god. His ungodliness, his imperfections, are hard to miss. This is one rumpled icon. He's wearing street clothes, and his shawl is draped casually over the back of his chair. His hair is uncombed. His tie is askew. Even when he's being preserved for the ages, he can't pull himself together. His eyes aren't quite symmetrical, and his hands betray a fidgety disposition. He's really, really big, but he's still a man.

But *why* is he so big? Why has he been made an icon? Harding gave a hint: "This memorial," he said, "matchless tribute though it is, is less for Abraham Lincoln than for those of us to-day, and for those who follow after." Americans made him an icon not because he deserved it but because they needed it—a persistent reminder of something larger than a man, even a good man.

Yet it was left to the third speaker at the dedication ceremony to explain the icon in terms that maybe even an age of self-styled iconoclasts can understand.

He was Robert Moton, the president of Tuskegee Institute and a son of slaves. He wore a swallowtail coat and striped pants, and he approached the microphone with great deliberation. Moton opened his speech with a brief sketch of American history. From the arrival of

the first settlers, in Virginia and in Massachusetts, the country had
been the site of contending ideas, between the "pioneers of freedom"
and the "pioneers of bondage." The Founders, in 1776, took sides:
they "set up their altars in the name of liberty" and in so doing
"started on these shores the great experiment of the ages—an experiment in human relations, where men and women of every nation, of
every race and creed, are thrown together." It was inevitable that "in
the process of time these great forces of liberty and the forces of
bondage [would meet] in open conflict." By Lincoln's time it had
fallen to Americans to "demonstrate whether the principles of freedom were of universal application."

Moton addressed directly a belief common then as it is now: that
Lincoln's greatness lies in his preservation of the Union. Judged simply
as a historical claim, much less a moral one, this struck Moton, as it should
strike us, as small potatoes. The nineteenth century, after all, was a century
of consolidators. Bismarck, in Germany, saved a union; so did Garibaldi,
in Italy. Moton and the men who designed the Lincoln Memorial recognized that Lincoln had done something much greater. Whoever honors
Lincoln simply because he saved the Union, Moton said, misses the larger
portion of his achievement. Lincoln saved the Union but it was a *particular kind of Union* he saved: a Union dedicated to a proposition.

"When the last veteran has stacked his arms, when only the memory
of high courage and deep devotion remains, at such a time the united
voice of grateful posterity will say: The claim of greatness for Abraham
Lincoln lies in this, that amid doubt and distrust, against the counsel of
chosen advisers, in the hour of the Nation's utter peril, he put his trust
in God and spoke the word that gave freedom to a race and vindicated
the honor of a Nation conceived in liberty and dedicated to the proposition that all men are created equal."

Moton's logic is the simple logic of the icon. If Lincoln had failed,
the country would have ceased to exist. The founders would have lost
their bet that ordinary people could govern themselves, and the principle they were betting on—that all men were created equal—would

have slipped into darkness, and no one can say when it might have been revived.

But Lincoln didn't fail. The Union was saved, and the proposition was preserved. That's what the memorial says. That's what the icon, solid and unmoving on the banks of the river, stands for. The rest is just nuance.

POSTSCRIPT

The Springfield Hilton, like many notable works of architecture, evokes the great landmarks that surround it, in a kind of homage to the aspirations and dreams that have shaped its environment. Unfortunately for the Hilton, its environment is farm country, and the aspirations and dreams that have shaped it involve corn and soybeans. Thus the Hilton rises like a silo for an improbable thirty stories in the middle of the low-rise downtown, where no other building tops 250 feet. Just as improbably, it rises and rises and then swells outward at the top, so that the twenty-ninth and thirtieth floors are more bulbous than the shaft leading up to it. A restaurant is up there, and a bar, where you can stare down every night on the lit-up dome of the state Capitol building and then the fathomless pitch beyond. Locals call the Hilton the "Penis on the Prairie" or the "State Stiffy"; also, blasphemously, "Lincoln's Log" or "Abe's Appendage." Some locals do, anyway.

I was in the lobby of the Hilton one spring day, waiting for a cab, when I met Frank Walker. Frank is the hotel's manager of guest services. He asked what brought me to town and we struck up a conversation about Lincoln.

"Let me ask you something," Frank said. When he talks to you, Frank gets up close. He's an imposing figure, with wide shoulders and wide-set eyes beneath a wide forehead. He fills out his gray blazer. His shoes gleam. He speaks slowly, and when he does he places the tips of his fingers together.

"What, in your opinion, were Lincoln's true feelings about slavery?"

I told him it was a question I was still wrestling with myself. I started into my pedant's mode, telling him I thought the scholarly consensus had shifted over the years and that now most students believed Lincoln's views had changed as time went on, but Frank cut me off, not unkindly.

"Well, see, here is where I experience problems, because the work of scholars makes me very skeptical. People who write, they have their own attitudes and their own viewpoints and what have you. I have read Frederick Douglass and W.E.B. DuBois and some of the biographies, and I have not reached any conclusions about Mr. Lincoln, but I do think he was not completely antislavery the way some people say. He was always qualifying. You could never quite tie him down. He never came out and said, we're going to stop this, right now. I wonder why he didn't do that."

He told me he'd heard about the local Lincoln all his life, having grown up in Jacksonville nearby, but had only recently started thinking about him seriously.

"I'm reticent to condemn Mr. Lincoln out and out. I'm interested in him, and I keep my mind open. And whatever my opinion about the man, I can tell you a story that perhaps makes our own views irrelevant."

Frank told me he'd moved to Springfield four years ago with his three daughters, the oldest of whom was now in high school. "I wanted them to get a better start in life. Jacksonville is a town of seventeen thousand. Springfield has a hundred and ten thousand people. There's more opportunity to get ahead, just so long as I can keep them away from these gangbangers and the knuckleheads out there." His original hope was to get a job with the state government. "Hopefully somewhere I could use my personality and my people skills. I prefer a job that's people-intensive." Unable to find a government job, he went to work at the Hilton, hoping the flow of politicians and officials in and out all day would give him contacts that might eventually pay off.

"It hasn't happened yet. And I think sometimes, well, why? Now I think I know why. Last Tuesday morning, I'm at my desk here, and there's some kind of commotion at the front desk. I ventured over to see if I could be of assistance. A tall gentleman was standing there, very old, very feeble. It appeared to me that he was suffering from Parkinson's disease or a disease of that kind. He was having trouble conversing. He spoke in broken English. The girl behind the desk says to me, 'Frank, we cannot understand what this gentleman is saying. We're having trouble here.'

"Well, if you listened closely and concentrated hard, pretty soon you could put two and two together and understand some of what the man was saying. He was experiencing difficulty entering his room, so I escorted him to the elevator and we were able to use the key to get him in the room. He asked me in. He was very grateful that I had been able to be of assistance and said he wanted to show me something."

Frank said the man walked over to the bed and picked up a piece of yellowing paper.

"It was a letter, dated April 1965," Frank said. "It was from the mayor of Springfield—the mayor at that time. It was addressed to this gentleman in Prague, Czechoslovakia. That's where he was from, Czechoslovakia. The letter from the mayor thanked him for his interest in Abraham Lincoln and invited him to Springfield, as a guest of the mayor. It said, You come here and see the home and the tomb and the Lincoln shrines as our guest, and we'll give you the key to the city. Well, apparently, it took him forty years to save up enough money to get here. But he made it.

"Then the man tells me his story. Suddenly he stands up straight as can be while he tells me. He said he'd been in the concentration camp. He pulled up his sleeve when he said this. Every time he mentioned the concentration camp he pulled up his sleeve, and you could see the number there. He said he knew about Abraham Lincoln and George Washington from when he learned about them in school as a boy.

"Now here's what's interesting. When he was in the concentration camp, and he was all alone in his cell, it was the worst time in his life and he didn't think he could go on anymore. And he said Mr. Lincoln came to him.

"Mr. Lincoln stood right in front of him, just like I'm standing here in front of you. And Lincoln said to him, 'You never forget: All men are created equal. This is true for all men for all times. And these men who would do this thing to you, who put you here, they're no better than you. You are their equal, because *all men are created equal*. You keep remembering this, and you persevere, you'll be all right.'

"Well, this is what the gentleman said, in his broken English. I don't know about ghosts. I'm skeptical. But this is what the man said. I get a chill thinking about it."

I told him I did too.

"Well, from this time onward, the man says he knew he was going to be all right. He knew he was going to persevere. And he vowed if he ever got out of that concentration camp, he would come to Springfield, to thank Mr. Lincoln, he was so grateful. He'd written a poem for Lincoln and he had to recite it for him. That's what he said. He had three flowers on the bed, they were the plastic kind, two red, one white. Carnations. He said he had to go to Lincoln's tomb to give him the flowers and recite this poem.

"Then he recited the poem for me, right there in the room. I didn't understand it, of course. He was hunched up in the back, but he stood up straight as he could when he said it, this old man. He put his hand over his heart. He was shaking."

Frank left him and went down to his post in the lobby and called the mayor's office. The opening of the Lincoln museum was a week away, and everyone on the mayor's staff was busy. Someone suggested Frank call the convention and visitors' bureau, and a woman named Alicia Erickson, who specialized in dealing with foreign tourist groups, arrived a few minutes later. "I told her, you have to help this gentleman, but be careful, because I'm thinking he's on some kind of death walk, Alicia, I think this is his final trip. This is something he's got to do before he dies."

Alicia told me later what happened after that.

"His name was Mr. Dubin, Henri Dubin," she said. "He was sweet and very gentle, but he was frail, very thin, and kind of hunched over— and very hard to understand. Only Frank could really understand him, I think. And he was just insistent that he had to visit Lincoln's tomb right then, that day. He couldn't wait because he had to fly back home the next day.

"So I got him in my car and we drove out to the tomb. He was carrying his flowers in his lap. I don't think he could hear me that well, because when I'd ask him something he didn't really answer. So we didn't do too much talking.

"At the tomb he walked around the outside very slowly. Then we went inside. You know how at the tomb you kind of go down a hallway and turn, then you go down another hallway and turn again, before you get to the actual tomb?"

I told her I did. At every turn is a small Lincoln statue, modeled after the more famous statues around the country. There's Anna Hyatt Huntington's *On the Circuit,* and the Saint-Gaudens from Chicago, and of course French's from the memorial in Washington.

"Well, he had to stop at every statue. He'd put his hand on it and study it, stare at it. By the time we got to the grave he was crying. He was very emotional. He took one look at the tomb and let me tell you: that man got down on his knees and he kissed the ground. Then he laid the flowers there, and he got back up, and he stood straight as he could and he recited his poem. Tears were streaming down his face. His voice was very strong and clear. Then he looks at me and he kind of sighs and he says, 'Yes. Now it's over.' He says, 'We can go.'"

Mr. Dubin slept most of the day and then through the night.

"The next morning," Frank told me, "we got him to the airport. I made sure my friends at the airlines understood how feeble this man was, that they had to take special care of him. When I got him to the check-in, he couldn't help himself. He was crying again. He turned to me and he said, 'Frank, God sent you to me to help me find Lincoln. You are an angel.' And he hugged me."

Standing there by his desk in the Hilton lobby, Frank didn't say anything for a while. "I told a lady friend about this last week, after it happened. She said to me, 'Frank, you want to know why you haven't got your job in the government yet—that's why. You had to be there, at the Hilton.' She said, 'God wanted you to be there to help this man!' Maybe so. I'm skeptical. I'm a skeptical man.

"I say I get skeptical about Lincoln. I am. But to me, you see, I don't care what you say about Lincoln, this was very reflective of the man, this story. He's bigger than Springfield. Lincoln transcends the whole United States even. He's all over the world. That gentleman was all alone over there, in that cell. But Lincoln was with him. Or he thought Lincoln was with him. I don't know what it was. But that is some kind of power."

ACKNOWLEDGMENTS

I'm just a journalist, not a scholar, so in trying to understand Lincoln and the world that's been built around him I have relied heavily on the pros. In several instances, my debt to an individual scholar or book is noted in the text. Wary of cluttering the page with too much academic machinery, however, I thought it best to cite others here, in an endnote.

For chapter 1, I greatly benefited from Nelson Lankford's *Richmond Burning: The Last Day of the Confederate Capital*, which is the definitive work on the subject and one of the great books written about that lovely city. Some of the essays in David Herbert Donald's *Lincoln Reconsidered* tell charming stories about the strange uses to which Lincoln's memory has been put, including the Lincoln-Lenin celebrations of the 1930s. *Lincoln in American Memory* by Merrill Petersen remains the nonpareil.

Donald also wrote the biography of William Herndon, *Lincoln's Herndon,* which is still, more than fifty years after its first publication, the touchstone for anyone who hopes to figure out that sad but strangely inspiring character, as I tried to do in chapter 2. In recent years, our understanding of Herndon has been immeasurably deepened by the painstaking scholarship of Douglas Wilson and Rodney Davis, particularly in the introduction and notes to their *Herndon's Informants*. Davis and Wilson spent a wintry afternoon generously talking Herndon with me in the office they share at Knox College in Galesburg, Illinois. Wilson's two studies of Lincoln, *Honor's Voice* and *Lincoln's Sword*, have taken their place on the shelf of books that no Lincoln buff can live without. Benjamin Thomas covered the progress of Lincoln's biographers in *Portrait for Posterity*. My account of John Hanks and the New Orleans episode comes from Richard Nelson Current's *The Lincoln Nobody Knows*, and the essay I cite by Don E. Fehrenbacher is in his *Lincoln in Text and Context*.

What I know about Jane Addams's relationship to Lincoln comes from two biographies, Jean Bethke Elshtain's *Jane Addams and the Dream of American Democracy* and *Citizen* by Louise W. Knight. In addition to Catherine Lewis's informative book about the Chicago Historical Society, cited liberally in chapter 3, I got lots of stuff from Paul A. Angle's *The Chicago Historical Society, 1856–1956: An Unconventional Chronicle*, as well as from a publication of the Society issued in conjunction with Northwestern University, "Wet with Blood," about the Society's Lincoln collection, and from Russell Lewis's pictorial essay, "Abraham Lincoln and the Chicago Historical Society," which appeared in the magazine *Chicago History*.

Angle, busy fellow, also wrote the indispensable book about Lincoln's Springfield, *Here I Have Lived*, which helped me a great deal with chapter 4. As for chapter 5, anybody who wants to know about collecting Lincoln has to consult (who could've guessed?) *Collecting Lincoln* by Stuart Schneider, as well as the essential magazine for Lincoln collectors, *The Rail Splitter*, edited by Jon Mann, who also generously sat with me one morning in a Greenwich Village diner while I peppered him with questions, until a short-tempered short-order cook chased us out. I heard about Willie Clark from Osborn Oldroyd's *The Assassination of Abraham Lincoln*, and learned lots about Laura Keene from *Manhunt* by James Swanson. Though his many writings are not autobiographical, my understanding of Lincoln collecting, and of Lincoln himself, was enriched by the work of the Chief, Frank J. Williams, particularly his *Judging Lincoln*.

The many writings of Dale Carnegie are often very autobiographical indeed, and they helped me tell Carnegie's story in chapter 7, along with *Dale Carnegie: The Man Who Influenced Millions* by Giles Kemp and Edward Claflin. For the accounts of Lincoln's home and his birthplace in chapters 8 and 9, I relied, respectively, on two excellent papers that haven't enjoyed general circulation: Tim Townsend's "The Site Adrift in the City," and "An Administrative History of Abraham Lincoln Birthplace National Historic Site" by Gloria Peterson. Tim was particularly helpful and generous with his time, though I'm sure he disagrees with my view of his employer, the National Park Service. The quotes in chapter 10 about the Lincoln Memorial, both for good and ill, are found in two books. The first is *The Lincoln Memorial,* a memorial book, if you don't mind the redundancy, printed in 1927 by the Director for Public Buildings and Public Parks of the National Capital. The second is Christopher A. Thomas's *The Lincoln Memorial and American Life,* which tells the story of how the building was put together and how the rest of us reacted to it once it was done.

In addition to these, I am indebted to the work of the great Lincoln biographers, both the dead and the living. Happily among the latter whose books I've devoured are Michael Burlingame, Allen Guelzo, Harry Jaffa, Wayne Temple, Richard Nelson Current, and David Donald.

Sooner or later, though, a journalist needs to stop reading and actually start talking to people, and I give my warmest thanks to all those whose interviews and conversations are recorded in this book. I need to thank others, too, who were kind enough to spend time with me and talk about Lincoln—and, even better, about themselves and Lincoln—though their reflections aren't included here, at least not directly or by name.

Wayne Temple, deputy archivist of the state of Illinois, may well be, as people say, the greatest living Lincoln scholar; what's beyond dispute is that he is a resource of infinite patience and wisdom for anyone who wants to learn about Abraham Lincoln. Hundreds of historians and writers are in his debt, and I have the honor to count myself among them. Richard Norton Smith, from whom I stole the title of chapter 3, helped me navigate the wilds of Lincolnworld, as did John Rhodehamel, Shelby Cullom Davis, Charles Kesler, Donna McCreary, Clark Evans, Bob Willard, Catherine Clinton, James Swanson, and a few old Lincoln hands who asked to remain anonymous. Brian Lamb understood what I was trying to do from the first and, having spent a lot of time in the Land of Lincoln himself, pointed me to several sites of interest. George Will gave me encouragement at a crucial moment and introduced me to the work of Don Fehrenbacher. Michael Burlingame steered me clear of many errors and became a valued friend. Harry Jaffa, author of *Crisis of the House Divided*, which Guelzo (incontestably) calls "incontestably the greatest Lincoln book of the twentieth century," gave me a full afternoon of his time at his office in Claremont, California.

I'm grateful to all these, my fellow buffs, and to one buff above all. Among the most rewarding and unexpected consequences of my sojourn was meeting Michael F. Bishop, former executive director of the Abraham Lincoln Bicentennial Commission. With typical generosity Michael resolved to help the book get going, and a word from him opened countless doors that would have otherwise remained shut. Without his aid and friendship the book couldn't have been written.

I do have friends who are not buffs—a few indeed who show no buff tendencies whatsoever but who nevertheless offered a swift, encouraging kick at a decisive point or shagged down an interesting quote, or just listened patiently while I prattled on. I'm grateful to Paul Lindblad and Joanne Innis, and to P.J. and Tina O'Rourke and Nick and Mary Eberstadt, for not yelling "Stop!" or making throat-slashing motions whenever I mounted my Lincoln horse during the many cocktail hours we shared. As a matter of fact, my debts to P.J. are so large and various that it's not a workable idea to start listing them, lest these acknowledgments swallow up the book.

Thanks also to my agents Glen Hartley and Lynn Chu, and to my editors Morgan Entrekin and Jofie Ferrari-Adler; to Joel Achenbach, Chris Buckley, Patrick Cooke, Dave Shiflett, and Dail Willis; to Carol Alexander, Monte Siegrist, and John Curtin, in the Shangri-La town of Taylorville, Illinois, home to the world's only statue of Lincoln with a pig; to Tom Mallon, Matt Labash, Jack Shafer, Christopher Hitchens, Jon Yardley, Gary Schmitt, Grant Miller, and Scott Walter; to my colleagues at the *Weekly Standard*, especially to Bill Kristol, Fred Barnes, Terry Eastland, Richard Starr, and Claudia Winkler, for their forbearance; and to my brothers Rick and Stan. Gratitude is too feeble a word to describe what I owe my father and my late mother, who started me on the Trail.

This book is dedicated to Denise. I hope she knows why.

PHOTO CREDITS